D1522841

THE
MODERN STAGE
IN
LATIN AMERICA:
SIX PLAYS

THE MODERN STAGE IN LATIN AMERICA: SIX PLAYS

AN ANTHOLOGY
Edited by George Woodyard

E. P. DUTTON & CO., INC., NEW YORK, 1971

A Dutton Paperback

Published simultaneously in Canada by
Clarke, Irwin & Company Limited, Toronto and Vancouver

SBN 0-525-47296-7

Individual Copyrights and Acknowledgments

René Marqués: *The Fanlights*. Translated by Richard John Wiezell.
Copyright © 1971 by René Marqués. Published by permission of the
author and translator.

Alfredo Dias Gomes: *Payment as Pledged*. Translated by Oscar
Fernández. Copyright © 1971 by Alfredo Dias Gomes. Published by
permission of the author and translator.

Osvaldo Dragún: *And They Told Us We Were Immortal*. Translated
by Alden James Green. Copyright © 1971 by Osvaldo Dragún. Published by permission of the author and translator.

Jorge Díaz: *The Place Where the Mammals Die*. Translated by
Naomi Nelson. Copyright © 1971 by Jorge Díaz. Published by permission of the author and translator.

José Triana: *The Criminals*. Translated by Pablo Armando Fernandez
and Michael Kustow; adapted by Adrian Mitchell. Copyright © 1967
by José Triana. Originally published in *The Drama Review*, Winter
1970. Published by permission of the author and translators.

Emilio Carballido: *I Too Speak of the Rose*. Translated by William I.
Oliver. Copyright © 1971 by Emilio Carballido. Published by permission of the author and translator.

CONTENTS

INTRODUCTION

Within the past several years the impact of Latin American letters upon the English-speaking world has become increasingly evident. Pablo Neruda is now a recognized figure, as are various fiction writers ranging from Mariano Azuela and Jorge Luis Borges to the Nobel Prize-winning Miguel Angel Asturias, not to mention the generation of "new novelists" headed by Julio Cortázar and García Márquez. Other artistic and cultural phenomena of Latin America are equally well known—in art, the Mexican muralists; in architecture, Oscar Niemeyer and Brasilia; in music, the *bossa nova*; in dance, the cha-cha or the rumba. Curiously, an area of the arts that remains obscure, even to relatively sophisticated literary minds or theatre specialists, is that of the Latin American theatre. It is therefore the purpose of this anthology of plays in translation to bring to the attention of the English-speaking world this very vital and important theatre of Latin America.[1]

Although the drama of Latin America has developed slowly in relation to other literary genres, less attention has been devoted to its study or performance outside Latin America than the richness of the material merits. Marked by a long and frequently arduous process of formation, it has been constantly in the ascendant in spite of the many factors that have conspired to keep it in a position of secondary

[1] It should be observed that the term "Latin America" will be used here with full realization of its limitations. In short, no expression exists that adequately combines the historical, linguistic, and cultural implications of such a diversified area. Some critics maintain that the complexity of the area defies a comprehensively unifying term. Not unaware of the controversy, I have adopted the term because I feel that the advantage afforded by a common denominator in discussing similar trends and experiences outweighs the objections to its imprecision.

importance within the arts. One factor commonly noted is the relationship of cultural sophistication to the development of an active theatre movement in emerging countries. Since a sizable and dependable theatregoing public is essential to foment good theatre, such conditions are favorable only in a few metropolitan areas of Latin America. The various forms of explicit and implicit censorship—political, religious, moral, etc.—have also had their effect. The greatest factor, however, has been the feeling of cultural dependence upon areas of the world with a more established and flourishing theatrical tradition.

Theatre existed in the Americas even in pre-Columbian times. The *Rabinal Achí*, a Maya-Quiché dance drama, has survived through several centuries, together with other indigenous works whose authenticity has been more seriously challenged. During the early colonial period, the missionary priests used dramatic forms familiar to the Indians to aid in proselytizing. A secular theatre that employed American themes, personages, and environment was not long in developing, but it was still never far removed from the dominant Iberian patterns. The concepts and techniques of playmaking reflected the current trends in the western European theatre throughout the Baroque and Neoclassical periods, and produced in some cases dramatists such as Juan Ruiz de Alarcón and Manuel Eduardo de Gorostiza who properly belong to both Spain and Mexico. Even the political and economic rupture precipitated by the nineteenth-century wars of independence did little to break the cultural or dramatic alliances with the mother country, and Romanticism set the style for a movement that lasted throughout the century. The realism that characterizes the Spanish *alta comedia* has only sporadic manifestations in the Americas, and Modernism, the personal creation of the Nicaraguan poet Rubén Darío, had little or no impact on the general theatre trajectory. The fact is that until the twentieth century, the theatrical traditions of Latin America remained closely linked to the Spanish patterns.

The twentieth century has witnessed a different evolution, one that marks an unprecedented period of independence. In the River Plate area, impoverished European emigrants began to deluge Argentina before 1900, in search of prosperity in a land of opportunity. The atmosphere created by the fusion of the picturesqueness of the recent arrivals in contact with the established atmosphere provided the raw material for the modernized costumbristic play. The emphasis upon local color and types, in the manner of the nineteenth-century Bretón de los Herreros plays, now focused upon the gaucho types and the conflict of cultures. In 1886 the gaucho novel *Juan Moreira* of Eduardo Gutiérrez was adapted for pantomime and produced by the circus with the Uruguayan clown José Podestá in the principal role. The old Spanish picaresque forms, fused with the European realistic-naturalistic influence, were assimilated into local elements, and the new style *sainete criollo*, produced on the stages of Buenos Aires and Montevideo, took on a moralizing purpose in interpreting the destiny of the country and the values, social problems, and ethnic complications of her people. The culmination of this theatre lies in the production of the Uruguayan-born master, Florencio Sánchez. During the Golden Decade of Argentine theatre (1900–10), the self-taught Sánchez was a faithful observer of the daily life and customs of his people. Although his weaknesses in psychology, philosophy, and sociology often resulted in simple solutions and stereotyped characters struggling against enormous odds, he understood the principles of dramatic construction sufficiently well to produce such masterworks as *La gringa* (1904) and *Barranca abajo* (1905). In the process, he set in motion a style of theatre adopted by Gregorio Laferrère, Ernesto Herrera, Robert J. Payró, and Alberto Vacarezza that remained popular for years and that showed the picturesqueness of certain atmospheres and exalted some popular types, often in caricature, for both serious and humorous effects.

Other parts of Latin America were dominated during the same period by a similar costumbristic theatre mixed with a liberal sampling of farces, operettas, and revues, which inhibited the expansion of serious theatre. During the first decade of this century in Mexico, the peace and economic progress proclaimed by the regime of Porfirio Díaz did little to foment the development of national dramatic art. The theatre seemed little more than a prolongation of the usages of the previous century, with the exception that the decade of the Mexican Revolution saw the rise of some insignificant political drama. If the period of the Mexican Revolution produced only second-rate theatre, it did, nevertheless, pave the way for the theatrical revolution that was to shake Mexico and eventually the other theatrical capitals of Latin America. The period following World War I had generated a feeling of despair that ruptured conventional literary forms and spawned an endless number of avant-garde movements that attempted a new vision of reality. The intellectual elite of Mexico, closely attuned to the vanguard manifestos of their European brothers, Tristan Tzara, Filippo Tommaso Marinetti, Pierre Reverdy, etc., initiated a period of poetic experimentation that quickly infiltrated the theatrical circles. In 1928 Xavier Villaurrutia and Salvador Novo, under the guidance of Antonieta Rivas Mercado, established the Teatro de Ulises. The Ulises accomplished the reform that earlier groups such as the Union of Dramatic Authors and the Group of Seven Authors had been unable to effect; and although the Ulises soon ceased to exist, other groups continued the spirit of the movement. Collectively, they rebelled against the stifling conformity to previous, now outdated, styles of acting, directing, and scene design, to plays written for an egocentric principal actor or actress, to the concept of the prompter's box, and to the inflexible design of theatre architecture, lighting, and sound equipment. Instead, these experimental groups, dedicated to searching out the best theatre on a world scale, introduced the techniques currently in vogue, following the models of their European masters—Gordon Craig, Max Reinhardt, Konstantin Stanislavski, and Erwin Piscator. The public was offered a panoramic view of universal theatre, with increased importance given to the director's role in creating a total performance through his control over its multiple aspects. This tendency toward universality and the attempt to deal with cultural values of other countries still resulted largely in an imported theatre, but exercises in translation to Spanish stimulated the translators themselves. From Sophocles and Shakespeare and Shaw they passed to their own original creations: *Parece mentira* (1933) by Xavier Villaurrutia, *Ifigenia cruel* (1934) by Alfonso Reyes, *Ser o no ser* (1934) by Celestino Gorostiza. The host of small experimental groups that succeeded the Teatro de Ulises, especially Gorostiza's Teatro de Orientación (1932–39), resulted in a new theatre public, new actors and directors who controlled their material and were able to interpret and balance a performance, and the establishment of many small new theatres, most with a very limited capacity.

A unique phenomenon in the Mexican theatre is the contribution of another dramatic giant, Rodolfo Usigli, who does not properly belong to the experimental movement. A prolific dramatist, a professor of theatrical history at the National University, and in recent years his country's ambassador to Norway, Usigli has captured the historical, sociological, and political problems of Mexican reality in such plays as *El gesticulador* (1937) and *Corona de sombra* (1943). In the tradition of his idol, Bernard Shaw, Usigli presents the ideas implicit in his dramas in explicit prologues and epilogues.

Throughout the history of the Americas, the lines of communication among the various Latin countries have been notably tenuous. Latin Americans have always been more closely attuned to the life-styles of Madrid, Paris, or New York than they have been to the cultural or political events in their own hemisphere. Recent evidence would indicate that this pattern may be in the process of change. In any event, the independent theatre movement that began in the River Plate area almost simultaneously with the Mexican movement is most likely related only through a common source of inspiration. The first group formed was the Teatro del Pueblo in 1930, which began as the work of one man, the writer Leónidas Barletta. Espousing the same ideals of bringing fresh life to techniques of stage performance and in the training of theatrical personnel and a new public, this group inspired the formation of some fifty subsequent independent groups. The usual foreign authors were presented—Luigi Pirandello, Jean Cocteau, Eugene O'Neill, etc.—which led to the introduction of more than twenty Argentine authors. Of these, Roberto Arlt is the only avant-garde author to have produced an organic body of work. The beginning of the Peronista regime marks the decline of the independent theatres, at which time the professional companies turned to the relative success of popular Broadway productions instead of continuing the valiant struggle of the "independentistas" in nurturing national themes, atmosphere, language, and characters.

The same spirit of experimentation characteristic of this internecine period also motivated the theatre in other areas of Latin America. In the Puerto Rico of the 1930s, road companies traveled around the island performing a popular *commedia dell'arte* theatre based on local types. Emilio Belaval created the nationalist movement in the island's theatre by staging Puerto Rican works and thereby developing an interested public. A drama contest of the Ateneo and the formation of Belaval's group Areyto in 1940 brought to prominence Manuel Méndez Ballester, Luis Rechani Agrait, and Fernando Sierra Berdecía, the precursors of the current Puerto Rican playwrights concerned with the problems of insular identity.

In Brazil, the *teatro ligeiro*—musical revues, operettas, etc.—had dominated the stage since the era of Artur Azevedo. Although the Week of Modern Art in 1922 brought postwar avant-garde material in literature and the arts to Brazil, Alvaro Moreyra and Oswalde de Andrade were unable to achieve public acceptance with their incomprehensible plays. A partial renovation occurred during the economic crises of the 1930s when Joracy Camargo advanced his sociopolitical theories revolving around class struggle in plays such as *Deus lhe Pague* (1932), but the new orientation did not take shape until Os Comediantes was formed in 1938. This group's production of Nelson Rodrigues' *Vestido de Noiva* (1943), under the direction of the Polish refugee Zbigniew Ziembinski, used expressionistic techniques of lighting, rhythm and movement to present the psychic disassociations of a moribund woman. For the first time, Brazilian theatre began to reflect the aesthetic revolution of the period.

This fifteen year period (1928–43) of frenetic activity on the part of experimental, amateur, and university groups saw the Latin American theatre break the grip of European traditions, and launch a new pattern of independent activity. The renewed interest in classical motifs and American themes combined with modern views on psychology and the surrealists' interest in fantasy and the dream world. With concepts of multiple staging, fractured time elements, and expressionistic moods, the theatre broke from its simple realistic or costumbristic styles and entered a new period of maturity.

The post-World War II era, then, presents a new level of theatrical sophistication, which places Latin America in serious competition with the world stage. Frivolous theatre continues to exist in Latin America, just as it does in other modern countries, and a public in search of light entertainment continues to make it a successful commercial venture. But a substantial serious theatre exists, committed to commentary on contemporary values and problems. Much of the sensationalism, melodrama, and sentimentality of earlier periods has been suppressed through improved control over dramatic structure and technique. The conflicts of reality and illusion and the concepts of alienation and absurdity have found a Latin American expression through young playwrights eager to show themselves as valid interpreters of the human condition. In line with the prevalent attitudes of the period, the general tone of their works is one of disillusionment. Man is seen to be incapable of adjusting to a changing environment and to the corrosive effects of time; he is a victim of an insensitive society, or simply of his own imperfect nature. His identity crisis reveals the multiple implications of the eternal question, "Who am I?" To extract meaning from a chaotic world may appear to be futile, but the attempt at least connotes a guardedly optimistic view. Analysis creates awareness, and throughout Latin America, the playwrights explore the social, political, religious, racial, sexual, psychological, and metaphysical aspects of the Latin American ambiance.

The young generation of writers often subscribes to a liberal political policy, which serves as a useful point of departure in criticizing real or potential evils. To obviate governmental censorship, it is frequently expedient to adopt a classical theme or a historical figure to disguise the contemporary issue at fault. From Brazil, a country that has endured a succession of erratic administrations, Augusto Boal's *Revolução na America do Sul* (1960) suggests the ubiquitous revolutions that substitute one oligarchy for another. Through his Teatro de Arena, the adaptations of Zumbi[2] and Simón Bolívar have revealed an increasingly militant posture. The Caribbean islands have felt the strong hand of dictatorships or the vested interests of North American enterprises. René Marqués' *La muerte no entrará en palacio* (1957) criticizes the Puerto Rican commonwealth arrangement, Abelard Estorino's *El robo del cochino* (1961) deals with pre-Castro Cuba, and Luis Rafael Sánchez in *La pasión según Antígona Pérez* (1968) attacks a military dictatorship. The unfortunate tendency of this kind of committed theatre is that the playwright's political ambitions tend to override aesthetic considerations to the extent that the play is in danger of becoming a political diatribe. Only an extremely skillful dramatist can handle the two elements successfully.

Social conditions are equally susceptible to a leftist treatment, in which the inequities of the system and the exploitation of the lower classes by a comfortable bourgeoisie are denounced. The conflict may take the form of the eternal class struggle between the have's and the have-not's, as in Egon Wolff's *Los invasores* (1962), or the struggles of the Brazilian *favelados* (slum dwellers) in Gianfrancesco Guarnieri's *Eles não usam black-tie* (1958) or Alfredo Dias Gomes' *A Invasão* (1962). Again, it may take the form of the hapless individual at the mercy of an exploiting society that usurps his rights and his personal freedom, as in Agustín Cuzzani's *Sempronio* (1962), in which the victim is dehumanized and depersonalized in order to serve the ends of the state.

A favorite theme with the Latin American playwrights has been the depiction of the North American, either as an imperialistic intruder upon Latin soil, or as a model of cor-

[2] The adopted African name of a runaway Brazilian slave; later a symbol of the Brazilian abolitionist movement. (Cf. English "zombie.")

ruption in his own territory. The Mexican Usigli has observed with relief that the imposition of North American culture upon Mexico is impeded by the language barrier. Federico S. Inclán in *Espaldas mojadas* (1951) and J. Humberto Robles in *Los desarraigados* (1956) are concerned with prejudice and discrimination toward the *braceros* and *pocho* families in the Southwest. In Puerto Rico, several plays by René Marqués, Manuel Méndez Ballester and others, have dealt with the adulterating effect of North American political and economic policies upon the Hispanic tradition of the island, as well as the problems created by the mass migrations of Puerto Ricans to the *barrios* of New York. North American geographic and political proximity with Mexico and Puerto Rico creates a normal source of conflict; what may be more surprising is that the Yankee appears throughout Latin American dramatic literature. El Salvador's Walter Béneke sets his *Funeral Home* (1956) in the United States, apparently in order to capture an environment of alienation. The renowned poet Pablo Neruda has ventured into drama with *Fulgor y muerte de Joaquín Murieta* (1966), a play that presents a rather biased view of the Chilean hero within the hostile climate of the California Gold Rush.

The topic of racial discrimination is not the exclusive province of the United States, however, despite the implications of such plays as the Mexican José Revueltas' *Israel* (1948). Other perceptive writers, observing a similar situation within their own areas, show the injustices, narrow-mindedness, guilt, and tragedies of lives torn by indecision or racked by suspicions about their racial heritage. Celestino Gorostiza examines a Mexican business family for racial considerations in *El color de nuestra piel* (1952). Francisco Arriví's *Vejigantes* (1958) dramatizes the problem through three generations of Puerto Rican woman. Demetrio Aguilera Malta, virtually the only important dramatist of Ecuador, has created an unforgettable horror in *Infierno negro* (1967), a piece that continues the Expressionistic orientation of his earlier works.

The declining importance of the church as the panacea for all personal, social, or metaphysical ills has brought organized religion and the clergy under attack with increasing frequency.

In *Versos de ciego* (1961) Luis Alberto Heiremans of Chile maintained an orthodox position in presenting the Three Wise Men searching for a new symbolic level of meaning in a modern world. More commonly, however, the church is seen as an oppressor, an irrelevant institution that victimizes man and destroys his freedom of thought and expression. Carlos Solórzano, Guatemalan-born but a long-time Mexican resident, presents in *Las manos de Dios* (1956) an inverse view of traditional Christian symbolism, couched within an existential ethic; Dias Gomes in *O Santo Inquérito* (1966) decries the inquisitorial tactics that deny a young girl's right to live.

Problems of sexuality have also become common fare. From the middle-class marital farces of Silveira Sampaio in his *Trilogia do Héroi Grotesco* (1948–49), subjects traditionally considered taboo—incest, prostitution, etc.—have been treated with increasing boldness. Many authors have dealt with homosexuality, such as the Brazilian authors Walmir Ayala in *Nosso filho vai ser mãe* (1959) and Nelson Rodrigues in *O Beijo no Asfalto* (1961), and the Argentine duo Juan Bautista Devoto and Alberto Sábato in *Tejido de sueños* (1962). As a ploy to Latin *machismo*, homosexuals appear frequently for comic relief, either as legitimate characters or as a whim of the director. But plays such as José Vicente's *O Assalto* (1969), also from Brazil, indicate more insight than the previous views.

In addition to those mentioned, other themes also express a Latin American conception of life—the decay of the old social order, the problems of youth, the generation gap, the conflict between provincial and urban life-styles, and many more. Regardless of theme, the serious contemporary plays exhibit a better control of technique than at any previous period in the history of the Latin American theatre. These playwrights with a poetic vision of their material correlate structure, character, and dialogue with the thematic importance of the work. Symbolic lighting and sound effects enhance the total experience, and the new dimensions provided through the inventive use of stage space and the manipulation of time elements create a vital and complex theatre.

Although Latin America was not physically ravaged by

the world wars, the effect on its moral climate was debilitating. Contemporary plays reflect feelings of alienation, anguish, desperation, and futility similar to those expressed by the existentialists and absurdists. Camus' influence has been noted in the plays of René Marqués, Carlos Solórzano, and Osvaldo Dragún. More recently, the Theatre of the Absurd has had a limited impact upon the area. In Cuba, the Revolution has produced, among other things, a new interest in theatre, but both Antón Arrufat and Virgilio Piñera were writing Theatre of the Absurd pieces before the time of Fidel Castro. Arrufat has been censured by the present regime for writing absurdist plays such as *La zona cero* (1959) while remaining aloof from a position of political commitment. Jorge Díaz of Chile in *Cepillo de dientes* (1961), Griselda Gámbaro, the young Argentine author of *Los siameses* (1967), Mexico's Elena Garro in *El árbol* (1967), and Piñera in *Dos viejos pánicos* (1968) all serve as solid evidence of a Latin American interest in the techniques and vision of the Absurd. These two-character plays are violent, grotesque games, the rules of which seem to be a substitute for the religious or moral conventions of an earlier epoch. Language, distorted from normal sequential dialogue, reflects the lack of verbal communication, and parallels the physical violence of interpersonal relationships shattered by feelings of contempt, hatred, and despair. While drawing freely from Samuel Beckett, Eugène Ionesco, Harold Pinter, Edward Albee, and the Spanish absurdist Ramón María de Valle-Inclán, these playwrights proceeded to fashion a uniquely Latin American product.

Theatrical development over the past few years has been greatly assisted by the formation of theatre contests and festivals on a regular basis. In 1946 the Mexican government established the National Institute of Fine Arts to foment national art in a professional and practical way through training actors and directors in artistic centers, and through the organization of professional theatre seasons. Puerto Rico instituted its first annual Festival of Puerto Rican Theatre in 1958. A similar situation prevails in Argentina, Chile, Cuba, etc., where national and international festivals encourage playwrights, actors, directors, and the theatregoing public.

Perhaps the most promising trend is the intercommunication that now exists among the various Latin countries. The first Latin American Festival of University Theatre was celebrated in October, 1968, in the beautifully modern theatre of Manizales, Colombia. In this annual event, university theatre groups from all areas of Latin America present both national and international productions. The forums, conferences, and round-table discussions that accompany this festival, and others, have resulted in a useful exchange of ideas. Theatrical personnel are presently very mobile, traveling extensively throughout the free world and some into the socialist countries. The playwrights represented in this collection, as well as such directors as Jorge Lavelli, Alexandro Jodorowsky, and Juan Carlos Uviedo, are well-informed people, sensitive, alert to change, and inventive. Latin America is no longer a one-way street, receiving but not giving. On the contrary, not only is the best European and American fare presented on the Latin American stage, but Latin American plays are now produced in New York, in university theatres across the United States, in Madrid, Paris, Berlin, and behind the Iron Curtain. This interchange has promoted good international relations, created an awareness of one's neighbor's problems and activities, and sustained the search for a Latin American reality and identity.

Practical considerations have precluded my presenting a complete range of all types of plays in this collection. The selection is obviously quite small, considering the extension of the area and the vast body of material available. The six plays in this anthology, chosen as the best and most representative examples of current themes and techniques, do, however, reveal admirably the trajectory of the current movement, indicate solid points of comparison, and attest to the refinement and sophistication of the contemporary Latin American theatre.

GEORGE WOODYARD

THE FANLIGHTS

RENÉ MARQUÉS

Translated by Richard John Wiezell

In memory of
Arthur and Esther Wiezell

Born in Puerto Rico in 1919, René Marqués has, since the start of his career in 1948, shown himself to be not only a uniquely capable writer but also extremely sensitive to the particular problems of Puerto Rico. Although his early plays fit a realistic-naturalistic category, at the same time they reveal an affinity for experimentation and an inclination toward symbolic theatre that pervades his later production. Strongly imbued with the values of Puerto Rican culture, Marqués is a staunch defender of his heritage and a dedicated nationalist, attempting to prevent, or at least to retard, the erosion of *lo puertorriqueño*, especially as it is threatened by the "colossus to the north." His widely-known *La carreta* (The Oxcart, 1952), written in the Puerto Rican vernacular, exemplifies social concerns and the conflict of the two cultures through the progressive disintegration of a rural Puerto Rican family unit in the slums of San Juan and New York. The preoccupation with political and cultural liberty becomes increasingly evident in *Un niño azul para esa sombra* (1959) and *La muerte no entrará en Palacio* (1959). In his more recent plays, Marqués deals with different levels of alienation: in a political framework in which people exist in a sociopolitical vacuum without valid commitments to life; in a metaphysical sense in which they play out senseless games in a search for salvation; or within a biblical reference of myth and legend with analogies to contemporary life. Marqués' themes demonstrate vital problems of the modern world, and he carefully coordinates plot with dramatic action. These features are, in turn, accented and enhanced by his control of technique and special effects—light, sound, symbolic objects and actions, and the particularly effective and integral usage of time.

Based upon an earlier short story by Marqués called "Purificación en la calle del Cristo," *The Fanlights* (*Los soles truncos*, 1958) dramatizes the interior world of three sisters, a world that touches upon external reality only tangentially through the ingenious use of symbolic lights and sounds. An exaggerated sibling rivalry and a series of cultural crises have produced disastrous results, and the three are committed to a life-style characterized by petty jealousies, envy, greed, and hatred. In expiating their sins, they tolerate each other until the final redemptive purification by fire. Throughout the play, chronological time is the corrosive and ultimately destructive element, yet time is also poetically manipulated to permit the apparitions of the mysterious Hortensia. The play serves, ultimately, as a dramatic metaphor of Marqués' conception of the present-day Puerto Rican. The guilt complex caused both by insularity and conformity manifests itself through subservience or escapism rather than through heroic resistance to the demands of an ever changing world. *The Fanlights*, although an early play within the context of Marqués' dramatic production, remains not only one of his best but also among the most successful of the entire Latin American theatre repertory.

Characters

INÉS
EMILIA
HORTENSIA

Scene

An old house on Cristo Street in San Juan, Puerto Rico.

Time

The present

ACT I

Large sitting room on the second floor of an old house on Cristo Street, Old San Juan. Upstage are three shuttered, double doorways that face out on the balcony. The doors are shut. Above each of the doors is a fanlight made of three panes of colored glass, one red, one blue, and one yellow; the shape of the fanlights suggests the ribbing of a Spanish fan or the rays of the setting sun. At one time these panes were transparent, but now they are covered with a dingy patina of dust, the salt air, and time. The shutters in the doors are also closed, and the only daylight filters into the room through the fanlights.

The house is in a state of near ruin. The sitting room is papered with a floral pattern in green and rose, now much faded and worn. The wallpaper is torn and ragged in several places. On the right wall an enormous water stain has spread out from the ceiling to the floor. Its shape suggests a map of two continents joined by an isthmus.

Downstage right is a bedroom door tightly closed. Above the door is another oval fanlight, sealed off with wooden paneling. Upstage right a mahogany stairway leads to the bedrooms on the floor above.

Stage left, running downstage from the middle of the room, an arch frames the entry hall that leads to the rest of the house. The floor of the hall is on a higher level than the sitting room, a series of steps joining the two. A part of this floor, a semicircle in form, juts into the sitting room. From the center of the arch hangs a badly faded damask drape, gathered together on the downstage side by a frayed silken cord that ends in a cluster of tassels. A part of the entry hall, half hidden in the darkness, is visible from the sitting room.

Random remnants of furniture from an age that knew refinement and elegance stand scattered about the room. A rosewood piano upstage center, and slightly stage right, gives ample room for action around it. A marble dresser, topped by a huge mirror with a gilt rococo frame, stands against the wall between the arch and the back wall of the sitting room. In the center of the room is a Louis XV armchair and a huge Viennese rocking chair. Against the right wall, between the stairway and the closed door, stands an Empire chair. A crystal chandelier, one arm and several prisms missing, hangs from the ceiling, dust-covered and no longer functional. A candelabrum with three sockets, only one of which contains a candle, stands on the dresser. The base of the candelabrum is badly tarnished. A Manila shawl, covered with huge pale roses, made even paler by time, lies across the piano like a tapestry. The silk of the shawl is frayed and worn. On the shawl stands a kerosene lamp. The entire scene has a lackluster, timeworn air. The kerosene lamp and the candle are lighted, despite the bright light of day filtering through the fanlights. The time is early morning of a summer day. Inés enters from the left, carrying a bucket of water and a mop. She is seventy years of age, tall, gaunt, withered, yet filled with energy. She wears an outmoded black dress. She places the bucket and the mop on the floor, downstage left. Then she goes to the doorways and opens one of the shutters. She goes to the dresser and puts out the candle, then to the piano and puts out the kerosene lamp. Rolling up her sleeves, she crosses to the foot of the stairway.

INÉS (*looking up the stairway*): Emilia! Emilia! (*She goes to the bedroom door on the right. About to open the door, she thinks better of it, and picking up the bucket and mop, she leaves them at the foot of the stairway.*) Emilia, here's the water. (*In a shrill, irritated voice.*) Emilia!

EMILIA (*calling down from the rooms above*): Wait a moment, Inés. The sun won't let me comb my hair.

INÉS: The water's ready.

EMILIA: It's the sun, I tell you. I'm not to blame. It's the sun . . .

INÉS (*impatiently*): Come down this minute!

EMILIA: I'm coming! I'm co—oo-ming . . .

Inés goes stage right, opens the door, and goes into the bedroom, closing the door behind her. Emilia slowly descends the stairs. She is a woman of sixty-five, wrenlike, fragile, and yet endowed with a face that reflects a vague, spiritual beauty. Her indecisive gestures frequently betray a deerlike timidity. Her left foot is crippled. She is wearing a gray, turn-of-the-century housecoat, badly worn, but clean and neat.

With the sun coming through that broken shutter and hitting the mirror as it does, you just can't get your hair combed! That's why I've told you, so many times, if we could just fix that shutter . . . (*She interrupts herself, seeing that the room is empty. Leaning against the bannister, she calls sharply.*) Inés. (*She looks into the entry hall and toward the door on the right. Then she calls again, more sharply this time.*) Inés! (*Receiving no answer, she turns, smiles to herself, and hobbles up the stairs as quickly as her lame foot will allow.*)

Suddenly, from the bedroom on the right, the pained voice of Inés.

INÉS (*from the bedroom*): Can you ever forgive me, Hortensia? Can you ever forgive me?

Emilia stops, startled, by Inés' voice. She turns around, her face filled with fear. Her fist clenched at her mouth, and supporting herself against the wall, she totters down one step.

EMILIA (*her fearful voice*): Inés! (*Hearing no reply, she gingerly hobbles down another step.*) Are you asleep, Hortensia? (*Pausing for a moment, she backs up one step.*) Are you still asleep, Hortensia? (*She strains to listen, and hearing nothing, relaxes. Finally she smiles, turns, climbs the stairs quickly, and exits. From the street wafts the crooning of a vendor that slowly fades away in the distance.*)
VOICE: Evil beams . . . love powders . . . coconut kisses . . . try them, lady! Love powder, coconut kisses to sweeten the soul, buy them, lady! Love powder, pretty little coconut kisses . . .

As the Voice of the vendor dies away, Inés enters through the door on the right holding a dishpan of water with a towel over her arm. She closes the door behind her, quickly crosses stage left, and exits through the entry hall. As she does so, Emilia appears at the top of the stairs. She is hiding something behind her back. She glances furtively around the sitting room and, finding it empty, comes down the stairs. When she reaches the bucket of water and the mop, she stops, glances about apprehensively, and takes a tiny chest from behind her back, pressing it to her breast as

*if to protect it from some strange contamination. Then she
gathers up her skirts with an elegant flourish of her fingers
and gracefully circles the bucket to avoid brushing her dress
against it. She notices that one of the blinds is open and
covers her eyes with her forearm to shield them from the
injurious light of day. Still in this position, she edges upstage, like one moving cautiously amidst flames. Squinting
her eyes, she shuts the blinds. Opening her eyes with a sigh
of relief, she hobbles to the piano. She lifts the piano cover
and hides her tiny chest inside. Then she goes to the dresser
and lights the candle put out by Inés a few moments
earlier. As she is about to turn, she notices her reflection
in the mirror and stops, transfixed. She arranges a few stray
hairs, while humming the strains of a Chopin waltz. About
to turn away, she stops again. Still humming, she straightens the collar of her housecoat. She steps back to look at
her reflection, then moves closer to the dresser again for
a better look. Satisfied at last, she turns away from the
mirror and comes downstage center. Suddenly she stops,
wondering what to do next. She glances around and
notices the pail of water. Her humming begins to die
away as she approaches the pail. She stops in front of it,
a questioning look on her face. Her humming stops. At
last she makes her decision, and bending over awkwardly,
she plunges the mop into the pail and gives a few licks to
the first step of the stairway. Then she straightens up and
drops the mop into the pail. Picking up the pail, she
carries it upstage. She sets it on the floor and looks about
her vacantly. Suddenly her eyes catch sight of the piano.
She begins to hum the waltz again and hobbles to the
piano. She fingers the cover over the keys absently, then
opens the back of the piano halfway. Suddenly she starts,
as if awakening from a dream, drops the piano cover, and
rushes upstage. As she approaches the pail, her humming
gradually fades away. She stops in front of the pail, takes
out the mop, and brushes it indifferently along the floor.
She straightens up, drops the mop into the pail, which she
then carries downstage left. She places the pail on the
entry hall ledge. Then she looks around uneasily for
something to while away her boredom. She notices the
Louis XV chair, and, assuming a dignified air, quickly
arranges her hair. Then she smiles and approaches the
empty chair, trying desperately to hide her limp. She*

*curtsies neatly before the chair and seats herself in the
Viennese rocking chair opposite. The Chopin waltz from
offstage accompanies her spoken reverie.*

EMILIA: Forgive me for having made you wait, sir. (*She
arranges the skirt of her dress carefully and begins to rock
gracefully.*) It's the sun, you know. Why, thank you. That's
the way they taught us to walk at the boarding school in
Strasbourg. No, no, my foot was injured at our plantation in
Toa Alta. I was very small at the time. Long before
boarding school, of course. Hortensia was always the most
beautiful. (*She laughs.*) Thank you, you're too gallant.
But really Hortensia is more beautiful than I. (*She stops
rocking, alarmed.*) No . . . please . . . don't let Inés hear
you say that. Inés hates my poetry. She has the same dark
hair as Mama Eugenia. Dark and thick like Málaga wine.
That's what Papa Burkhart says. But that doesn't really
describe her, because Mama Eugenia brought a kind of
beauty from her Andalusia that belonged to the Greeks.
Why, you must have seen her at the last reception given
by the Governor General. She was the lady wearing the
diadem of diamonds and sapphires. (*Adopting the tone
of a footman announcing important guests.*) Doña Eugenia
Sandoval de Burkhart! Yes, she does have a certain regal
air, doesn't she?—just like a queen in a palace. (*She sighs
and goes on rocking.*) You know how those things are!
Inés has probably sold it . . . or pawned it, perhaps, which
amounts to the same thing. And the ruby necklace and
the diamond ring, and the pearl ring, and our silver, too
. . . (*She interrupts herself and stops rocking.*) please don't
ever let Hortensia find out about what's happened! She
thinks that the plantation at Toa Alta is still ours! That
sun is bothering you, isn't it? Let me close the shutters (*She
gets up and goes upstage, continuing her conversation.*)
No, no, it's no trouble at all! I've always said that the
sun bleaches out the rugs. (*She pretends to close the
shutter.*) Mama Eugenia says the same thing over and
over: Close the shutters, girls, or the upholstery on the
furniture will lose its color. Of course, Papa Burkhart gets
furious and opens the shutters one by one, shouting: "Let
the sun in, girls, let the sun in!!" (*She smiles softly and
returns to her chair.*) Why, thank you so much for saying
that. It is true, though. We're an enchanting family. (*With*

a mysterious air, stopping her rocking.) The truth is that the doors stood open until Hortensia said "NO" to life. Yes, she did, even though the lace veil had already arrived from Strasbourg. (*She closes her eyes and rocks, as if in a trance.*) No, no, don't ask me why—I only know that she said "NO" to life—that's all.

INÉS: Emilia!

EMILIA (*startled*): Oh, excuse me, please! I think someone is calling me.

INÉS (*calling offstage*): Emilia! What's going on out there?

EMILIA: Oh! Excuse me, excuse me, please! (*Gets up and crosses stage left, replying in a high, shrill voice.*) I'm . . . why . . . I'm working. (*She stops, retraces her steps, and stops the rocking of the chair, then she crosses left again, complaining softly to herself.*) You can't even carry on a conversation in this mad world, I declare! (*She takes the mop out of the pail and lightly drags it across the entry hall ledge.*)

Inés enters stage left.

INÉS: You haven't done a thing, as usual.

EMILIA: Why, what do you mean, Inesita? Can't you see I'm finishing up? The room is very large. I'm not one of those machines they have nowadays, you know. I'm only a weak old woman. And my foot . . .

INÉS: All right, all right—let's not start that business of your foot all over again—

EMILIA: But, Inesita, I was just explaining all about my foot— and how I fell from that horse at the plantation in Toa Alta, I was very young then, of course, as you know very . . .

INÉS: And to *whom* were you explaining all this?

EMILIA: I? Explaining to someone? Why, I wasn't explaining anything to anyone. Did you say explaining something to someone?

INÉS: Were you talking to yourself again?

EMILIA (*indignantly*): Talking to *myself*? *Me*, talking to myself? Why, of course not! I won't allow you to say such things about me. I wasn't alone. I was speaking to . . . (*She starts to point to the Louis XV chair, then draws her hand back absently.*) to . . . I was speaking . . . (*She drops the mop, walks upstage, and stands facing the closed shutters, her back to Inés. She is silent for a few moments, then speaks with finality and decisiveness.*) I'm sorry I can't help you, Inés.

Inés falls heavily into the Louis XV chair.

INÉS: I didn't ask for your help. I *never* ask anyone for help. I've spent a hellish night. I just brought some water up from the cistern. I'm going out now.

EMILIA (*half turning around*): I hate to see you go out . . . like that . . .

INÉS (*getting up*): That's my business.

EMILIA: Perhaps if I . . .

INÉS: When you're through mopping, take the pail out in the kitchen. (*She goes to the stairway, stops, and looks back.*) And Emilia, don't let the candle in Hortensia's room go out.

EMILIA (*going toward the stairway, with anguish in her voice*): No, Inesita, not that!

Inés stops, turns, and stares coldly at her sister. Emilia bows her head confusedly.

I'm afraid.

INÉS: Afraid?

EMILIA: Did I say afraid, no, I'm not explaining it properly. Grief mixed with fear, but I feel the grief most. Oh, my God, how terrible Time is! Hortensia had on her blue satin dress and had just danced a mazurka with the Governor General. Do you remember? (*Defiantly.*) Inés! Inesita! How can you face Time and not die of horror?

The sound of a mazurka being played is heard offstage. The stage lights dissolve to a soft lavender.

(*Emilia continues in a narrative tone.*) That was when the Spanish officer came up to her and said, smiling, "Your beauty is the most dazzling at this reception, Miss Hortensia."

Inés turns brusquely away and begins to go up the stairway.

And they danced another mazurka. Time wasn't horrible *then*. It hardly seemed to go by at all!

The lavender glow and the music both intensify.

It was at the Governor General's residence. And poor
Emilia with her hair pulled tight against her head—how I
hated that hair!—sitting primly next to Mama Eugenia.
"Thank you sir, but Emilia is still too young for dancing.
However, if you would care to dance with my other
daughter, Inés"—And Papa Burkhart, with his icy, defiant
smile: "Strasbourg will never belong to France, my lord!"
And time *didn't hurt* us and Strasbourg *didn't* belong to
France. And the ballroom was ablaze with lights, and
Hortensia laughed in her officer's arms, and they whirled
about, he in his magnificent uniform and Hortensia in her
dress of blue satin. (*In a muffled shout, as if to dispel
the vision.*) How can you face the horrible image of *Time*,
Inés?

*The music stops suddenly and daylight returns. Inés has
disappeared from view at the top of the staircase.*

(*Emilia looks around wildly, then crosses to the left, picks
up the pail, and exits through the entry hall.*)

*The stage is empty for a brief period. Then Inés appears at
the top of the stairs. She has on an old-fashioned hat and
carries an old black purse trimmed in tassels over her
arm. She puts on her gloves as she comes down the stairs.
As she reaches the bottom, she notices that the blinds are
shut and that the candle is lighted again. She opens the
blinds, then goes to the dresser and snuffs out the candle.
As the flame goes out, a strange sound is heard, like the
breaking of a violin string. At the same time, the morning
light coming through the fanlights and the open blinds
fades out. There is a moment of complete darkness and
then the right side of the room begins to glow in eerie blue
light.*

*Hortensia appears at the top of the stairway. She is a girl
of nineteen, with a splendid Nordic beauty and the haughty
bearing of a queen. She is wearing an elaborate, fin-de-
siècle housecoat. She is languidly combing her long blonde
hair.*

HORTENSIA: Were you calling me, Inés?
INÉS (*in the shadows to the left, in front of the dresser, her
back to Hortensia*): Yes, Hortensia.

HORTENSIA: Well then?

INÉS: The lace for the veil has arrived from Strasbourg.

HORTENSIA: Yes, I saw it. Mama Eugenia and I opened the box.

INÉS: Do you like it?

HORTENSIA: It's not bad . . .

INÉS: You deserve the *best*.

HORTENSIA (*slowly beginning to descend the stairs, still combing her hair*): Thank you, Inés. I suppose that *was* the best Papa Burkhart's relations could get.

INÉS: You deserve the best in a husband too—

HORTENSIA (*laughing*): I have the best in a fiancé—

INÉS: *No.*

HORTENSIA (*sits down in the Empire chair and begins to tie a ribbon in her hair. Speaking good-naturedly*): Now *really*, Inesita, you never think anything is good enough for me! But, after all, San Juan isn't Paris, you know, nor is it Berlin or Madrid. Mama Eugenia is happy. And even poor Papa Burkhart . . .

INÉS: Why did you say poor?

HORTENSIA: Just a manner of speaking. But you know as well as I do, a German naturalist stuck with farming in the tropics . . .

INÉS: And doing very well.

HORTENSIA: Did I say otherwise?

INÉS: And he *loves* you—more than anyone.

HORTENSIA: Because I resemble him. Sheer masculine vanity, my dear.

INÉS: He has the looks of a Nordic god.

HORTENSIA: Which makes me out to be a Valkyrie, at the very least. (*She laughs.*)

INÉS: No one can deny that you're beautiful.

HORTENSIA (*as if she hadn't heard her*): You have Mama Eugenia's hair.

INÉS: But not her face.

HORTENSIA: And the same bearing of a Moorish queen.

INÉS: There is *no* Moorish blood in our veins.

HORTENSIA: That's just an expression, my dear. I'm quite aware that we're Celtic Iberians through the Málaga branch. But now, when I marry, we'll have—

INÉS (*bursting out as she hits her fist on the marble top of the dresser*): He isn't worthy of you, Hortensia!

HORTENSIA: What a foolish thing to say! Papa Burkhart has studied his background, his whole family. . . . His blood is . . .

INÉS: It isn't the *blood* of your officer I'm talking about!

HORTENSIA (*suddenly sober*): Why do you always call him "your officer"? (*Getting up.*) Why don't you ever mention his name?

INÉS (*disturbed*): I've never thought it was important.

HORTENSIA: Perhaps not, but it does seem strange that you never call him by name. After all, he'll soon be my husband.

INÉS (*stifling a scream*): No!

Pause.

HORTENSIA (*going toward the piano, speaking slowly and deliberately, with her gaze fixed on the back of Inés' neck*): Or perhaps you'd rather that he weren't?

INÉS (*straightening up before the mirror*): What do you mean?

HORTENSIA: I'm not really sure—What do *you* mean, Inés?

INÉS: Why nothing really . . . I only wanted to . . . warn you.

HORTENSIA: About him, you mean?

INÉS: I don't want to say any more about it.

HORTENSIA: But you've already said *something*—if you really didn't want to tell me, you should have kept silent. Why did you call me just now? What is it that you've been wanting to tell me all along?

INÉS: I *won't*, Hortensia! I *won't* destroy your happiness.

Pause.

HORTENSIA (*leaning on the piano*): Then it has to do with my *happiness*. Nothing less than my happiness. And it seems you have the power to destroy it!

Brief pause.

(*Wistfully.*) Do you intend to use that power, Inés?

INÉS (*still with her back to Hortensia*): No, you don't understand at all—I only wanted to tell you . . .

HORTENSIA: Don't say it! (*She turns and goes quickly toward the stairway.*)

INÉS: But you just asked me—

HORTENSIA (*stops, without turning back. Sharply*): That's

not so! I didn't ask you to destroy a dream. Just the opposite, Inés. I'm asking you *not to!*

INÉS: But you *can't* be happy if you don't know the truth!

HORTENSIA (*rushing toward the stairs*): I prefer that risk to the other. I don't want to hear any more!

INÉS (*firmly*): It's my duty to tell you.

HORTENSIA (*starting up the stairs*): I don't *want* to know. I don't want to know!

INÉS (*in a shout that mingles triumph with hatred*): He has a mistress, Hortensia! And a son by her!

The shout freezes Hortensia on the stairway. A tense silence follows.

HORTENSIA (*without turning*): Who is she?

INÉS: The herb-seller in Imperial Street.

HORTENSIA (*turning, in a terrible voice*): You're lying!

INÉS: I've never lied to you, and I'm not lying now!

Brief pause.

That Spanish officer may be able to swear his love for you. But that doesn't deny the fact that he has given the blue of his eyes to the urchin offspring of an herb-seller.

Hortensia, her emotions shattered, descends the stairs slowly and crosses to the Empire chair. She sinks into it with a sob.

HORTENSIA (*in a low voice*): Are you sure, Inés?

Pause.

How did you find out?

INÉS: Nanny told me. She didn't even dare tell Mama Eugenia. But don't think for a moment that I only took her *word* for it. I made sure myself, later. I went to Imperial Street . . .

HORTENSIA (*slowly lifting her head, without turning to Inés*): You had the courage to do that?

INÉS (*standing proud and erect in front of the mirror*): You know there isn't *anything* I wouldn't do for you.

HORTENSIA (*after a brief pause, bitterly*): Yes, I know. (*She rises and goes toward the stairway. She goes up the first step and stops, her voice filled with pain.*) You've done your "duty" now, Inés. You've destroyed a dream. I don't know what your punishment will be. But I'm sure that it will be terrible. (*Struggling to control her emotions.*) Of course I won't marry him now. (*She climbs two steps more and stops.*) And really, it's much better that way. Because I could never *share* his love with another woman, never! (*She goes up another step and stops. Leaning heavily on the bannister, her voice a near whisper.*) Not with *anyone*!

INÉS (*her voice trembling*): Then, you know that Emilia loves him? You've read Emilia's poetry?

HORTENSIA (*coldly*): I'm not talking about Emilia. Our sister may be capable of loving and of writing poetry, but capable of destroying, *never*!

INÉS (*flustered*): I don't . . . I don't understand you, Hortensia.

HORTENSIA: Take a good look at the ugly reflection in that mirror, Inés. (*She continues up. When she reaches the top of the stairs, she stops and wheels around.*) Inés, do people know about it? Do they know about his . . . with this . . . woman?

Inés remains silent.

Very well. What I didn't know couldn't hurt me. But now, I could never face the looks—and the gossip!

Pause.

I'll never set foot out of this house again!

The blue light begins to dim.

(*Hortensia turns to exit, then half turns back, speaking in a soft, calm voice.*) Inés, I ask you, please, never open the shutters in the sitting room again.

The blue light fades out. In the darkness Hortensia's voice can still be heard as she exits.

From this day on, the pure sunlight of Cristo Street must never reach us.

The darkness is pierced by the strange sound of a breaking violin string followed by the thud of a falling body. The bright morning light rushes through the open shutter and the fanlights. Hortensia is gone. Inés lies unconscious on the floor in front of the dresser. Emilia enters left. She

*is eating a half-peeled banana. As she comes down the
steps from the entry hall, she notices Inés. Her first, child-
like reaction is to hide the banana behind her back. Then,
realizing that Inés is in no condition to scold her, she puts
the banana in the pocket of her housecoat and gingerly
approaches the inert body of her sister.*

EMILIA: Inés! Inesita! Inés! (*She bends over her, takes off
her sister's hat, and slaps her hands.*) My Lord, she's
fainted again. I'll just bet she's had nothing to eat, as usual.
You're going to die of hunger, Inesita. And here I am,
eating the only piece of fruit . . . (*She takes the banana
out of her pocket.*) Here, Inesita, have a bite. No, no,
what she needs are the smelling salts. That's it, those
English smelling salts! Now where *are* those smelling salts?
(*She gets up, the banana still in her hand.*) The smelling
salts. (*She goes to the bedroom door.*) The English smelling salts. (*About to put her hand on the knob, she stops,
looks at the door, dread etched on her face, turns quickly
away.*) No, no, all we need is the smelling salts, just the
smelling salts. (*She climbs the stairs to the bedrooms
above, while Inés begins to regain consciousness.*) She's
always fainting—you're going to die of hunger, Inesita—
I've told you so many times. A nice chicken broth. A
nourishing consommé. A fried chicken. If only we still had
our poultry runs at the plantation in Toa Alta!
INÉS (*weakly*): Emilia . . .
EMILIA (*turns and descends the stairs*): Here I am! I was
going to look for the smelling salts. They always help.
Though I still insist your trouble is hunger, Inés. (*She
remembers the banana and slips it into the pocket of her
housecoat.*) Thank the Lord you're all right now. The
awful thing Time can do! Time is horrible, truly it is! (*She
helps Inés to her feet.*) Come here and sit down for a
minute. (*She helps Inés to the Viennese rocking chair.
Inés sits down.*) I'm going to make you some orange
blossom tea . . . (*She crosses stage left, then stops.*) But I
wonder if there's any sugar left?
INÉS: Forget about it, I'm all right.
EMILIA: I don't think there's any sugar. There's never any
sugar.
INÉS (*getting up*): I must go now. (*She goes to the mirror
and replaces her hat.*)

EMILIA (*pleadingly, after a moment of silence*): Does it have to be today, Inés?

INÉS: Yes.

EMILIA: Couldn't we . . . couldn't we find a spot for her here, in our patio?

INÉS (*sharply*): Out there, in the world, there are stupid men who make rules and laws, Emilia.

EMILIA: But we don't live in *that* world.

INÉS: That doesn't make any difference.

EMILIA: Yes, it *does* make a difference. They may attack us from out there with hunger, and with Time. But here they have no power. They have no control over us here.

INÉS: Don't be too sure—

EMILIA: You wouldn't let them! Just like always. . . . You'd pretend to be mad as you've done before, to keep them out. The creditors and the real estate people. And the tourists— fending off the prying and poking noses of strangers who would like to wallow in our degradation and our misery.

INÉS: And just how long do you think we'll be able to call this place ours? It will be lost the same as the plantation was. There'll be an auction if there hasn't been one already. (*Irritated.*) Do you think I can keep track of everything? And then—

EMILIA: And then?

INÉS: Why, they'll turn us out of course!

EMILIA (*terrified*): No, Inés! Not that!

INÉS: What difference will it make *what* they do! Hortensia is no longer with us. They'll take us to an institution—

EMILIA (*shouting*): Stop it! Stop it!

INÉS (*a bitter irony in her voice*): They'll take *good* care of us, Emilia.

EMILIA: I don't want anyone to take care of me! What I want is to die if this house isn't going to be ours any longer!

A pause. Inés looks at Emilia intently. She approaches her sister and, running her hand along Emilia's cheek, asks softly.

INÉS: Do you really mean that?

EMILIA (*clutching her*): I swear I do.

INÉS (*holding Emilia tightly, a strange smile on her face as she continues to stroke her cheek*): It isn't easy to die

when one wants to. (*A brief pause. In an ominous voice.*)
Or perhaps it is. (*Suddenly pulling away from Emilia.*)
Very well then—forget about the house for now. After all,
it's still ours.

EMILIA: It must always be ours. This is the house that Hortensia loved, the house where we destroyed Hortensia's
dream, the house where we've suffered for our crime for
these many long years. (*In a low voice.*) The house should
suffer *with* us. It's our accomplice. No one must save it
from its suffering. We *will* struggle to keep it, won't we?

INÉS: Of course, just as long as we can . . .

EMILIA: And we *can*, Inés! (*Adopting her childish tone.*) We
shall keep the shutters closed tight. I've told you so many
times, Inesita! Don't open the shutters! Don't *ever* open
them. And as for Hortensia—

INÉS: I have to go now. (*She starts rapidly to the left. Emilia's
voice stops her.*)

EMILIA: But don't let them take Hortensia away. I told you
already, perhaps, right here in our patio—we could dig it
ourselves—

INÉS: Stop that! (*She goes out through the entry hall.*)

EMILIA (*crossing stage left quickly*): Inés. Inesita! (*Speaking
from the arch to the entry hall to Inés, listening from
offstage left.*) Please make sure that it's beautiful. It
doesn't have to be like Papa Burkhart's, of course—just so
it's not ugly. I beg you, Inesita. Hortensia deserves the
best. I know it's a gift from the Welfare people. But do
what you can, Inesita. Just so it's not ugly!

The street door in the entry hall slams shut behind Inés.

*Emilia turns, heaves a sigh, and shaking her head as if
to clear it of unhappy thoughts, crosses to the piano. She
smiles, opens the back of the piano, and takes out the
tiny chest. She looks at it tenderly, presses it against her
breast and begins to rock it to and fro, humming the same
Chopin waltz. She goes through the motions of a few
dance steps. As she whirls about, she notices that the
shutter is open again. She stops her dancing and shields
her eyes with her arm. She gropes her way upstage and
closes the shutter. Then she goes to the dresser, places the
chest on the marble top as if she were laying an offering
on an altar, and lights the candle.*

As she does so, the same sound of a breaking violin string is heard, the fanlights dim, and the room begins to swim in a blue glow. A muted piano offstage takes up the Chopin waltz.

(Emilia opens the chest and takes out a small book of poems. She opens the book and reads, her voice fraught with emotion.)

> I am the tiny pebble between your hands of musk
> Archangel's wings for your love's abandon . . .
> The Paschal Lamb for your shining sword,
> And the Valley of the Echo for the sound of your
>   voice . . .

Hortensia appears in the entry hall. She is now a woman of thirty. She wears a severe black dress, appropriate for mourning. She is even more lovely than she was at nineteen, but now there is a cold aloofness in her beauty.

(Emilia presses the open book against her breast, closes her eyes, and, lifting her head, recites ecstatically.)

> The Paschal Lamb for your shining sword,
> And the Valley of the Echo for the sound of your
>   voice . . .

HORTENSIA (*simply*): You loved him too, Emilia.

Emilia lets out a shriek and doubles forward on the dresser as if stabbed in the stomach.

Hortensia moves slowly into the blue glow that bathes the left side of the sitting room.

Don't be afraid. I know about your poetry. Your book of poems in the sandalwood chest.

A brief pause.

You always did write poetry, Emilia, ever since we were at boarding school in Strasbourg. But your poems were different then.

EMILIA (*still crumpled up on the dresser*): Hortensia . . .

HORTENSIA: No, they were different from these. You began to write this kind of poetry after we returned to San Juan. In fact, right after the reception at the Governor's residence.

EMILIA (*still hunched over the dresser*): Hortensia, you were so lovely in your blue satin dress.

HORTENSIA: "Who is that girl with her hair worn so severely, Miss Hortensia?" "That's my sister Emilia." "Doesn't your sister *ever* dance?" "No, the poor thing has a crippled foot."

EMILIA (*beginning to straighten up*): But you knew I could dance, Hortensia. Despite my crippled foot, I could still dance!

HORTENSIA (*reciting*): "Your faunlike foot standing upon a word: 'love.'" Another one of your images, Emilia. And you thought that a sandalwood chest could hide your poetry.

EMILIA (*replacing the book in the chest*): This sandalwood chest is where I hide my heart. (*She closes the chest.*)

HORTENSIA: It's a poor excuse for a heart then.

EMILIA (*turning toward her, imploringly*): Don't be cruel to me, Hortensia!

HORTENSIA (*sweetly*): Forgive me, dear sister. I didn't mean to be, really.

EMILIA (*noticing Hortensia's dress*): But . . . but . . . you didn't put on your blue dress . . . I should have liked . . . You know . . . The blue satin . . .

HORTENSIA: I'm in mourning, Emilia.

EMILIA: In mourning? But it's too early . . . for that . . . I mean, no one . . .

HORTENSIA: Mama Eugenia died when the century did . . .

EMILIA: That's true.

HORTENSIA: And Death fell in love with us then. Papa Burkhart—and then Nanny. And our aunts and uncles in Málaga. And our relations in Strasbourg. It seems to me now that I've always been in mourning.

EMILIA: But Mama Eugenia was the first to go. (*She goes to Hortensia and kisses her tenderly.*) You poor thing! How grieved you must be! How much pain her death caused us all! (*Maternally.*) Come and sit down—You must be all worn out, poor thing. (*She helps her sister to the Louis XV chair. Hortensia has a look of complete exhaustion mixed with suffering.*) It *was* a beautiful funeral, though, wasn't it? That's some comfort!—and how lovely Mama Eugenia looked!

HORTENSIA: Just as she always did.

EMILIA: Yes, just like always. (*She strokes Hortensia's hair fondly.*)

HORTENSIA: Though she was a little more pale than usual. Did you notice?

EMILIA (*goes to the Viennese rocking chair and sits down*):
She began to feel ill when the invasion came.

Muted sound of a bugle from offstage.

HORTENSIA: "It's the barbarians, my girls, the barbarians have
arrived!"

EMILIA: We always call the ones who change the world we
love "barbarians." "They're shelling Saint Joseph's Church!
Just look, Eugenia, old girl!" But they didn't only shell a
church, they bombarded the very *foundations* of our world.
That's why Mama Eugenia called them "barbarians." And
a short while later she began to feel ill—

HORTENSIA: The doctors called it pernicious anemia.

EMILIA: And Papa Burkhart called their diagnosis nonsense.

HORTENSIA: Because Mama Eugenia was really dying of grief.

EMILIA: The grief of seeing a foreign flag flying where her
own pennant had always waved before. "That's why your
mother is dying, my girls."

The sound of the bugle dies away.

HORTENSIA: But it *was* a beautiful funeral.

EMILIA: That's just what I was telling you. All of San Juan
came to the cathedral. The bishop . . .

HORTENSIA: Was that when our world began to fall apart?

EMILIA: No. Time was set loose later.

HORTENSIA: If that's so, why did you want to see me in
my blue dress?

EMILIA: I don't know. That's the way I loved you best. Then
too, today is—

HORTENSIA (*sharply*): Where is Inés?

EMILIA (*perplexed*): Inés? Why, she went out.

HORTENSIA: Tell me the truth, has she gone out to pawn
something? Some more of our jewels? (*Suddenly her voice
breaks into a childish whine.*) Last year she sold the ruby
bracelet. That was a cruel thing to do. She knew very well
that I'd rather die than see us lose our jewels. (*Pleadingly.*)
Don't let her do it, Emilia.—The jewels are the only things
that give security to my life. There's so much ugliness—

EMILIA (*breaking in quickly*): Yes, there is much ugliness,
in the world outside—

HORTENSIA: No, no, in ourselves, Emilia. Jealousy, envy,
pride, selfishness, anger—

EMILIA (*reproaching her violently*): Don't mention those things, Hortensia! Such things can't exist in our world!

HORTENSIA: Dream of our world in any way you wish—I know the ugliness within us, that rises up and stalks us despite your dreams.

EMILIA: Time is to blame for bringing us all that ugliness.

HORTENSIA: Well, I guess it really doesn't matter now—But the jewels—they *are* beautiful—with a beauty that nothing can destroy, not even Time itself. When I'm hidden away in my room, I put on Mama Eugenia's diadem and suddenly all the ugliness disappears. Your frustration, Emilia, and Inés' envy and jealousy, my terrible hatred, our poverty—they all disappear.

EMILIA: And Time itself—

HORTENSIA: Yes, and even Time itself. (*Recovering her authoritarian tone.*) And so, you see you must tell me truly —has Inés gone to pawn something?

EMILIA (*getting up nervously*): No, she can't have done that. There's nothing left to pawn.

HORTENSIA (*getting up haughtily*): Then she's begging, I suppose?

EMILIA: Not exactly, but—

HORTENSIA (*disdainfully*): A beggar!

EMILIA (*almost crying*): What can you expect! If she doesn't . . . you have your pride. And I, I can't stand the sun. I keep on telling her that. "Close the shutters, Inés." But you know Inés. She has a will of iron. And now, ever since we lost the plantation at Toa Alta—

HORTENSIA: What are you saying?

EMILIA: Yes, it's true! The plantation is gone. You weren't supposed to know. We never told you—but that's the reason. That's why Inés has to go out and beg. Death and Time—But she's not out begging today—I can promise you that . . . not today. And it really doesn't matter any longer that you know—about her begging, I mean. I can't allow you to go on torturing her. You know how well she's treated you, how she's spoiled you, without one complaint—And last night . . . she did everything . . . up to the very last moment . . . And now today . . . I wouldn't have the courage!

HORTENSIA: So the plantation at Toa Alta is lost! (*Her voice harsh with hatred.*) You've sold our lands!

EMILIA: We didn't want to do it, Hortensia. They were

confiscated, I think, though I really don't understand it all very well. We owed so many years of back taxes. Our old notary warned us of that a long time ago: "They'll just sell the plantation at public auction"—that is, he warned *Inés*. And you see, he knew what he was talking about . . .

HORTENSIA: That miserable traitor!

EMILIA: But, Hortensia, what else could we do?

HORTENSIA: We could have fought on! That's the key, Emilia! To fight tooth and nail! In the face of hunger, Time and misery. That miserable old fox could come whining to me as often as you please: "Now's the time to sell, Miss Hortensia. The Americans will pay well." And do you think I'd finally tell him: "Go ahead, go ahead, you old rascal, sell, sell, sell, for when hunger is staring you down, can money be put to good use"? Never, Emilia, never! Twenty, a hundred, a thousand times, I'll tell him the same thing: "Our lands will never belong to the barbarians." (*Pausing, noticing that Emilia is sobbing.*) Why are you crying, my dear?

EMILIA: I shouldn't have told you. Inés would kill me if she knew—

HORTENSIA (*maternally, embracing Emilia*): Cheer up, cheer up—stop that crying! We won't say anything about this to Inés. Dry your eyes. We don't want her to see you've been crying. Hmmm, let's see if we can cheer you up. Do you want me to put on my blue dress?

EMILIA (*calmer now, smiling childishly*): Would you? Would you put it on *for me*? Just for me?

HORTENSIA (*kissing her on the forehead*): Of course, child, of course! Of course, I will—just for you!

A horn honks in the street. The blue glow is extinguished immediately, as well as the candle on the dresser—In the darkness, the sound of the piano ceases abruptly. Daylight suddenly streams through the fanlights. Hortensia is gone. Emilia sits in the Viennese rocking chair. She is rocking slowly, her eyes closed. The horn honks again. Emilia opens her eyes, stops rocking, and looks toward the shutters. She notices that the candle has gone out. She shakes her head in surprise. Then she gets up and goes to the dresser. She stares at the candle, then looks hesitantly around the room. Finally she lights the candle, then rests

*her hands on the sandalwood chest. She smiles at it fondly.
A sudden noise in the entry hall interrupts her reverie.*

EMILIA (*startled*): Is that you, Inés? (*She waits a moment,
then picks up the chest and hides it in the piano.*)

Another noise from the entry hall.

(*Emilia turns around.*) Inesita, is that you?

INÉS (*from the entry hall, offstage*): Yes, it's me, Emilia.
(*Speaking to someone else.*) You can leave it here.

*The sound of a heavy object being set down on the wooden
floor.*

Thank you very much. That will be all. Good-bye. Good-
bye.

Sound of footsteps and the street door closing. Inés enters.

Well, Emilia, there's the casket. (*She crosses center, takes
off her hat matter-of-factly, throws it on the sofa, and
starts to take off her gloves.*)

Emilia looks hesitantly toward the hall, then at Inés.

EMILIA (*in a low quavering voice*): Is it pretty, Inés?

*Inés doesn't answer. With her back to the hall she con-
tinues taking off her gloves.*

(*Emilia trembles as she approaches the arch. She hesitates.
Finally, she peers into the hall. She gives a shriek of horror
and clutches at the drape to shield herself from the terrifying spectacle in the hall.*) Inés,—It's horrible! . . . Horrible!

THE CURTAIN FALLS QUICKLY

ACT II

*The room is the same as in Act I. Early afternoon of the
same day. The daylight streaming through the panes of the
fanlights is more intense than in the preceding act. The stage*

*is empty. The bedroom door is shut. In the street the call of
the same vendor going by.*

VOICE: Evil beams, love powders, coconut kisses, try them,
lady! Evil beams, love powders, coconut kisses, to sweeten
the soul, buy them lady! Evil beams, love powders, pretty
coconut kisses . . . !

*Just before the call dies away completely, Emilia enters
stage left with a milk bottle filled with water in one hand
and a bunch of flowers in the other. She is mouthing the
vendor's call in a low croon. She crosses to the piano,
places the glass bottle on top of it, and begins to arrange
the flowers cut from the trellis in the patio.*

EMILIA: Evil beams, love powders, coconut kisses, try them,
lady! (*Angrily trying to straighten one of the branches in
the improvised vase.*) Coco-o-on-ut! Coco-oo-nut! (*She
steps back to observe her efforts. Satisfied, she goes back
to her task still crooning.*) Evil beams. Evil beams of love,
kisses of bile and the dust of time! Evil beams!
INÉS (*from the bedroom on the right*): Emilia! Emilia! What
are you doing?
EMILIA: I'm arranging the flowers in the sitting room, Inesita!
INÉS: Do you have any powder left?
EMILIA: Powder! (*Frightened.*) No, my lord, no!
INÉS: That's all right. Forget it.

*Emilia recovers her composure. She puts the finishing
touches on her improvised vase. Then she takes two
candles out of her pocket and inserts them in the two
empty sockets in the candelabrum atop the dresser, again
humming the Chopin waltz. She lights the candles and
steps back to judge the effect. She wrinkles her brow, then
places the candelabrum on top of the piano. She takes
the kerosene lamp from the piano and puts it on top of
the dresser. She lights the lamp, and deciding that she
likes it there, limps stage center and rearranges the Louis
XV chair and the Viennese rocker. Crossing stage right,
she then takes a small handkerchief from her breast and
wipes the dust from the back of the Empire chair. Shaking
the dust from the handkerchief, she replaces it. She returns to the center of the room to observe the total effect*

*of her efforts. She stops the rocking of the Viennese rocker,
which is still moving slightly.*

EMILIA: The only thing we need now is some chocolate.
INÉS (*from the bedroom*): What did you say?

*Emilia gets up, crosses to the bedroom door, and states in
a loud voice.*

EMILIA: I said, if we only had some chocolate!
INÉS: Chocolate?
EMILIA (*quietly*): If we only had some, I said. (*Getting no
answer, she becomes flustered, and looks around in confusion. Finally she crosses stage left, murmuring half to
herself.*) I'll make a little orange blossom tea.

*As she reaches the arch, the bedroom door opens and Inés
appears. She has the sleeves of her black dress rolled up.
She begins to roll them down.*

INÉS: All right. Now you can bring down the wedding dress
and the veil. (*She stops short, noticing the lighted candles.*)
Not *again*, Emilia! (*She crosses to the piano and puts out
the candles.*) Burning candles again, and in broad daylight!
What will we have left to light the room tonight? (*Emphat-
ically.*) And the kerosene . . . (*She goes to the dresser
and puts out the lamp.*) For the sake of that which you
love most, for Hortensia's sake, I beg you to act sensibly
today! I have too many things to do to be wasting my
time with your childishness.
EMILIA (*lowering her head, like a naughty child, then adding
softly*): You're not wasting your time, Inés. It's Time itself
that has been wasting you.
INÉS: Very well, very well, then—but do as I say.
EMILIA (*crossing stage center*): If it hadn't been for Time,
Strasbourg would never have been lost—You may not
believe it, but it was Time who lost Strasbourg.
INÉS (*impatiently*): It was the Germans who lost Strasbourg.
EMILIA: Ah, no, my child, no, the Germans didn't lose it!
Not while we were there. It was the following year. I keep
good track of Time, Inés. If a century were cut from Time
itself, the Germans couldn't lose Strasbourg. But Time
insists on passing through each century. Time is to blame—
INÉS (*with energy*): That will be enough, Emilia.

EMILIA (*going to the right, sweetly*): Inés, don't be hard on me today—You see, I've arranged the sitting room. I even dusted the furniture. (*She caresses the back of the Empire chair.*) The Empire furniture was in the entry hall. (*She sits down in the chair.*) Do you remember? The Viennese rocking chair didn't really belong in the sitting room. "Who brought this rocker into the sitting room, Nanny?" "Missy Eugenia, sir." "Put it out on the porch!" "But what will Missy Eugenia say?" "All I want here is my Louis XV furniture!" But in the end the Viennese rocking chair was brought back into the sitting room. (*Laughing softly.*) Nanny brought it in on the sly while Papa Burkhart was away.—Why don't you sit down, Inés? Why don't we have a little chat? Today is a good day for memories.

INÉS (*ironically*): Time itself is just a memory for you.

EMILIA (*brightly*): There, you see, you mentioned Time!

INÉS: Yes, so I did, but before I'd mentioned something else— something I wanted you to do, Emilia.

EMILIA (*getting up*): That's right. I'm sorry. (*She goes stage left.*) At times I forget. I'll make it right away.

INÉS: Where are you going?

EMILIA (*stopping with surprise*): Why, to make the orange blossom tea you wanted.

INÉS: The *wedding gown*, Emilia. And the *veil*.

EMILIA: Ah, that's right! That's what you told me! (*She retraces her steps, then asks timidly.*) Inés, couldn't we use the blue dress?

INÉS (*firmly*): No, Emilia. The white wedding gown.

Emilia starts up the stairs. She stops on the third step.

EMILIA (*timidly*): You know . . . the veil would look very nice with the blue dress. (*Continues up the stairs, then stops again.*) Anyway, I don't even know where the wedding dress is—

INÉS: It's in the chest in my room. It's the only thing in the chest, so you really couldn't make a mistake if you tried.

Emilia reaches the top of the stairs and exits.

Inés heaves a sigh of complete weariness, she rubs the back of her hand along her forehead, and falls heavily into the armchair. Her voice comes in a faint whisper.

INÉS: Hortensia, Hortensia, how tired I am! (*She places her elbow on the arm of the chair and presses her forehead into her open hand.*)

Strains of the wedding march play faintly. A bluish glow falls over the stairway. Emilia appears at the top of the stairway. The wedding dress, the lace veil, and the crown of orange blossoms in her arms. Folds of the dress hide her worn housecoat, while the lace floats out around her. The wedding march increases in volume as Emilia slowly descends the stairs, valiantly hiding her limp. She seems almost made whole in the blue glow.

Inés raises her head slowly as Emilia descends the stairs. When she has a full view of her sister, she rises from her chair, fascinated, yet somewhat horrified, with her eyes riveted on the small figure so quaintly garbed in nuptial finery.

Emilia reaches the stage and draws near her sister. The blue glow on the stairway begins to fade away, but as Emilia approaches, the wedding march rises to a violent, deafening crescendo.

Inés draws back involuntarily, until she is stopped by the armchair. Emilia stretches out the wedding garments to her. Inés turns away and buries her face in her hands.

No!

The music ceases. A brief silence. The blue glow vanishes and daylight streams in through the fanlights.

EMILIA: Here is the dress, Inés.

Inés tries desperately to control herself. She straightens up. Without turning around she says.

INÉS: Please, please take it . . . take it into the bedroom. I'll come in a little while.

Emilia turns and goes to the bedroom door. When she reaches it, she stops, looks at the knob with dread and half turns to Inés.

(*Not seeing, but sensing Emilia's hesitation, in a sharp voice.*) Go on in, Emilia!

Emilia opens the door and exits into the bedroom. Inés goes slowly upstage. She approaches one of the shuttered doors and, leaning her forehead against it, she stretches out her arms in an empty embrace. Standing there sobbing, she seems crucified upon the doors that will never open again. Emilia enters from the right, closing the door behind her. She goes upstage to Inés, then stops confusedly. She takes a few, indecisive steps back, then limps to the stairway. Stopping on the first step, she sinks slowly until she is sitting hunched up on the step itself. She remains there quietly, like a frightened child, biting her nails and looking at Inés through the railing. Inés begins to compose herself, turns, goes to the piano, and leans on it. She dries her eyes with her fingertips. She looks at the candelabrum, then toward the dresser. Emilia gives her a pouting look of disapproval. Then Inés takes the kerosene lamp and puts it back on the piano. Another disapproving look from Emilia. Inés smoothes out the Manila scarf on the piano. She notices that one corner of the scarf is caught in the piano lid. She moves the vase and lifts the piano lid to free the scarf. As she does so, she notices Emilia's sandalwood chest. She picks it up. Emilia struggles to her feet. Inés opens the chest and takes out the book of poems. She comes downstage, then opens it.

(*Reading*) "Only your hand will purify my heart." (*She notices that Emilia is looking at her with dread.*) Your own verses, Emilia.

Emilia comes toward her pleadingly.

EMILIA: Don't take them away from me, Inés.

INÉS (*slowly going toward Emilia, holding out the open book*): I've never taken anything away from you, Emilia. (*She puts the book into Emilia's hands.*) Never. (*She steps away from Emilia.*) Nor have I ever liked your poems. No, never.

Emilia presses the book to her breast and goes toward the piano.

I remember all of them. There is something nameless in them. Something . . . indecent, Emilia.

EMILIA (*protesting*): My poetry is pure!

INÉS (*after a brief pause, as if reciting to herself*): "Your crippled foot standing upon one word: 'love.' "

EMILIA (*correcting her, offended*): "Your faunlike foot, Inés."

INÉS: Yes, that's what I meant. If you had written "your crippled foot" that would have been easier for me to understand—but, "a faunlike foot"—Really, that's almost obscene, coming from you.

EMILIA (*placing the book in the chest and the chest on the piano*): It's useless trying to talk to you, Inesita. You never did understand anything about poetry.

INÉS: You're wrong. I understand a great deal about poetry. I understand very well the poetry of long periods of silence, of hunger and misery, of pride. And childish words, and words that cut deeply. The poetry of old age and of darkness, of the merciless sun and hidden poverty. The poetry of Hortensia's cancer, and the monstrous multiplication of the cells in dear Hortensia's breast, and the deep pain that destroys quietly. And the horrible poetry of Time itself, I know that too, Emilia. I had to know all these poetries so that you might keep your own poetry intact—and so Hortensia might keep hers.

EMILIA (*with real surprise*): Inés . . . You're speaking . . . you're *speaking* in poetry!

INÉS: Poor little Emilia, who thinks she can lock poetry into her shabby verses—And she misses the poetry in our horrible day-to-day lives (*Smiling.*) "Only your hand will cleanse my heart." And did it ever cleanse your heart, Emilia?

EMILIA (*confused*): My . . . why, no, . . . that is, . . . I don't know.

INÉS (*with intense emotion*): Cancer cleanses . . . fire cleanses . . . love and jealousy and hatred cleanse . . . and then love cleanses again! And hell and perhaps even Death itself . . . they all cleanse . . . and purify.

EMILIA (*fearfully*): No, Inesita, don't talk like that.

INÉS: And why not, Emilia? I only mentioned the name of Death. And we have seen Death face to face, haven't we? Mama Eugenia. Papa Burkhart. Our Nanny.—Papa Burkhart! Don't you remember?

The lights begin to dim and the sound of a distant funeral march can be heard.

When Mama Eugenia died, he left the house of the three fanlights—the house of the setting suns—*our* three setting suns—and went to the plantation—where he rode his

horses through the fields of cane like a madman. And then
the day—it was an October afternoon—You and I were
in the sitting room. A short time later Hortensia came
down from her room.

*At this moment, Hortensia comes down the stairway, sud-
denly bathed in a blue glow. She is a girl of twenty-five,
dressed in a violet,* fin-de-siècle *housecoat.*

Suddenly we heard violent blows on the ausubo doors.

*From offstage blows rain on the ausubo doors that open
out on the street from the passageway below. Emilia and
Hortensia start at the sound of the blows. Inés shudders.*

And then, Nanny's terrible screaming.

*Hortensia rushes to Emilia and embraces her. They both
look fearfully to the left. All the stage lights have gone
out except for a faint bluish glow. Footfalls climb the
stairs from the passageway below, keeping time to the
heavy rhythm of the funeral march, which has increased
in volume. The footsteps come closer and closer. Four
Negro servants appear in the entry hall carrying a body
on a stretcher. They advance into the sitting room in
measured rhythm. Hortensia lets out a muffled scream.*

HORTENSIA: Papa Burkhart!

*The reactions of Hortensia and Emilia enable the audience
to visualize clearly what Inés is recounting.*

INÉS (*still motionless, her back turned*): The body carried on
the shoulders of four faithful servants. With its improvised
shroud of dust and blood. They've lowered the stretcher.
They are lifting the body. Now they are placing it in the
rocker.

*Hortensia and Emilia throw themselves on the floor and
embrace the leg of the Viennese rocking chair, racked with
sobs.*

HORTENSIA: Papa Burkhart!
INÉS: Here we were, the three of us, weeping. United as
always in the sitting room. The three doors facing out
on the balcony, shut as always. The three fanlights staining
the sunlight with blue, yellow, and red. And Time divided

in two: behind us lay our life of security. The present became the beginning of a future filled with disaster. As if Death were the keen blade of a knife that plunged into Time and let loose a whirlwind of unimagined terrors. That was when I began to bear my cross. (*Moving slowly toward Emilia and Hortensia.*) Feeding your dreams, Emilia; feeding your hatred and pride, Hortensia . . . (*She raises Hortensia and gently rests her sister's head on her own shoulder. Then she guides her maternally toward the stairway.*) On Inés' broad, strong shoulder. Poor ugly Inés. And all this without selling our lands to the barbarians. So that later the barbarians could simply take them away. (*She starts up the stairway, still supporting Hortensia.*)

The funeral march can still be heard.

"Never sell your lands, girls!" Papa Burkhart's dictum. How poorly you carried it out, Hortensia! Lands that lie fallow will always revert to the barbarians!

A pause followed by a change in tone.

And all the while, never telling me the words that would have relieved my horrible uncertainty. Our secret shared only in part. Because if we had shared it completely, I would have wounded your pride deeply—too deeply. Yes, you were aware of it—I *too* was in love with your Spanish officer. You found out about my love when I revealed to you his faithlessness. And how you enjoyed making me pay for my crime! The crime of ruthlessly destroying your happiness. How we hated each other, loving each other. How many long years of suffering for poor, ugly Inés! Day after day climbing my calvary.

They both disappear at the top of the stairs, but Inés' voice can still be heard.

Climbing it laden with my Emilia's dreams, and the burden of your pride, Hortensia.

As her voice dies away, a tremendous pounding rocks the ausubo doors below. The funeral march ceases, the bluish light drains away, and daylight rises quickly through the fanlights. Emilia is still stretched out on the floor, almost at full length, her face buried in the seat of the Viennese rocking chair. The pounding of fists and hands continues its tattoo on the door. Emilia raises her head in fright. She rises halfway, looks fearfully to the left, and staggers to her feet.

EMILIA: Inés. Inesita. (*She turns around, lost in indecision.*) Inés, Inés . . . (*In a louder voice.*) Inés. Inesita.

The blows continue to rain on the doors below. Emilia still hesitates.

I'm c-o-o-oming. (*She exits left.*)

Emilia descends the stairs to the passageway. Inés appears at the top of the stairs leading to the upstairs rooms. In her hands she carries a large porcelain powder box. She descends the stairs slowly. When she reaches stage level, she goes to the bedroom door, opens it, and exits, closing the door after her. Emilia's voice is heard below in the passageway.

No, no! You can't come in. This home is ours. No! You've made a mistake. Wait here. I'll call my sister. (*Calling.*) Inés! She doesn't answer. I'll go to look for her—No, no, you can't come up! Please, gentlemen, the sun is bothering my eyes. I'm not used to it . . . Inés! Wait here. I'll go and look for her—For God's sake, wait here! (*The heavy thud of Emilia's crippled foot sounds on the stairway. Her voice is panting and fearful.*) Ine-e-és! Inesita! Inesita! . . . (*Emilia's voice is heard in the hall.*) For God's sake, hurry! Come here! Inés! (*She comes hobbling into the sitting room.*) Inés! (*Seeing no one there, she shrieks out.*) For the love of God. Inés, where are you?

INÉS (*from the bedroom*): All right, Emilia!

EMILIA (*hobbling quickly to the door on the right, her voice cracked with emotion*): Inés!

Inés enters stage right.

INÉS: Emilia, what's wrong? Why are you screaming?

Emilia throws herself into her sister's arms, sobbing.

EMILIA: You're here, Inés! How good that you're finally here, Inesita!

INÉS: Calm yourself, my child. Why are you crying?

EMILIA: Those men! . . .

INÉS: Who? What men?

EMILIA (*gaining control of herself, and stifling her sobs*): The ones downstairs. I went to open the . . . since you weren't here. And the sun hit me full in the face . . . they were talking about the house . . . I told them they were mistaken . . . But they refused to be considerate . . . and the sun, hitting me right in the face like that . . .

INÉS: What house were they talking about?

EMILIA: The one on Cristo Street, the one with the fanlights—

INÉS: What did they say about the house?

EMILIA (*in a low voice, as if telling a secret*): It's no longer ours!

INÉS: What are you saying?

EMILIA (*moving away from Inés, pointing at the fanlights*): The house with the three fanlights . . . it's no longer ours. Another public sale . . . don't you understand? We've owed taxes for so many, many years. Time has tricked us once again! Just as it did at the plantation in Toa Alta! Just as it did when it gave Strasbourg to France! Another foul trick of Time! It's no longer ours! They said so, Time's messengers—Instead it will become a fine hotel for the tourists, and the bankers, and the officers of the fleet that shelled San Juan. It's no longer our house. We shan't be able to struggle against Time any longer, Inés! We no longer have a house!

INÉS: Are the men still downstairs?

EMILIA: Yes, I wouldn't let them come up. (*Cheering up.*) They're waiting for you, Inés. You'll know what to do, won't you? Just as you always have before. The house isn't lost, is it? (*Shaking her.*) You'll fight for it . . . You'll pretend you're mad as you've done before.

INÉS (*stepping back from Emilia*): This time it won't be necessary to do that, Emilia. (*She crosses determinedly to the left. Grimly.*) I swear to you . . . that won't be necessary! (*She exits left.*)

EMILIA (*going to the left*): That's right, Inés. Defend your house. Mama Eugenia's house! Papa Burkhart's house. The house of our nanny who wept for us, sang to us, and rocked us, unaware of Time. Hortensia's and Emilia's house! Our house!

The voice of Inés from the passageway below.

INÉS: Get out of this house! Get out of here!

EMILIA (*gripping the drapery that hangs from the arch*):

God bless you, Inés! God bless you!

INÉS (*from the passageway*): No one has the right to trespass here. (*Shouting furiously.*) It makes no difference to me if times do change! Time in our house is not your time! Burn those papers for all I care! Careful there! Don't you touch me!

EMILIA (*alarmed, she goes to the piano*): Don't let them in, Inés. Your nails, don't forget your nails . . . your long nails that have known Time well. (*As if she could see Inés struggling.*) Sink them in deeply. Like this! (*She digs her fingernails into the Manila shawl on the piano.*) Until you draw blood and their smiles disappear.

INÉS (*from the passageway*): Get out! (*Her voice muffled in the struggle.*) Get out of this house, I said! There is no law that makes a person sign over his life! None of you can come in! None of you! Out of my house! Get out! Get out, I said!

EMILIA (*moves upstage toward the shuttered doors. As Inés says "None of you can come in," she begins to speak softly so as not to drown out Inés' voice. When Inés finishes speaking, Emilia's voice rises like a continuation of her sister's*): Hit them without mercy, Inés! Like this! With the same fury you used to strike out at life! Like this! Against misery, and men, and the world. Get out! Get out! (*Beating on the door as she speaks.*) Against life, and Time, and Death itself—

The whole house shudders as Inés finally succeeds in slamming shut the huge ausubo doors. Emilia stands motionless, fists clenched against the door. After a brief pause, Inés enters stage left, breathing heavily and showing visible signs of the savage struggle below. Emilia turns around slowly.

Inés! You've won!

INÉS: No—They've won!

EMILIA (*her voiced choked with emotion*): Then, my God . . . They'll destroy the house!

INÉS: Worse than that, Emilia, they'll keep the house, profaning it so that it will no longer be the purifying instrument of our sin. They say they'll reconstruct it. They'll mock the past by masking with their new oldness the ruins of the house of the fanlight windows. (*Crossing to the right, her eyes begin to focus on the great stain on the wall, next to the stairway.*) And their time will enter our house, and the house will be filled with strange voices that will drown out our words, all of the words of our lives. Over our pain, Hortensia's and yours, Emilia, and mine, will rise the laughter of the tourists, the loudness of the bankers, the filthy drunkenness of those who shout—

EMILIA: No Inés, no—

INÉS: In the luxury hotel of Cristo Street.

EMILIA: Then, all is lost—There's nothing more that can be done?

Pause.

INÉS (*pointing at the water stain*): Do you see that stain, Emilia? Do you know what it is?

EMILIA (*approaching Inés*): It's the stain left by the rainstorm on St. Philip's Day. Don't you remember? The wind lifted the ceiling right off the room . . .

INÉS: It's a map drawn by Time . . .

EMILIA: So it is, Inés. I never thought of that—It *is* a map.

INÉS (*pointing at it again*): Do you see? One world above: ours. Another world below: theirs. With an isthmus joining the two worlds . . . (*Her face aglow.*) We must destroy the isthmus.

EMILIA: That's right, Inés. We must destroy the isthmus. But I . . . How can we do that?

INÉS: We'll do it together. . . . Do you have enough courage?

EMILIA: Enough to do whatever *you* say, Inés—All the courage in the world!

INÉS: Come, then, you must swear to it before Hortensia. (*She takes her sister to the door on the right.*)

EMILIA: I'll swear to it, Inés. Hortensia would have had the courage too. I'm sure of it.

Inés opens the door.

Inés, how beautifully you have her arranged!

They both exit, closing the door after them. A brief interlude. The music of Wagner's "Ride of the Valkyries" is heard. Emilia enters stage right, leaves the door open, then turns and looks back into the bedroom. She smiles. Her face reveals an inner peace and happiness.

Yes, Inés, you are right! The three of us ought to be united here once again, in the sitting room, as always. (*She goes*

*to the piano and lights the three candles in the candelabrum.
Turning to the piano, she arranges the flowers. She opens
the piano lid, removes the chest, and places it next to the
vase. Then she moves the Viennese rocking chair so as to
leave an empty space almost in the center of the room.
She goes slightly stage left to judge the effect. Then she
smiles, turns toward the bedroom, and calls out.)* All right,
Inés!! All right!

*The lights begin to dim, as the "Valkyries'" music rises
dramatically. Hortensia glides out through the bedroom
door. She lies in a rough coffin provided by the Municipal
Welfare Agency. The coffin, which has no cover, rests
on a wheeled cot. Hortensia is arrayed in her wedding
finery. Her head, crowned with a lace veil intertwined with
orange blossoms, lies on a richly embroidered and decorated cushion. The folds of the dress and lace veil almost
hide the casket from view. Inés has taken tremendous care
with every detail, as if she had never meant for the coffin
cover ever to be put in place. Death here seems a poetic
dream—not a macabre vision. Hortensia lies dead, at sixty-
eight. The footprints of time and the ravages of cancer
have not completely erased the beauty of the loveliest of
the Burkhart sisters. Inés comes into view pushing the cot,
and wheels it reverently to the space cleared by Emilia. A
blue glow rises around the casket. Emilia goes to Hortensia,
as the music dies away.*

How beautiful she looks!

INÉS *(smiling sweetly)*: As always.

*Emilia takes her chest of poetry from the piano and places
it at Hortensia's feet.*

EMILIA *(tenderly)*: My heart at your feet, Hortensia.

*A lavender hue begins to rise above the blue glow around
the casket and the light of the lamp and the candles. Daylight has completely died away. Emilia and Inés smile
tenderly at Hortensia.*

(Raising her eyes to Inés.) Are you ready, Inés?

INÉS *(smiling)*: There is no hurry, Emilia. Now, for once,
Time belongs to us. *(She crosses to the bedroom door and
exits.)*

Emilia sits in the armchair.

(*Inés returns with a jewel case in her hands. She goes to the casket and places the jewel case upon Hortensia's breast. She opens it.*) Your pride, Hortensia!

EMILIA (*rising in amazement*): Inés, you kept the jewels!

INÉS: Only the ones that Hortensia loved most. I always kept them for her. Despite the misery and the hunger. One last dream for her pride to feed on. The only beautiful thing that the cancer could not destroy. She smiled when she saw them, just before she died. (*Changing tone.*) And Mama Eugenia's fan, do you remember? (*She takes a tiny mother-of-pearl and lace fan from the box. The fan is attached to a long, gold chain.*) It's yours, Emilia. (*She places the chain around Emilia's neck.*)

EMILIA (*stroking the open fan tenderly*): Eugenia Sandoval de Burkhart.

INÉS: And now the pearl ring. (*She starts to place it on Emilia's fingers, but Emilia stays her hand.*)

EMILIA: No, no, not the pearls!—They bring bad luck.

INÉS (*placing the ring on Hortensia's finger*): Hortensia was never afraid of pearls. (*She takes out a diadem encrusted with diamonds and sapphires.*) Nor was she afraid of diamonds.

EMILIA (*with awe*): Mama Eugenia's diadem.

INÉS: The most beautiful of all our jewelry. (*She places the diadem on Emilia's head.*)

EMILIA (*crestfallen*): But, Inés . . .

INÉS: Today it belongs to you, Emilia.

Emilia falls into the armchair. The jewels burn brightly under the soft light.

INÉS (*taking out the last jewel from the case, a thick ring with a large diamond*): And Papa Burkhart's ring. Of all the jewelry, the only thing I want for myself. (*She puts on the ring, closes the jewel case and puts it on top of the piano.*) The time has come, Emilia.

The lavender light begins to fade.

The time has come to destroy all our ugliness: what was once beautiful and what has always been ugly and horrible. To destroy them both—To cleanse them both!

EMILIA (*fanning herself, in a serious tone*): Yes, Inés. It is time.

Inés takes the kerosene lamp and climbs the stairway. The music increases in volume. Emilia follows Inés with her eyes until her sister exits above. Then she gets up, goes to the marble dresser, takes the candelabrum with the lighted candles, and exits stage left.

The stage is empty for a moment. Then Inés appears at the top of the stairway, still carrying her kerosene lamp. As she starts down, the lavender glow fades out completely. Above her, a reddish glow appears from the rooms above. As Inés reaches the stage, Emilia appears from the left still carrying the candelabrum. They smile at each other. Inés goes to the open bedroom door and exits. Emilia crosses to the dresser and places the candelabrum on it.

A reddish glow is rising in the entry hall. Emilia comes stage center, smiles at Hortensia, and sits down in the Louis XV chair. She fans herself gracefully.

The glow from the stairway intensifies as smoke begins to filter down from the upper rooms. Inés enters from the right. She is no longer carrying the lamp. She goes to the casket. A reddish glow rises from the bedroom. Flames flicker from the entry hall amid wisps of smoke. Inés smiles at Hortensia.

INÉS: Purification, Hortensia, purification!

Flames now flicker from offstage right, and smoke begins to pour out from the bedroom. Vivid flames flicker through the fanlights and mount in brightness until the fanlights blaze like three setting suns. Emilia leaps to her feet.

EMILIA (*with an exultant shout*): Inesita, the fire has made you beautiful! (*She tears the diadem from her head and places it on Inés' forehead. Then she leads her sister to the Louis XV armchair, seats her in it, and kneels at her feet.*) We've conquered Time, Inés! We've conquered it! (*She kisses Inés' hand tenderly, on which Papa Burkhart's diamond glows strangely.*)

Inés smiles.

The Wagnerian music rises to a crescendo, as the whole sitting room swims in a cleansing and purifying inferno, a purgatory of flame.

SLOW CURTAIN

PAYMENT AS PLEDGED

ALFREDO DIAS GOMES

Translated by Oscar Fernández

To Janete, with love

To Pascoal Longo and Édison Carneiro

Alfredo Dias Gomes was born in 1922 in Salvador, Bahia, a region of Brazil rich in the folk traditions, customs, and legends that form an essential part of his work. After abortive careers in law, engineering, and the military, he found success as a playwright with *Payment as Pledged* (*O Pagador de Promessas*, 1960). The winner of various Brazilian drama awards and, in its film version by Anselmo Duarte, winner of the International Film Festival of Cannes in 1962, the play is one of the milestones of Brazilian dramaturgy. That mankind is continually threatened by the forces of a disinterested or exploitative society is a source of constant concern to Dias Gomes. He deals with the vicissitudes of slum-dwellers struggling against venal politicians, he inveighs against the military, and he laments the effects of hyperreligiosity in the form of fanaticism, cultism, superstition, or the extremist tactics of the Inquisition. Within the fabric of contemporary life in a Brazilian ambiance, he is a deeply committed liberal who opposes establishment policies, or rather, any system that paradoxically mouths freedom for its people yet methodically destroys their right to individual human dignity.

The conflict of *Payment as Pledged* (*O Pagador de Promessas*) develops between an ingenuous peasant bent on fulfilling a religious promise and an intransigent priest who thwarts his objective by denying him entrance to the church. The resulting scene in the village square piques the curiosity of all, the sympathy of only a few, and the profit motive of most of the villagers. Joe Burro's deliberate indiscrimination between the pagan Yansan and the Catholic Saint Barbara reveals the curious syncretism of the region. With touches of *capoeira*[1] and *candomblé*,[2] the play captures the flavor of the

---

[1] The *capoeira* is a traditional dance and music form characteristic of Bahia. When fighting among the Negroes was prohibited by law, this highly stylized fight-dance form developed. Another aspect of the *capoeira* is the recitation of extemporaneous verses, using forms ranging from the simple to the highly complex. A *capoeirista* can perform alone but the excitement is greater when two performers challenge each other to a verbal duel.

[2] A term now in widespread use to refer to the Afro-Brazilian religious complex practiced by a large proportion of Brazil's black and mulatto population. Although many of the saints have been syncretized

customs, the speech patterns, and the value system of northeastern Brazil. It presents a simple man as a symbol of almost mythical purity, with an unswerving dedication to his conscience and his principles, and with a firm belief that right *must* win—without regard for the deceptive forces acting to destroy him. Ironically crucified, he achieves in death what is denied to him in life.

Dias Gomes has intimate knowledge of the Brazilian psyche and the cultural traditions of the Northeast, but his plays easily transcend a limited regional appeal. The antireligious and anticlerical elements of *Payment as Pledged* are, after all, only small parts of the greater problems of exploitation, inhumanity, and deprivation of freedom.

---

with those of the Roman Catholic hierarchy, and indeed many of its practitioners also consider themselves Catholics, *candomblé* rites are still performed in parts of Brazil with linguistic, magical, and ritualistic survivals of African origin. (Cf. *macumba* in Rio de Janeiro and *xangô* in the Brazilian northeast.)

Characters

JOE BURRO
ROSA
MARLI
PRETTY BOY
PRIEST
SEXTON
POLICEMAN
RELIGIOUS WOMAN
GALICIAN
AUNTIE
REPORTER
PHOTOGRAPHER
RAY-THE-RIMER
SECRET POLICE AGENT
POLICE COMMISSIONER
MASTER COCA
MONSIGNOR
MANNY *and the Capoeira* GROUP

Scene

City of Salvador in Bahia, Brazil

Time

The present

ACT I

Scene 1

As the curtain rises, the stage is almost completely dark. Only a stream of light, from the right, brings some illumination to the stage. Nevertheless, after becoming accustomed to it, the audience will easily make out a small village square into which two streets run. One is to the right, following the line of the footlights; the other to the left, upstage, facing the audience, rising, sloping, curving up a hill, against the outline of some old colonial houses. On the corner of the street, to the right, we see the façade of a relatively modest church, with four or five steps leading to its entrance. On one of the street corners, on the hill, on the opposite side, there is a café-bar where coffee, refreshments, brandy, etc., are sold; on the other corner, on the side of the hill, there is a colonial-type building, its previously unseen upper floors protruding somewhat like a slight paunch. The pavement on the hill is irregular, and some of the tiles on the front of the buildings have deteriorated with time. In short, it is a typically Bahian scene, of old colonial Bahia, which even today resists the avalanche of modern urbanism.

It must be about four-thirty in the morning. Both the church and the café have their doors closed. In the distance one hears the sound of the drums of a far-off candomblé *(voodoo session), and the call of Yansan (voodoo idol). After a few seconds, Joe Burro appears in the street at the right, carrying on his shoulders a very large and heavy wooden cross. Slowly, tired, he comes into the square, followed by Rosa, his wife. He is a man still young, some thirty years of age, thin, of medium height. His expression is restrained, contemplative. His features convey kindness and tolerance, and there is a certain boyishness in his face. His movements are slow, lazy, as is his way of speaking. He has a two- or three-days growth of beard and is dressed properly, but simply, although his clothes fit him loosely; furthermore, they are wrinkled and covered with dust. Rosa seems to have little in common with him. She is a pretty woman, although her features are a little rough, as are her manners. Contrary to her husband, she is "warm-blooded." One immediately notices in her a lack of sexual satisfaction and a suppressed desire to break with a*

47

*situation in which she feels stifled. She is dressed like a
country girl going to the city, but also like a woman who
does not want to conceal her best features.*

*Joe Burro goes to the center of the square and puts down his
cross, balancing it on its base and on an arm. He is exhausted.
He wipes the perspiration from his forehead.*

JOE (*looking at the church*): That's it. It has to be.

   *Rosa also stops, near the steps, tired, irritated, revealing the
   revolt which is growing in her.*

ROSA: And what do we do now? It's closed.
JOE: It's too early. We'll wait until it opens.
ROSA: We'll wait? Here?
JOE: There's nothing else we can do.
ROSA (*looks at him angrily and sits down on one of the steps.
   She takes her shoe off*): My blisters are killing me.
JOE: So are mine. (*Twists his body in pain. Takes an arm
   out of one of the sleeves of his jacket.*) I think my shoul-
   ders are raw.
ROSA: It serves you right. You wouldn't cushion them like I
   told you to do.
JOE (*convinced*): It wouldn't be right. When I made the
   promise, I didn't say anything about padding.
ROSA: OK. So you didn't. That's why you could've used it;
   the saint wouldn't care.
JOE: It wouldn't be right. I promised to carry the cross on
   my back, like Jesus did. And Jesus didn't use any padding.
ROSA: He didn't use any because they didn't let him.
JOE: No. When it comes to miracles, you have to be honest.
   If you cheat the saint, you lose your credit. The next time
   around the saint takes a look, consults the book, and says:
   "Oh, you're Joe Burro, that fellow that put one over on me!
   And now you come to me with another promise. Well,
   you can go to the devil with your promise, you dirty
   swindler!" And that's not all: a saint is like a gringo;
   you trick one and all the others know about it.
ROSA: You mean you are thinking of making another promise
   after this one? Isn't this enough? . . .
JOE: I don't know . . . you never know when you're going
   to have to. That's why it's a good idea to have your ac-
   counts up to date. (*He goes up one or two steps. He*

examines the façade of the church looking for an inscription.)

ROSA: What are you looking for?

JOE: For some identification . . . so I can tell if this is the church of St. Barbara.

ROSA: Man, have you ever seen a church with a shingle on the door?

JOE: Well, it's just that this might not be it . . .

ROSA: Of course it is. Don't you remember what the priest said? A small church, on the square, near a hill . . .

JOE (*looks around*): If I could just ask somebody . . .

ROSA: At this ungodly hour everybody is still in bed. (*She looks at him, almost in anger.*) Everybody . . . except me. Unfortunately, I'm married to a guy who would disrupt his whole life in order to keep a promise. (*She gets up and tries to convince him.*) Now listen, Joe . . . since the church is closed, we can go find a place to sleep. Haven't you thought how good a bed would feel now?

JOE: And what about the cross?

ROSA: You can leave the cross there and tomorrow, in the daytime . . .

JOE: Somebody might steal it.

ROSA: For heaven's sake, man, who's going to steal a cross? What can they use a cross for?

JOE: There's so much evil in the world. I'd be running a great risk, and after having almost completed my vow. And have you given it a thought: if my cross was stolen, I'd have to make another one and come here again with it, on my back, all the way from the country: twenty-five miles.

ROSA: But why? You'd simply explain to the saint that you'd been robbed. She wouldn't insist.

JOE: That's what you think. When you're going to the store to pay a bill and you lose your money on the way, does the storekeeper cancel your debt? I'll say he doesn't!

ROSA: But you've already kept your vow. You brought a wooden cross all the way from our farm to St. Barbara's church here in the city. There you have the church, and here you have the cross. OK. It's done. Now, we can leave.

JOE: But St. Barbara's church is not here. The church is beyond that door.

ROSA: Come now! The door is closed and it isn't your fault. St. Barbara must know that, for heaven's sake!

JOE: If I could only talk to her and explain the situation . . .

ROSA: Well then . . . talk to her!

JOE (*lifts his eyes toward heaven, timidly, and opens his lips as if to speak to the saint, but he loses his courage*): No, I can't do it . . .

ROSA: Why not, man?! St. Barbara is such a good friend of yours . . . Aren't you on good terms with her?

JOE: I am, but this business of talking to a saint is very complicated. A saint never answers in everyday language . . . You don't know what he's thinking. And besides, it isn't right. I promised to take the cross into the church and I have to do it. I walked twenty-five miles. I'm not going to get in bad with the saint on account of a few feet.

ROSA: And so that you won't get in bad with the saint, I'm going to have to sleep on the ground of the Lord's "hotel." (*She looks at him angrily and then lies down on one of the church steps.*) If only all of this were for something worthwhile . . .

JOE: You didn't have to come. When I made the promise I didn't mention you, only the cross.

ROSA: Now you tell me. Why didn't you tell me before? . . .

JOE: I didn't think of it. Besides, you didn't object . . .

ROSA: I'm your wife. I have to go where you go . . .

JOE: Well then . . .

Rosa makes herself as comfortable as possible on the steps, while Joe Burro, also quite tired, makes a superhuman effort to stay awake. He dozes, guarding his cross. Suddenly, Marli and Pretty Boy break out into the square. She is actually twenty-eight years old, but seems ten years older. She is excessively made up, but nevertheless one can make out her greenish-yellow complexion. She has some of the features of a sickly beauty, a sad and suicidal beauty. Her dress is very short and low cut, somewhat worn and out of style, but nevertheless it looks good on her. Her gestures and movements reveal the conflict within a woman who wishes to free herself from a tyranny that is, nevertheless, necessary for her own psychic well-being— her exploitation as a victim of Pretty Boy in part satisfies a frustrated maternal instinct. In her love, her abjection, in her voluntary degradation, there is much maternal sacrifice; also, a certain pride. Pretty Boy is indifferent to all of this. He is cold and brutal in his "profession." He looks

upon the exploitation to which he submits Marli and other
women as a right to which he is entitled, or better yet, a
gift that nature has given him together with his physical at-
tributes. In his way of thinking, his masculine good looks
and his sexual vigor, together with the natural right to
subsist, completely justify his way of life. He is a little
taller than average, strong, and of mulatto complexion.
His black heritage is apparent, although his hair is quite
straight, shining from hair oil, and his features regular,
except for his thick and sensual lips and his nostrils, which
are quite dilated. He always dresses in white, with a high
collar, and two-toned shoes. They come down the hill,
she in front, walking rapidly. He follows her, as if they
had just had an argument.

PRETTY BOY: Wait. What's your hurry?

MARLI: We'd better talk about this at home.

PRETTY BOY (*catches up with her and makes her stop, twist-*
ing her arm violently): No, we're going to settle it right
here. I don't have anything to talk over with you . . .

MARLI (*frees herself with a jerk, but her face shrivels with*
pain): You beast!

PRETTY BOY: Come on, let's stop beating around the bush.
Fork over the money.

MARLI (*takes a roll of bills from her dress pocket and gives*
them to him): Couldn't you wait until we got home?

PRETTY BOY (*goes over to the light and counts the bills*
rapidly): Is this all you got?

MARLI: That's all. It wasn't a very good night. You saw. The
place was empty.

PRETTY BOY: And what about that Galician who was talking
to you when I arrived?

MARLI: Just a lot of talk. He wanted me, he said, but he
jabbered and fooled around and never did anything.

PRETTY BOY (*he suddenly thrusts his arm in Marli's bosom and*
pulls a bill out): You cow! (*He raises his arm to strike*
her, and she runs and takes refuge behind the cross.)

Joe Burro wakes up from his semidrowsiness.

MARLI: I need that money. To pay for my room, you know
that.

PRETTY BOY: I don't like to be tricked. Why didn't you ask
for it?

MARLI: And would you give it to me?

PRETTY BOY: Of course not. (*He puts the money in his wallet.*) That would knock the hell out of my budget. I've got obligations and you know well enough that I don't like to borrow money. It's a question of principle.

MARLI: And what am I supposed to do to pay my room rent? I'm already two months behind, and the old lady is giving me some dirty looks.

PRETTY BOY (*indifferent*): That's your problem. I've got a lot of other things to think about.

MARLI: I know. I know what you're thinking about . . .

PRETTY BOY (*smiling and with a shade of threat in his smile*): I'm thinking, for example, that you haven't been doing very good the last three months. Now, Matilde is doing almost twice as good . . .

MARLI (*understanding the threat, advances toward him shaken by jealousy and by the fear of losing him*): I know, you're chasing that bitch. She goes around telling everybody.

PRETTY BOY: I don't chase any woman. You know that. It's a question of principle.

MARLI: What you mean is that she's chasing you!

PRETTY BOY: She asked me if I needed some money.

MARLI (*anxiously*): And what did you say?

PRETTY BOY: I only asked for some information of a technical nature: daily take, etc. . . .

MARLI (*seizing him frantically by the arms*): Pretty Boy, you didn't take her money, did you?! You didn't take any money from that whore!

PRETTY BOY (*looking at her coldly*): And what if I did? I've got to live, don't I?

MARLI: But isn't what I give you enough?!

PRETTY BOY: You understand, don't you, that I've got certain ambitions. If I didn't have these special qualities, well, it would be different. But I know I do have them, and it's only right that I take advantage of them.

MARLI: But what do you need? Don't I give you everything you ask for? And if it's necessary, I'll give you even more. And don't think it's because I'm afraid that you'll abandon me for that Matilde woman, not at all. (*She smoothes out his jacket and looks at him maternally.*) You know I like to see you dressed in the clothes I gave you, wearing the shoes I bought you, and with your wallet full of bills I got for you. I'm proud of it, see?

PRETTY BOY (*breaks away from her*): Well then, next time don't hold back any money. I'm sure that Matilde wouldn't play a dirty trick like that.

MARLI: She'd do a lot worse. If you want to know, I'll tell you . . .

PRETTY BOY (*abruptly*): I don't want to hear it. What I want is for you to go home.

MARLI (*disappointed*): Aren't you going with me?

PRETTY BOY: No, I'm going to hang around here a while. Go on ahead; I'll be there a little later.

MARLI (*jealous*): And what are you going to be doing in the street at this time of day?

PRETTY BOY (*very seriously*): Come, woman, I've got to work! (*He lights a cigarette, walking away from Marli, who looks at him like a dog abandoned by its master. Only then does he show interest in the cross in the middle of the square. He looks at it curiously, and finally speaks to Joe Burro.*) Is it yours?

Joe nods his head affirmatively. Marli goes to the church steps, sits on one of them, without bothering Rosa, who is lying a little higher up, takes off her shoes and wiggles her aching toes.

(*Pretty Boy looks at the church, coming to a conclusion.*) An order?

JOE: No, a promise.

PRETTY BOY (*at first he doesn't seem to understand, then he laughs*): Very funny.

JOE: I don't think so.

PRETTY BOY: Oh, come, I didn't mean any harm. I'm also sort of religious. Why I even made a promise to St. Anthony once . . .

JOE: Marriage?

PRETTY BOY: No, she was already married.

JOE: And did you get your wish?

PRETTY BOY: I got it. Her husband went away for a week . . .

JOE: And you kept your promise?

PRETTY BOY: No, I didn't want to embarrass the saint.

JOE: You must always keep a promise. Even when it might

embarrass the saint. I'll bet that next time St. Anthony will turn a deaf ear to you. And I wouldn't blame him.

PRETTY BOY: You see, St. Anthony would end up in a bad light if people knew that he was the one that made the old fool take off. (*Noticing that Marli is still there.*) What are you still doing here?

MARLI: Waiting for you.

PRETTY BOY (*going over to her*): I told you that I'd go later. Are you going to stick around glued to me?

MARLI (*getting up*): Listen, Pretty Boy . . . couldn't you at least let me have that one bill?

PRETTY BOY: I already told you no. Don't insist.

MARLI: But I have to pay my room rent!

PRETTY BOY: It's your room, not mine.

MARLI: But it's my money. It's only right that I keep at least some of it.

PRETTY BOY: And why is it right?

MARLI: Because I'm the one that did the work.

PRETTY BOY: And since when does work give a right to anything? Whoever put those ideas in your head? (*He looks at her from head to foot with distrust.*) Are you turning communist?

Marli looks at him with hatred and leaves abruptly to the right. Pretty Boy follows her with his eyes and then smiles, takes the money from his pocket and begins to count it.

JOE (*naïvely*): That money . . . is it really hers?

PRETTY BOY (*putting his money away*): Well, that's one way of looking at it. Everything can be considered from at least two points of view: from the outside looking in, or from the inside looking out. You understand?

JOE: No . . .

PRETTY BOY: No point trying to explain it. It's a question of sensibility.

JOE: You're . . . her husband?

PRETTY BOY: No, I'm a sort of income tax collector. (*He goes up the hill, as if to leave, but he stops in front of Rosa, whose skirt, raised, reveals part of her thigh.*)

ROSA (*opening her eyes, feeling that someone is looking at her*): What's wrong?

PRETTY BOY: Nothing . . . I was just looking . . .

Rosa fixes her dress.

That bed can't be very comfortable . . .

Rosa looks at him angrily.

(*Pretty Boy looks at her a little more closely.*) And you know you really deserve something better.

ROSA: Tell that to him. (*Pointing to Joe Burro.*)

PRETTY BOY: To him?

ROSA: My husband.

PRETTY BOY: Oh, you also came to keep a promise . . .

ROSA: Not me; he did. And on account of him I'm sleeping here on the steps of a church like an old beggar. (*She sits up.*)

JOE: The church should be opening up soon. Do you know what time it is?

PRETTY BOY (*looking at his watch*): A quarter to five.

JOE: Do you know what time the church opens?

PRETTY BOY: No, that's not exactly my line . . .

JOE: But there must be a Mass at six o'clock. Today is St. Barbara's day . . .

ROSA (*resentful*): At six o'clock. I still have to spend at least an hour on these hard steps and it's not even my promise!

PRETTY BOY: The sacristy door might already be open.

JOE: Do you think so?

PRETTY BOY: The priest wakes up early . . .

JOE: At five o'clock?

PRETTY BOY: Of course: he has to get ready for the six o'clock Mass.

JOE: That's right . . .

PRETTY BOY: Why don't you go and find out?

JOE: I'll do that . . . (*He hesitates a little.*)

PRETTY BOY: The door is on the other side . . .

JOE: Rosa, you look after the cross; I'm going over there . . . I won't be long. (*He leaves.*)

PRETTY BOY: You don't have to worry. I'll help take care of your cross . . . (*After Joe Burro leaves.*) of both of them.

ROSA: Except that one of them he carries on his back, and the other . . . it can follow him, if it wants to. (*She gets up.*)

PRETTY BOY: And you're not a woman to go after any man . . . on the contrary, you're a cross that anyone would carry with pleasure . . .

ROSA (*cautiously, but a little vain at heart*): Come on, leave me alone.

PRETTY BOY: On my word. Your husband doesn't treat you right. That's not the way to treat a woman . . . even a guy's wife.

ROSA: Well, if he doesn't treat me right, what about it? I'm his.

PRETTY BOY: True enough. But I don't think you're the type of woman to be sleeping on church steps. You have qualities which demand much more: a good bed, with a mattress and better company.

ROSA: Don't mention the word bed to me. I'm completely worn out.

PRETTY BOY: Are you really that tired?

ROSA: Two nights without sleep, following him for twenty-five miles . . .

PRETTY BOY: Twenty-five miles?

ROSA: Twenty-five times I cursed the day I went to steal cashew nuts with him out at the priests' farm . . .

PRETTY BOY: Ah, so that's the way it was . . .

ROSA: People do such crazy things . . .

PRETTY BOY: How long ago was that?

ROSA: Eight years ago . . .

PRETTY BOY: And you married him?

ROSA: I married him.

PRETTY BOY: Without loving him?

ROSA (after a pause): I loved him, yes. You know, out in the country, the men are ugly, skinny, dirty, and poorly dressed. But he was one of the best. He had a farm . . .

PRETTY BOY: And?

ROSA: And, I felt he guaranteed everything I wanted out of life: a man and a home. When a girl's still a young chick, if you'll excuse the word, she's got a lot of crappy ideas in her head.

PRETTY BOY (rather interested): So he's got a farm, right?

ROSA: He had one, but now he's only got a piece of one. He divided the rest among some poor farmers.

PRETTY BOY: Why?

ROSA: It was part of the promise.

PRETTY BOY: What's he trying to do? Become a saint?

ROSA: Don't joke. On the way here there were quite a few people who wanted him to perform a miracle. And don't doubt it. He may end up doing it. If it weren't for the ungodly hour, I tell you he'd have a pilgrimage right here, with people following him all over the place.

PRETTY BOY: After he carries out this promise, is he going to go back to his farm?

ROSA: He is.

PRETTY BOY: And what about you?

ROSA: Me too. Why?

PRETTY BOY: If you came to the city, I could guarantee you a good future . . .

ROSA: Doing what?

PRETTY BOY: You'd find out later.

ROSA: I don't know how to do anything.

PRETTY BOY (*taking her by the arm*): Women like you don't have to know how to do anything, except what nature taught them . . .

Rosa pulls her arm away abruptly, after maintaining, for a few seconds, a look of defiance.

ROSA: Don't do that! He could come back suddenly.

PRETTY BOY: He must have gone to wake the priest. (*He again approaches her.*)

ROSA (*breaks away from him again*): Let go of me. (*Sits down on the steps again.*) What I want is to sleep. I would give my life for a white sheet . . . and a tub of hot water where I could soak my feet.

PRETTY BOY: I can fix you up in a little hotel near here . . .

Rosa looks at him with a hostile expression.

And without any conditions . . . just so you could sleep and rest from this pilgrimage.

ROSA: I don't want to get into any trouble.

PRETTY BOY: But there's no danger of any trouble. I'm on very good terms with the hotel doorman and I get along fine with the police. Around here, everybody respects Pretty Boy.

ROSA (*almost sensually*): Pretty Boy . . .

PRETTY BOY (*proud*): It's a nickname . . .

Rosa looks him over from head to foot.

Pretty Boy sits down next to her.

ROSA: Don't come near me, I'm all sweated up.

PRETTY BOY: There's a bathroom in the hotel . . . for some-

one who has walked twenty-five miles, a shower, and then
a bed with a spring mattress . . .

ROSA: A spring mattress?

PRETTY BOY: That's right . . .

ROSA: I've never slept on a spring mattress. It must be wonderful.

PRETTY BOY: It's out of this world . . .

Joe Burro comes in from the right.

Pretty Boy gets up.

JOE: Everything's closed. It doesn't make sense.

ROSA (*disturbed*): And so I'm to stay on these hard steps
until God knows what time.

JOE: Patience, Rosa. Your sacrifice will be worth it.

ROSA: To who? To St. Barbara? I didn't make any promise.

JOE: Come now! So much the better. Tomorrow, when you
make a promise, the saint will already be in debt to you!

ROSA: I never saw a saint pay a debt. (*She again sits down
on the steps.*)

PRETTY BOY (*assuming as ecclesiastical an air as possible*):
You are wrong in having so little faith. For all you know,
St. Barbara may already be paying back that debt. And
for all you know, she may have chosen me to be her agent.

JOE (*very naïvely*): Didn't you say you were an income tax
collector? Now you say you're St. Barbara's agent . . .

PRETTY BOY: My dear friend, with the cost of living going
up every day, one has to do a little moonlighting. But
that's not the point. What I'm saying is that St. Barbara
must already be trying to pay off the debt contracted today
with your wife, because she made me pass by here this
morning.

JOE: I don't see what that's got to do with it.

PRETTY BOY: Because you don't know that in five minutes I
can fix you up with a fine bed, with a spring mattress, in
a hotel nearby.

JOE: Fix *her* up?

PRETTY BOY: And you too.

JOE: I can't go. I've got to wait here until the church opens.
If I knew that nobody would steal my cross . . .

PRETTY BOY (*rapidly*): Oh no, the cross should not be left
here unattended. This place is full of thieves. That's a
wooden cross and wood is very expensive.

JOE: That's what I'm thinking. I've got to stay here.

PRETTY BOY: But I can stay here and take care of it while you and your wife go and rest.

JOE: You?

PRETTY BOY: Why not?

JOE: But it might be some time before the church opens. At least an hour.

PRETTY BOY: I'll wait. Your wife told me of the long trip you've made, carrying that cross on your back mile after mile, in order to keep a promise. This has moved me.

JOE: But it isn't right. You didn't make the promise.

ROSA: He's trying to help, Joe.

JOE: But it isn't right. I promised to keep my vow myself, without anybody's help. And this sleeping in a hotel isn't part of the bargain.

PRETTY BOY: And is your wife in the bargain?

JOE: Rosa? No, she can go.

PRETTY BOY: In that case, if you want me to take your wife . . . at least she can rest while she waits for you.

JOE: Do you want to, Rosa? Do you want to wait for me in the hotel? (*He turns to Pretty Boy.*) Is it a respectable hotel?

PRETTY BOY (*pretending he is offended*): Come now, do you think I would recommend . . .

JOE: I'm sorry, it's just that I've always heard that here in the city . . .

PRETTY BOY: You can trust me.

JOE: Is it far from here?

PRETTY BOY: No, you just go up the hill . . .

JOE: What do you say, Rosa?

ROSA (*sensing Pretty Boy's game*): I don't want to, Joe. I'd rather stay here with you.

JOE: Why, just a few minutes ago you were complaining.

PRETTY BOY: Of course. She must be exhausted. Twenty-five miles.

JOE: After all, you're right, it's my promise and not hers. (*Turns to Rosa.*) Go with the young man, don't be timid about it.

PRETTY BOY: I'll go with her that far, I'll introduce her to the doorman, who is a good friend of mine—yes, because a woman by herself, you know, they won't let her in—then I'll come back and tell you her room number. In a little while, after you have fulfilled your promise, you can go there.

JOE: If you would do that, it would be a great favor. I can't leave this spot.

PRETTY BOY: Nor should you. First, St. Barbara.

ROSA: Joe, I'd better stay with you . . .

JOE: What for, Rosa? This way you can go and rest in a good bed and you won't have to lie there on those cold steps . . .

PRETTY BOY: Why it's dangerous! She could catch pneumonia.

ROSA (*she begins to leave. She stops, hesitating. She senses the danger that lies before her. She tries, with her look, to make Joe Burro understand her fear*): Joe . . .

JOE: Oh, yes. (*He puts his hand in his pocket and pulls out a roll of bills.*) You may have to pay in advance . . .

ROSA (*she takes the money. She faces her husband*): Perhaps it would be better, after delivering the cross, to have a Mass offered in thanksgiving . . .

JOE (*without understanding the meaning of the suggestion*): That's right, that's not a bad idea.

Rosa goes up the hill and Pretty Boy follows her.

PRETTY BOY (*leaving*): I'll be back in a minute.

JOE: Good. (*He sits down at the foot of the cross and tries to find a way of resting his body on it. Gradually, he falls asleep. The lights go out.*)

Scene 2

The lights go on again, slowly, until we see a clear day. One hears, in the distance, occasional sounds of the city, now waking up: automobile horns, fireworks bursting, saluting Yansan, the African St. Barbara, and church bells announcing the six o'clock Mass. But none of this awakens Joe Burro. A religious woman enters from the hillside. She is dressed all in black, a veil on her head, as with short steps, she hurries, afraid of arriving late. She passes by Joe Burro and the cross without noticing them. She stops in front of the steps and mutters to herself a little.[3]

---

[3] The director may have various persons come down the hill and enter the church during this scene.

RELIGIOUS WOMAN: The door's closed. It happens every time.
You run, afraid of arriving late, and when you get here
the door is closed. Why don't they open the door first and
then ring the bells? No, first they ring the bells, and then
they open the door. That's that sexton for you. (*She stops
muttering on seeing the cross. She adjusts her glasses, as
if not believing her eyes. She goes and examines closely
the cross and its sleeping owner. Her expression is one of
great surprise.*) The saints be praised!

*At this moment, the door of the church opens and the
Sexton comes out. He is a man about fifty years of age. His
mentality, however, is closer to fourteen. He is nearsighted,
and wears thick-lensed glasses. His hair persists in falling
over his forehead, accentuating the appearance of one
mentally retarded. He seems groggy from sleep. He yawns
widely, loudly, after opening the first section of the door.
He stretches out and groans forcefully. After he has opened
the rest of the sectioned door, he leans back for a moment
on the door and dozes, not noticing the Religious Woman
who is approaching.*

(*She nudges him slightly with her elbow.*) Hey there,
fellow . . .
SEXTON (*awakening, quite startled*): Yes, Father, I'm com-
ing! . . .
RELIGIOUS WOMAN: Father, my eye . . .
SEXTON: Oh, it's you . . .
RELIGIOUS WOMAN: I'm going to complain to Father Olavo
about this crazy habit of yours of ringing the bells before
you open the church door. I hear the bells, I come running
with my tongue hanging out, I get here, and the door is
still closed.
SEXTON: Then why do you come to the six o'clock Mass?
Why don't you come later?
RELIGIOUS WOMAN (*ill-manneredly*): Because I want to.
Because it's none of your business. (*She points to the cross.*)
What's that?
SEXTON: What's what?
RELIGIOUS WOMAN: Can't you see? A big cross in the middle
of the square . . .
SEXTON (*straining to see better*): Oh, yes . . . I see it now
. . . it's a wooden cross . . . and it looks like there's a man
sleeping next to it . . .

RELIGIOUS WOMAN: What wonderful eyesight you have! Of
course it's a wooden cross and of course there's a man
next to it. What I want to know is what's it all about?

SEXTON: I don't know. How do you expect me to know? Why
don't you ask him?

RELIGIOUS WOMAN (*roughly*): I'm not going to ask him anything!

SEXTON: Perhaps he's a straggler from the procession . . .

RELIGIOUS WOMAN: What procession? St. Barbara's? The
procession hasn't even started. And did you ever see anybody carry a cross in a procession? Not even on Good
Friday. (*She makes the sign of the cross and hurries into
the church.*)

*The Sexton approaches Joe Burro, quite curious. At this
point Pretty Boy comes in from the hill. He sees the church
open and is surprised.*

PRETTY BOY: Well, I'll be . . .

SEXTON (*he looks at him puzzled*): It *is* a cross . . .

PRETTY BOY: And what did you think it was? A gun? (*Goes
over to Joe Burro.*) He's sound asleep . . . not even the
St. Barbara fireworks woke him up. Well, they say that's
the way people sleep who have a clear conscience and a
light heart . . . (*Cynically.*) That's the way it is with me.
When I hit the sack I'm dead to the world. (*He shakes
Joe Burro.*) Friend . . . hey there, my friend! . . .

JOE (*waking up*): Oh, it's already daylight . . .

PRETTY BOY: Yes, it is. And the church is open. You can
deliver your load.

JOE (*getting up with difficulty, his muscles asleep and painful*):
That's right . . .

PRETTY BOY: I came back here to give you your wife's room
number. It's 27. It's a nice room on the second floor.
(*Quickly.*) At least, that's what the doorman told me.

JOE: Oh, thanks very much . . .

PRETTY BOY: The hotel is that one over there, the first one,
just after you go up the hill and turn to the right. The
Ideal Hotel. I'm a little late, because I stayed behind to
play a little . . . to play a little checkers with the doorman.

SEXTON (*very interested*): Did you win?

PRETTY BOY: It was a tie.

SEXTON: I'm crazy about that game!

PRETTY BOY (*looking at him from head to foot*): Frankly, no one would believe . . .

Father Olavo appears in the church door.

SEXTON (*as if he had been caught in some act*): Father Olavo! . . .

JOE: I've got to talk to him.

The Sexton hurries back to the church. He stops at the door, before the intimidating glance of Father Olavo. The latter is a rather young priest. He should not be over forty. His religious conviction verges on fanaticism. Perhaps, at heart, this is proof of a lack of conviction and a form of self-defense. His intolerance—which leads him at times to go against principles of his own religion and to confuse as enemies those who are really on his side—is perhaps no more than a defense with which he protects himself against a conscious weakness.

PRIEST (*to the Sexton*): What were you doing there?

SEXTON (*defending himself*): I was talking with those men.

PRIEST: And me there inside waiting for you to assist with the Mass. (*He notices Pretty Boy and Joe Burro.*) Who are they?

SEXTON: I don't know. One of them wants to talk to you.

JOE (*advancing*): It's me, Father. (*He bows, respectfully, and kisses his hand.*)

PRIEST: It's time for Mass now. Later, if you wish . . .

JOE: But I've come a great distance, Father. I've come twenty-five miles.

PRIEST: Twenty-five miles? To speak to me?

JOE: No, to bring this cross.

PRIEST (*looking at the cross, very closely*): And how did you bring it . . . in a truck?

JOE: No, Father, on my back.

SEXTON (*giving childish vent to his admiration*): Man alive!

PRIEST (*casting a stern look at him*): Hush! Be quiet! (*His interest in Joe Burro increasing.*) Twenty-five miles with that cross on your back! Let's have a look at your shoulder.

Joe Burro takes off one side of his jacket, opens up his shirt and shows him his shoulder. The Sexton stretches out

*as far as he can to take a look and indicates how impressed
he is.*

SEXTON: It's down to the flesh!

PRIEST (*he seems satisfied with the examination*): A promise?

JOE (*nods his head affirmatively*): To St. Barbara. I was
waiting for the church to open . . .

SEXTON: You must have received a very great favor from her!

The Priest waves the Sexton to be quiet.

JOE: Thanks to St. Barbara death did not take my very best
friend.

PRIEST (*he seems to meditate deeply on the question*): Even
so, don't you think the promise a little exaggerated? And
also a little pretentious?

JOE: Not at all, Father. A promise is a promise. It's like a
business deal. If you set a price, and get the goods, you
have to pay. I know a lot of welshing goes on. But not with
me. It's give and take. When Nicholas became ill, you
can't imagine how I felt.

PRIEST: And it was on account of that . . . Nicholas, that
you made the promise?

JOE: It was. Nicholas was injured, Father, by a tree that fell
during a storm.

SEXTON: The saints be praised! The tree fell on top of him?!

JOE: Just a branch, that struck him a glancing blow on the
head. He came home, bleeding all over the place! My wife
and I took care of him, but no matter what we did, we
couldn't stop the bleeding.

PRIEST: A hemorrhage.

JOE: And it didn't stop until I went to the stable, took a bit
of cow dung and applied it to the wound.

PRIEST (*nauseated*): But my son, what a backward thing to
do! Filthy!

JOE: That's what the doctor said when he arrived. He ordered
me to take that filth from the wound or else Nicholas would
die.

PRIEST: Undoubtedly.

JOE: And I took it off. He cleaned the wound well and the
blood began to run again like a waterfall. And what about
the doctor's efforts to stop the bleeding? He sopped it with
cotton and more cotton, but to no avail. It was a bleeding
that just wouldn't stop. Finally, the little man turned to me

and shouted: Hurry, my good man, go get some more cow dung or else he will die!

PRIEST: And . . . the bleeding stopped?

JOE: Immediately. It is an excellent remedy. Did you know that, Father? And if not from a cow, from a castrated horse will also do. But there are some who prefer spider webs.

PRIEST: Go on, go on. I am not interested in that kind of medicine.

JOE: Well, the bleeding stopped. But Nicholas began to tremble with fever, and the following day something happened that had never happened before: I went out of the house and Nicholas stayed home. He couldn't get up. It was the first time this happened in six years. I left, I went shopping in town, went into Jacob's bar to have a shot of brandy, went by Zèquinha's pharmacy to get the latest news—all this without Nicholas. Everybody noticed it, because if anyone wanted to know where I was, all he had to do was to look for Nicholas. If I went to Mass, he waited for me at the church door . . .

PRIEST: At the door? Why didn't he go in? Isn't he a Catholic?

JOE: Having such a good heart, Nicholas can't help being a Catholic. But that's not the reason he doesn't go into the Church. It's because the priest doesn't allow it. (*Very sadly.*) Nicholas had the luck to be born a burro . . . a four-legged one.

PRIEST: A burro? Then that . . . that one you call Nicholas is a burro?! An animal?!

JOE: My burro . . . yes, sir.

PRIEST: And it was for him, for a burro, that you made this promise?

JOE: It was . . . Of course, the truth of the matter is that I didn't know it would be so difficult to find a church dedicated to St. Barbara, that I would have to walk twenty-five miles before I would find one, here in Bahia . . .

PRETTY BOY (*who has been witnessing the entire scene, from the side, bursts out laughing, roughly*): He got stuck . . .

Father Olavo, surprised, looks at him, as if just now noting his presence. Pretty Boy stops laughing almost at once, disarmed by the priest's forceful glance.

JOE: But even if I had known it, I would still have made the promise. Because when I saw that even Black Zeferino's prayers had no effect . . .

PRIEST: Prayers?! What prayers?!

JOE: Forgive me, Father . . . but I tried everything. Black
  Zeferino is a very famous praying man where I live: dog
  itch, worms, cattle disease, he can cure all this with two
  prayers and three doodles on the ground. Everybody says
  so . . . and I myself, I once had a terrible headache which
  I couldn't get rid of by any means . . . I called Black
  Zeferino, and he said I had the sun inside my head. He
  put a towel on my forehead, poured out a bottle of water,
  said a prayer, and the sun left me and I was well again.

PRIEST: You did wrong, my son. Those prayers are the
  prayers of the devil.

JOE: Not of the devil, no sir.

PRIEST: Yes, of the devil. You were not able to distinguish
  good from evil. All men are like that. They live for miracles
  instead of living for God. And they don't know whether
  they are on the road to heaven or to hell.

JOE: To hell? How can it be, Father, if the prayer talks about
  God? (*Reciting.*) "God made the Sun, God made the light,
  God made all the illumination of the grandiose universe.
  With His Grace I bless you, I cure you. Sun, leave the
  head of this creature and go to the waves of the Sacred Sea,
  through the holy powers of the Father, of the Son, and of
  the Holy Ghost." Then he said an Our Father and my
  headache was gone at that very moment.

SEXTON: Unbelievable!

PRIEST: My son, that man was a witch doctor.

JOE: What do you mean a witch doctor, if the prayer is
  used to cure?

PRIEST: It is not to cure, it is to tempt. And you fell into
  temptation.

JOE: Well, all I know is that I got well. (*Changing his tone.*)
  But with Nicholas there was no praying that could make
  him get up. Black Zeferino put his foot on the poor burro's
  head, said a string of prayers, but nothing happened. I was
  already beginning to lose hope. Nicholas, all dried up, so
  thin that one could count his ribs. He wouldn't eat anything,
  drink anything, nor would he swish his tail anymore to
  drive away the flies. I could see that never again would I
  hear his steps behind me, following me everywhere, like a
  dog. They even gave me a nickname on account of that:
  Joe Burro. And it doesn't bother me. I don't consider it
  offensive. Nicholas isn't a burro like other burros. He's

a burro with the soul of a man. And he does this out of friendship, dedication. I never ride him; I prefer to walk or to go on horseback. But one way or the other, he always comes behind me. If I go into a house and stay there two hours, he'll wait for me for two hours, right there at the door. Now I ask you, Father, isn't a burro like that worth a promise?

PRIEST (*dryly, still holding back his indignation*): Go on.

JOE: It was then that comrade Miúda reminded me: why didn't I go to Maria Yansan's *candomblé*, her voodoo session?

PRIEST: *Candomblé*?! Voodoo?!

JOE: Yes, it's a voodoo ceremony held about seven miles from my farm. (*With the conscience of one who has committed a sin, but not a serious one.*) I know that you're going to get angry with me, Father. I too was never one to attend voodoo ceremonies. But poor Nicholas was dying. It wouldn't cost anything to try. And if it didn't do any good, it wouldn't do any harm. So I went. I told the priestess about my situation. She said that indeed it had to do with Yansan, goddess of lightning and thunder. It was Yansan that had injured Nicholas . . . It was to her that I should make reparation, that is: make a vow. But it had to be quite a big promise, because Yansan, that had injured Nicholas with a bolt of lightning, was not going to turn back for any old thing. And then I remembered that Yansan is St. Barbara and I promised that if Nicholas got well I would carry a wooden cross from my farm to her church, on her feast day, a cross as heavy as Christ's.

PRIEST (*as if annotating the words*): As heavy as Christ's. You promised that to . . .

JOE: To St. Barbara.

PRIEST: To Yansan!

JOE: It's the same thing . . .

PRIEST (*shouting*): It is not the same thing! (*Controlling himself.*) But continue.

JOE: I also promised to divide my land among the poor farmers, poorer than me.

PRIEST: To divide? Equally?

JOE: Yes, Father, equally.

SEXTON: And Nicholas . . . I mean, the burro, did he get well?

JOE: He got well in two shakes. A miracle. Indeed a miracle. The next day he was up, braying. And a week later every-

body was pointing to me in the street: "There goes Joe
Burro with his burro behind him!" (*He laughs.*) And I
didn't tell anybody. And, of course, neither did Nicholas.
Only he and I knew about the miracle. (*As if correcting
himself.*) He and I and St. Barbara.

PRIEST (*trying at first to control himself*): In the first place,
even admitting the intervention of St. Barbara, it would
not be a miracle, but merely a favor. The burro could have
been cured without divine intervention.

JOE: But, Father, he got well from one day to the next . . .

PRIEST (*as if he hadn't heard him*): And besides, St. Barbara,
if she were to grant a favor, would not do it at a voodoo
session!

JOE: It's because in my town's chapel there is no statue of
St. Barbara. But in the *candomblé*, they have a statue of
Yansan, who is St. Barbara.

PRIEST (*exploding*): She is not St. Barbara! St. Barbara is a
Catholic saint! You went to a fetishistic ritual. You invoked
a false divinity and it was to her you promised this sacrifice!

JOE: No, Father, it was to St. Barbara! It was to the Church
of St. Barbara that I promised to come with my cross!
And it is before the altar of St. Barbara that I am going
to fall on my knees in a short while to thank her for
what she has done for me!

PRIEST (*walks back and forth, his hand on his chin, and
finally stops in front of Joe Burro in an inquisitorial
manner*): Very well. And what do you intend to do after
. . . after keeping your vow?

JOE (*not understanding the question*): What do I intend to
do? Return to my farm, in peace with my conscience and
on even terms with the saint.

PRIEST: Just that?

JOE: Just that . . .

PRIEST: Are you sure? Aren't you going to try to be taken
for a new Christ?

JOE: Me?!

PRIEST: Yes, you. You who have just repeated the Way of
the Cross, suffering the martyrdom of Jesus. You who,
presumptuously, try to imitate the Son of God . . .

JOE (*humbly*): Father . . . I did not try to imitate Jesus . . .

PRIEST (*cutting him off sharply*): You lie! I marked your

words! You yourself said that you promised to carry a cross *as heavy as Christ's.*

JOE: Yes, but that . . .

PRIEST: That proves that you are being submitted to an even greater temptation.

JOE: What's that, Father?

PRIEST: To make yourself equal to the Son of God.

JOE: No, Father.

PRIEST: Why then do you repeat the Divine Passion?! To save humanity? No, to save a burro!

JOE: Father, Nicholas . . .

PRIEST: A burro with a Christian name! A quadruped! An animal!

The Religious Woman comes out of the church and witnesses the scene from the top of the steps.

JOE: But Father, wasn't it God that also made burros?

PRIEST: But not in his likeness. And it wasn't to save them that he sent his son. It was for us, for you, for me, for humanity!

JOE (*very distressed, trying to explain*): Father, I must explain that Nicholas is not an ordinary burro . . . you don't know Nicholas, that's why . . . he's a burro with the soul of a man . . .

PRIEST: Well even if he had the soul of an angel, you are not going into this church with that cross! (*He turns his back to him and goes toward the church. The Sexton follows him immediately.*)

JOE (*desperately*): But Father . . . I promised to take the cross up to the main altar! I must keep my promise!

PRIEST: You should have made it then in a church. Or in any place other than in a voodoo den.

JOE: But I already explained . . .

PRIEST: You cannot serve two masters, God and the Devil!

JOE: Father . . .

PRIEST: A pagan ritual, which began in a voodoo session, cannot end in the nave of a church!

JOE: But Father, the church . . .

PRIEST: The church is the House of God. Voodoo is the cult of the Devil!

JOE: I didn't walk twenty-five miles to turn back here. You

can't keep me from entering. The church is not yours, it's God's!

PRIEST: You are going to disregard my authority?

JOE: Father, between you and St. Barbara, I choose St. Barbara.

PRIEST (*to the Sexton*): Close the door. Let those who wish to hear Mass enter through the door of the sacristy. That cross cannot pass through that door. (*He goes into the church.*)

The Religious Woman also enters rapidly behind the priest. The Sexton, promptly, begins to close the door of the church, while Joe Burro, in the middle of the square, his nerves tense, his eyes wide open, with an air of incomprehension and revolt, seems disposed not to move from there. Pretty Boy, a little to the side, looks on with an ironic smile on his lips. The door of the church closes completely, while a tremendous display of fireworks salutes Yansan.

THE CURTAIN FALLS SLOWLY

ACT II

Scene 1

About two hours later. The café has opened and the Galician is seen standing on a box, tying a cord with red and white streamers that extends from the door of his café to the building on the opposite side. Joe is still in the middle of the square with his cross. A cry is heard: "Sweets . . . Come buy my sweets!" A little later, a Negress in typical bahiana dress, and with a tray on her head, appears at the top of the hill. She comes down the hill and on passing the Galician greets him.

AUNTIE: May Yansan give you a good day.

GALICIAN (*he speaks partly in Spanish*): *Gracias*, Auntie.

Auntie walks up to the church and stops there, near the steps.[4]

---

[4] During the entire act, people can cross the square, as long as they do not interfere with the action.

AUNTIE (*addressing the Galician*): Would you come over here and give your Auntie a hand, white man?

The Galician hurries over to help her. First he takes the stand which is on the tray, opens it, then he helps her take the tray from her head and put it on the stand.

May St. Barbara reward you. (*Noticing Joe Burro.*) Saints alive! What's that?

GALICIAN: I don't know. He was already here when I opened the shop. I think he's *loco*, a nut. (*He goes back to his streamers, while Auntie gets her small burner ready, trying to light it.*)

Ray-the-Rimer is seen coming down the hill, lazily, at a slow pace. He is a mulatto, his kinky hair showing under a worn and dirty bowler—a necessary accessory for his occupation: poet-salesman. Under his arm he carries a big pile of pamphlets and books: popular poems and tales in verse. And two signs, one in front and the other behind. One says: "Story of the Mulatta Esmeralda—a masterpiece"; and on the other "Just Out, the Latest! 'What Blind Jeremiah saw on the Moon.' "

RIMER (*reciting*):
Good morning, my Galician friend!
A day like this has never come,
To greet the goddess our Yansan.
This calls for cash, a little sum,
Just as a loan, to mark the day;
Or failing that, a shot of rum.

GALICIAN: *Usted* with your rimes and verses, always end up talking me out of something. (*He goes into the café and walks behind the counter.*) Is that story about Blind Jeremiah really that good? (*He serves the rum.*)

RIMER (*very loudly and theatrically*): An epic. A new *Iliad*, where the moon is Troy and the Trojan horse is St. George's horse! (*He takes out a copy and puts it on the counter.*) That's to pay for the rum.

GALICIAN: *Sí*, but . . . *yo*, I prefer *la otra*, the other one about the Mulatta Esmeralda.

RIMER: That proves you've got good taste, Galician! (*He exchanges the pamphlets.*) It's also a masterpiece. All modesty aside, it brings to mind the great poet Castro Alves.

(*He drinks the rum with one gulp. Pointing to the streamers.*) Red and white streamers, Yansan's colors. They say
you don't believe in voodoo.

GALICIAN: *Yo,* I don't believe, but there are those who do.
And *yo soy,* I am a businessman . . .

RIMER: That makes two of us! (*Holds the glass out again.*)
Another shot. I'll pay you for it tomorrow.

*The Galician shows his displeasure but he fills the glass
again.*

*The Religious Woman enters from the right and stops
near Auntie on seeing Joe Burro. She is surprised and
angry.*

RELIGIOUS WOMAN: That's the limit! He's still there!

AUNTIE: Dearie, ain't they gonna open the church today? It's
St. Barbara's day . . .

RELIGIOUS WOMAN (*casting an accusing look at Joe Burro*):
Not as long as that character stays here.

AUNTIE: What's he done?

RELIGIOUS WOMAN: He wants to go into the church with that
cross.

AUNTIE: That's all?

RELIGIOUS WOMAN: Isn't that enough? Do you think Father
Olavo would allow it?

AUNTIE: The saints be praised! Why not? Was it a promise
he made?

RELIGIOUS WOMAN: Yes, it was. But a voodoo promise. To
some Yansan or other . . . may the Lord forgive me. (*She
makes the sign of the cross. She goes toward the left and
on passing Joe Burro insults him.*) Heretic! (*She goes up
the hill, as Joe Burro follows her with a look of pained
incomprehension.*)

RIMER (*having heard the conversation. Speaking to the Galician*): I'm going over and see if Auntie will give me some
of that bean specialty of hers. (*He crosses the square. On
passing Joe Burro, he shows great curiosity and interest.*)
Good morning, Auntie!

AUNTIE: Good morning, Master Rimer. (*Extending them
toward him.*) Beans, bean stew, sweets . . . Come on,
give them your blessing!

RIMER (*pointing*): Some of that beef dish. I'll pay you shortly,
when I get my first sale.

AUNTIE: I knew it . . . (*Hands him a serving, wrapped in a banana leaf.*)

RIMER (*indicating Joe Burro*): What's that all about?

AUNTIE: You heard?

RIMER: Yes, I heard.

AUNTIE (*respectfully*): A debt to Yansan . . . (*With the tips of her fingers she touches the ground and her forehead.*)

RIMER: Is that why the priest didn't let him in?

AUNTIE: That's why. Poor fellow.

RIMER: He even closed the door.

AUNTIE: You understand it?

RIMER: No, I don't.

AUNTIE: The priest is such a good man.

RIMER: You think so?

AUNTIE: Sure I do. He's such a good friend of the poor and does so much for them. I don't understand it.

The Policeman enters from the right. He goes straight to Joe Burro. He is a man who tries to evade problems that come up. His idea of duty fits in perfectly with his fear of responsibility. His main hope is that nothing will happen, so that he will not have to exercise his authority. At heart, this authority fetters him terribly, and even more so, his duty of carrying it out.

POLICEMAN: Hi there, friend.

JOE: Hello.

POLICEMAN (*pointing to the cross*): Is that for the St. Barbara procession?

JOE: No.

POLICEMAN: Because the procession doesn't start here. It starts at the marketplace not far from here and goes to the other church.

JOE: I'm not interested in that procession.

POLICEMAN: Then what are you doing here? Waiting for the celebration? It's too early. It's eight-thirty in the morning. It doesn't get going until the afternoon.

JOE: I've been here since four-thirty this morning.

POLICEMAN: Four-thirty?! (*He scratches his head, worried.*) You must be quite religious, and then some! But, it just so happens that you picked a bad place . . .

JOE: It's not my fault.

POLICEMAN: Yes, I know; you didn't originate this St. Barbara celebration. But, can I help it if I'm a policeman? It's my job to keep traffic moving as much as possible.

JOE: I'm very sorry, but I've got to stay here.

POLICEMAN (*his patience beginning to run out*): Oh, come now, . . . I'm trying to get along with you.

JOE (*also becoming a little angry*): I'm also trying to get along with you and with everybody. But I think nobody understands me.

Ray-the-Rimer, who has been witnessing the entire scene, is led by his curiosity to come closer. Auntie is also following everything with interest.

JOE: That woman called me a heretic; the priest closed the door of the church as if I were the Devil himself. Me, Joe Burro, a devotee of St. Barbara.

RIMER: But, what do you want?

JOE: I want them to let me put this cross in the church, nothing more. Then, I promise to go away. This whole business is beginning to get me down!

RIMER: It was a promise, a promise he made.

POLICEMAN (*thinking—a process which seems to require a tremendous amount of physical effort on his part*): A promise . . . to put the cross in the church . . . I don't see any difficulty in that. We'll talk to the priest and . . .

JOE: If you can get him to open the door and let me go in, everything will be solved.

POLICEMAN (*thinking a little more, and seeing that there is no other way of settling the problem, he comes to a decision*): OK, I'll go and talk to him. (*Walks toward the door of the church.*)

The Galician, Ray-the-Rimer, Auntie, all watch him anxiously.

RIMER: I'm not going over there to help him because the priest and I are not on the best of terms. (*He leaves.*)

POLICEMAN (*knocks on the door several times without any result, puts his head against the door, and calls out*): Father? Please open a moment!

A few seconds later, a small section of the door opens, and the Sexton's head appears, his uneasiness evident.

I want to talk to the priest.

SEXTON (*seeing that there is no danger, he opens the door a little*): Come in!

The Policeman takes off his cap and enters. The Sexton closes the door rapidly. Rosa comes down the hill. She is in a hurry, as if afraid of not finding Joe Burro still there. But when she sees him, she slows down, and becomes somewhat relieved. She still has, however, a certain air of guilt about her that she tries to conceal.

ROSA: You still here! (*Noticing that the church is closed.*) Didn't the church open yet?

JOE: It opened, all right. But the priest won't let me go in with the cross.

ROSA: Why not?

JOE (*shaking his head, most unhappy*): I don't know, Rosa, I don't know . . . For two hours I've been trying to understand . . . but I'm dizzy, as if I'd been kicked in the head. I don't understand anything anymore . . . It seems that I've been turned completely around and that I'm seeing things the opposite of what they are. Heaven in place of hell . . . the Devil in place of the saints.

ROSA (*thinking of her own experience*): That's it exactly. Suddenly, you find out that you're another person. That you were always another person . . . it's terrible.

JOE: But it's not possible, Rosa. I've always been an honest man. I've always feared God.

ROSA (*thinking of her own problem*): Joe, this is beginning to look like a kind of punishment!

JOE: Punishment? Punishment for what? Because I made such a great vow? Because it was made to Maria de Yansan at a voodoo session? But if St. Barbara wasn't for this, she wouldn't have performed the miracle.

ROSA: Joe, forget St. Barbara. Think a little about us.

JOE: About us?

ROSA: About me, Joe.

JOE: About you?

ROSA: Yes, Joe, about me, your wife.

JOE: What do you want? Didn't you get to sleep, to rest?

ROSA (*without looking at him*): Joe, let's get out of here.

JOE: Now?

ROSA: Yes, right now.

JOE: I can't. You know very well that I can't go back until I carry out my vow. It would bother me for the rest of my life.

ROSA: You believe in things too much.

JOE: It's because you don't consider what could happen.

ROSA: More than has already happened?

JOE: What's happened? The march, nights without sleep, and now to be cursed as if I were the Devil himself? All this is nothing, compared with the punishment that could still come.

ROSA: But if the priest won't let you go in with the cross, why are you still hanging around here?

JOE: The policeman went to talk to him. I'm waiting. (*As if excusing himself for not having thought about her situation.*) If you want to, you can go and eat something.

ROSA (*faced with the impossibility of communicating her problem to him*): I already had something at the hotel.

JOE: And wasn't that a good hotel that fellow fixed you up with?

ROSA: Very good. It even had a washbasin in the room and a spring mattress.

JOE: I was a little worried.

ROSA (*hurt by his lack of jealousy*): About me?

JOE: You in a hotel, by yourself. In a big city, one never knows. Although that young man did assure us that it was a respectable hotel.

ROSA: So you didn't have anything to worry about. The young man was completely reliable. So kind, so attentive . . .

REPORTER (*he enters with the photographer*): There he is. (*He goes over to Joe, while the photographer moves around trying out the various angles. The Reporter is lively and discerning. He greets Joe Burro enthusiastically.*) Good morning, my friend! (*He shakes hands warmly with Joe Burro.*) Congratulations! You're a hero.

JOE (*looking at him surprised*): A hero?

REPORTER (*enthusiastically*): Yes, twenty-five miles carrying this cross. (*He estimates the weight.*) Quite heavy, eh? Twenty-five miles . . . twenty-five miles. The largest hike I ever made was fifteen miles, in the service. And my rifle wasn't nearly so heavy. (*He laughs, but his laugh dissipates like a pricked balloon when he sees the look of distrust on the faces of Rosa and Joe Burro.*) Oh, excuse me . . . I know you made a promise. The comparison was not a very good one . . . (*To the photographer.*) Carey, you can take a picture now. (*He strikes a pose in front of Joe Burro, with his notebook and pencil in hand.*) Now just pretend you're speaking to me.

JOE (*beginning to become impatient*): Pretend I'm speaking . . . why?

REPORTER: And within a few hours all Brazil is going to know. You're going to be famous.

JOE (*annoyed*): But I don't want to be famous, all I want . . .

ROSA (*interrupting, in a tone of reproach*): What's the matter, Joe? Be a little more polite with the young man. He's from the gazette . . .

REPORTER: His wife?

ROSA: Yes. I also walked twenty-five miles. My feet are covered with corns that big.

REPORTER: Marvelous. And how long did it take you to cover the course?

ROSA (*not understanding*): How's that?

REPORTER: I mean: When did you leave your city?

ROSA: Our farm? We left yesterday, early in the morning. At five o'clock in the morning.

REPORTER: And when did you arrive?

ROSA: Before five o'clock.

REPORTER: Then you covered the course in twenty-four hours. Let's see now, with a cross that must weigh? . . . (*He looks questioningly at Joe Burro.*)

JOE (*disturbed*): I don't know, I didn't weigh it.

REPORTER: Well, no matter what it weighs, it's a record! From this standpoint alone, we can consider it a great sporting feat, a test of physical endurance . . . (*To Rosa.*) And of dedication . . .

Rosa smiles, flattered, considering herself a heroine.

But where did the idea come from for this . . . pilgrimage? (*His questions are directed at Joe Burro, but the latter refuses to answer them.*)

ROSA: There was no such idea. The burro became ill, was dying—he made a promise to St. Barbara.

REPORTER: The burro? What burro?

ROSA: Nicholas.

JOE (*angry*): Why? Are you also going to tell me that my burro is not worth a promise?

REPORTER: No, not at all . . . I . . . I just didn't know . . .

then, all this . . . twenty-five miles . . . the cross . . . all
on account of a burro . . . (*Suddenly, foreseeing the interest
his reporting will arouse.*)

ROSA: And that's not all. He also promised to divide his land
among a bunch of lazy bums.

JOE: What lazy bums? People who want to work and don't
have any land.

REPORTER: Dividing his land . . . Tell me, are you in favor
of agrarian reform?

JOE (*not understanding*): Agrarian reform? What's that?

REPORTER: It's what you've just done with your land. Redis-
tribution of land among those who don't have any.

JOE: And I don't regret it, young man. I've brought happiness to a few people, and what's left is more than enough
for me.

REPORTER (*taking notes*): He is in favor of agrarian reform.

JOE: Of course, it's true that if my burro hadn't become ill,
I wouldn't have done it . . .

REPORTER: But, what if all land owners did the same thing?
What if the government decided to expropriate the land
and divide it among the peasants?

JOE: Oh, that would be very good. Everybody should work
his own land.

REPORTER (*taking notes*): He is against the exploitation of
man by man. Do you belong to any political party?

JOE (*with a little pride, concealed behind a modest smile*):
Well, they wanted to make me a councilman . . .

ROSA: The burro threw a monkey wrench in the works.

REPORTER: The burro? But how?

ROSA: Wherever he goes, the burro goes behind. If he were
elected, the burro would also have to be . . .

REPORTER: I see, but this time, Mr. . . .

JOE: Joe Burro, at your service.

REPORTER: . . . Mr. Joe Burro, you'll be elected, burro and
all. (*Aside to him.*) Come now, isn't the story of this
promise merely a publicity stunt to impress the electorate?
. . .

JOE (*offended*): A publicity stunt?!

REPORTER: And a masterful one, I grant you! I can just
imagine the hubbub you created. As you went along the
streets, on your way here, tremendous crowds must have
gathered to see you pass by.

JOE: In fact, there were . . .

ROSA: A lot of riffraff too.

REPORTER: And just imagine your return! Your arrival in your town, in an open car, with a band of music, fireworks!

JOE: Are you crazy? There isn't going to be anything of the kind.

REPORTER: Of course, there will. There will because my newspaper is going to promote it. I only insist on one thing: that you give us an exclusive. That you not grant interviews to anybody else. (*In another tone.*) Of course, you'll have some compensation . . . (*He makes a significant gesture with his index finger and his thumb.*) And also publicity. Front page, with photographs, of you and your wife . . . we'll also have the burro photographed . . . in a few hours you'll be a national hero.

JOE (*very annoyed*): Young man, I don't believe you understand me. Nobody yet has understood me . . .

REPORTER (*without paying attention to him*): It's just too bad that you had to pick today for it. Saturday. Tomorrow is Sunday and there's no edition. Only on Monday. And our Promotion Department would have to prepare things. Now we'll have a real scoop in today's edition, but the big bang can't be until Monday. When do you intend to return?

JOE: If I had my way, I'd already be on my way back.

The door of the church opens a little. The Sexton lets the Policeman out and closes it again. The Policeman comes to speak to Joe Burro, who awaits him without much hope.

POLICEMAN (*shaking his head, discouraged*): I wasn't able to do anything.

JOE: You spoke to the priest?

POLICEMAN: I did; I argued . . . but it didn't do any good. And in addition, I had to listen to a long sermon. He's of the opinion that instead of asking him to let you in the church, I should arrest you. Of course, I'm not going to do anything of the kind, but you certainly could have made a less complicated promise.

ROSA: That's the way I feel about it.

POLICEMAN: And there's no point in your hanging around here. The priest said that he won't open the door, and he won't open it—I know him.

REPORTER: Excellent! That's very good! This gives us an excuse for postponing delivery of the cross until Monday.

It will give us time to organize everything. Interviews, radio introductions, and announcements . . . and your triumphal return with majorettes and a band!

JOE (*more and more annoyed and more unhappy*): Young man, I came on foot, and I'll return on foot.

ROSA (*she finds in the Reporter's words a vague possibility of liberation, as she listens to them with a growing enthusiasm*): For heaven's sake! Don't be stupid, man! The young fellow is trying to help us.

JOE: Then let him help me convince the priest to open the door . . .

REPORTER: I'm going to interview the priest. But you can be sure of one thing: whatever your objective is, a little publicity isn't going to do any harm . . . (*He winks at Joe Burro, who doesn't understand the insinuation.*) Carey, let's have another picture. (*To Joe Burro.*) Would you be kind enough to put the cross on your shoulder? (*To Rosa.*) You too.

Joe Burro remains undecided, not finding words to express his indignation.

ROSA: Come on, Joe! (*She pushes him under the cross and stands at his side, in a forced pose.*)

The Policeman also tries to slip into the photograph. The scene is ludicrous, with Rosa breaking out into a broad toothpaste-ad-type smile, Joe Burro bending over from the weight of the cross and his great unhappiness. And the Policeman, with his chest out, determined to take part in the event.

GALICIAN (*comes out of the café, and runs over to speak to the photographer*): Un momento! Usted, couldn't you get my café into the picture? You know . . . a little publicity . . .

The photographer takes a position that will show the café in the background. The Galician runs back to his counter and strikes a pose.

REPORTER: Excellent. Fire away, Carey.

The photographer puts in a plate and takes a picture.

REPORTER: Thank you. This will come out today on the front page. (*To the photographer.*) Let's go now and have an interview with the priest.

POLICEMAN: You better go by the door of the sacristy.

JOE: I'll take you there.

REPORTER (*not liking the idea*): No, I think it's better you stay here . . .

JOE (*determined*): But I want to go with you.

REPORTER (*gives in, unwillingly*): Very well. (*He goes out with Joe Burro and the photographer.*)

The insistent blowing of automobile horns is heard.

POLICEMAN: I guarantee that the priest will open the church now. Everybody is afraid of the press. (*He looks to the right.*) I'd better go over there, for things are getting worse. (*He leaves to the right.*)

Pretty Boy comes down the hill and stops at the café. Rosa sees him and cannot conceal her emotion.

PRETTY BOY (*to the Galician*): A double shot.

GALICIAN: Hi there, Pretty Boy. *Usted* here so early? . . . (*Pours him a drink of brandy.*)

ROSA (*she goes to the café and takes a position at the counter next to Pretty Boy*): Coffee, young man . . .

PRETTY BOY: Still here?

ROSA: Still here.

PRETTY BOY: I don't see how you can stand it.

ROSA: I don't either.

PRETTY BOY: Did he suspect anything?

ROSA: Nothing. He only thinks of his cross and of his promise.

PRETTY BOY: You know, I went home to sleep and I couldn't.

ROSA: Why not?

PRETTY BOY: I kept thinking of you.

ROSA: It's better you don't think of me.

PRETTY BOY: Are you sorry?

ROSA: Yes, I am.

PRETTY BOY: It's a little late now.

ROSA: No it isn't. One night can be wiped out.

PRETTY BOY: A lot of nights can be wiped out. No scars are left.

ROSA: It left one on me. I don't understand why he doesn't

notice it. It burns me up. It makes me want to tell him
everything.

PRETTY BOY: That's not a bad idea. He's not a violent man.
He might leave you here in the city and go to his farm
alone. That would take care of everything.

ROSA: Take care of what?

PRETTY BOY: Your life. You've got a future.

ROSA: It wouldn't do. That's my fate. Oh, it's true, at times
I feel like packing my things and hitting the road. But I
don't have the nerve. And if I did have, I wouldn't know
where to go . . .

PRETTY BOY: When I was a kid, I was a guide for a blind
man . . .

ROSA: Well, I'm not blind. And I knew very well what I was
doing. Just as I know that I'm capable of doing it again,
if he doesn't take me away from here. Even against my will.

PRETTY BOY: If you don't get away from him, you're going to
end up cracked just like him.

ROSA (*trying to justify her lack of courage*): He needs me.

PRETTY BOY: He has his burro.

ROSA: You stupid ass!

PRETTY BOY: I wasn't trying to make a comparison . . .

ROSA: He's very much a man, I'd like you to know!

PRETTY BOY: If that's true, why are you so hungry? . . .

ROSA (*she feels herself more and more drawn toward him, as
toward an abyss, lacking within herself the desire to resist
this definitive jump. There is merely that great weakness
that confronts a human being at the moment of a great
decision*): And why did you have to come back here?

PRETTY BOY: It was you who came to talk to me.

ROSA: You make me do things I don't want to do.

PRETTY BOY (*he laughs, conscious of his seductive power*): Is
it my fault that I was born with so many good qualities?

*She starts to return to the center of the square. He takes
her by the arm.*

(*Softly.*) Wait . . .

ROSA (*also softly*): Are you crazy?

PRETTY BOY: Apparently, he's going to be there a long time.
You understand?

ROSA (*breaks away from him with a jerk*): I don't understand
anything. You're mad and I'm beginning to go crazy myself.

PRETTY BOY: He can't leave his cross. But you can . . . you can go to the hotel to rest . . . or you can go and pray in another church, to ask another saint to help convince the priest that he should open the door . . . A little reinforcement always helps . . .

Joe Burro comes back. Rosa and Pretty Boy try to cover up.

AUNTIE (*stopping Joe*): So? . . .

JOE: They didn't let me go in. They think it's better to talk to the priest in private.

AUNTIE (*assuming an air of extreme complicity*): My son, I'm an assistant at Menininha's *candomblé*. Before long the voodoo session will be in full swing. You made a pledge to Yansan; Yansan will be there to receive it.

JOE (*not understanding*): What do you mean?

AUNTIE: I'll take you there! You take your cross and the saint receives it. You remain at peace with her!

JOE: Yansan . . .

AUNTIE: She was the one who granted your wish.

JOE: But the church . . .

AUNTIE: Tell the priest to go to the Devil. Take your cross to the voodoo session! I'll go with you!

JOE (*he hesitates a little and then reacts vehemently*): No, I didn't say I was going to carry the cross to a voodoo session, but to a church. To a church dedicated to St. Barbara.

AUNTIE: St. Barbara is Yansan. And Yansan is there! She's coming down on her horses! Let's go.

JOE: No. It's not the same thing. It's not the same thing.

The door of the church opens and the Reporter, the photographer, and the Sexton come out.

REPORTER (*to the Sexton*): You really think the priest will not let him go in?

SEXTON: Didn't you hear what he said? He's the Devil! The Devil in one of his many disguises!

REPORTER: The Devil disguised as Jesus Christ . . . I think that's a little strong. Anyway, that's his affair. I'll admit I'm not too well versed on this subject. What is important, however, is to keep him here at least until Monday. If necessary, I'll have some food and drinks sent here. Provided that he doesn't leave before Monday.

Joe Burro takes a step toward the church. The Sexton becomes frightened.

SEXTON: Excuse me, gentlemen, excuse me. (*He goes in and closes the door hurriedly.*)

The photographer goes over to the café.

REPORTER (*going over to Joe Burro*): It didn't do any good, my friend. The priest is like a rock. (*Trying to encourage him to resist.*) But he'll give up in the end. If you don't move from here, he'll have to open the church. I guarantee it. Now it's not only your cause but it's also our newspaper's cause. And being our newspaper's cause, it's the people's cause!

Joe Burro looks at him as if he were trying, unsuccessfully, to understand someone from another planet.

I advise you to resist. After all, it's your right. It's a right you earned on twenty-five miles of the "via crucis." I have faith in you. (*To Rosa.*) Read my newspaper this afternoon. It's going to hit like a bomb. (*He goes out followed by the photographer.*)

PRETTY BOY: Newspapermen, right?

ROSA: That's right. (*Proudly.*) They took my picture. Do you think they'll really publish it?

PRETTY BOY: If you were in the nude, I would guarantee it. This way . . . I don't know.

At this moment, Marli enters from the right. Seeing Pretty Boy near Rosa, she advances toward him in an aggressive manner.

MARLI: I knew it! . . . I knew you'd be after a piece of tail!

PRETTY BOY: What are you doing here?

MARLI: I came to find out why you didn't show up at the house last night.

PRETTY BOY: What house?

MARLI: My house!

PRETTY BOY: I was indisposed. I went to my hotel.

MARLI (*looking Rosa over from head to foot*): Yes, I see your "indisposition."

PRETTY BOY (*restrained, but forcefully*): Don't start any trouble!

MARLI: Why not? Are you afraid of her husband?

PRETTY BOY: I'm not afraid of anybody, and I'm not going to allow you to annoy the lady.

MARLI (*ironically*): The lady . . . if she's a lady, I'm a queen . . .

PRETTY BOY (*ordering her*): Marli, do what I tell you!

MARLI: Oh, you want to play the big he-man in front of her, don't you?

PRETTY BOY: I don't have anything to do with her!

MARLI: You spent the night with her!

Joe Burro's face clouds up and he seeks an explanation in Rosa's eyes. She avoids his glance.

PRETTY BOY (*he takes Marli by the arm, violently*): Let's go home!

MARLI: No! First, I want to clear all this up. I want that cow to know that you belong to me. (*Proudly.*) To me! (*She shouts at Rosa.*) These clothes were bought with my money! These clothes and all the clothes he has!

PRETTY BOY (*losing his patience and threatening her*): If you don't go home immediately, I won't ever let you give me anything again!

MARLI (*letting him drag her over to the right*): He's mine, you hear? Stick to your pious crackpot and leave my man alone! He's my man! He's my man!

There is a very long pause during which Joe Burro just looks at Rosa quietly, under the impact of the scene. One can see in his face doubt, disbelief, and especially fear before a world that is beginning to fall apart. The lights go down.

Scene 2

Three o'clock in the afternoon. Joe Burro and Rosa are still in the middle of the square. Auntie, with her stand, is at the door of the church, and the Galician is in his café. Ray-the-Rimer enters from the right.

RIMER: "The Story of the Mulatta Esmeralda," a complete

story relating Esmeralda's life from her birth in Innocents'
Lane until her death, victim of thirty knife-thrusts, on
Perdition Street. (*Offers a copy to Joe Burro.*) Five cents . . .

Joe Burro makes a sign of refusal.

(*He reads, reciting.*)
> Oh, my good Lord,
> Give me inspiration,
> Give me rhyme and meter
> To give good description
> Of Esmeralda's sorrows
> On the Street of Perdition.

(*To Joe Burro.*) I was just thinking . . . you know, your
wrangle with the priest offers a good subject for a story.
If you want, I'll write it.

JOE (*with determination*): No.

RIMER: Why not? The story in verse, it would be very good
. . .

JOE: No.

RIMER: Verses which, all modesty aside, are read by all Bahia.
(*Purposefully.*) Even by Father Olavo . . . and I don't want
to brag, my friend, but here as you see me, poet by the
grace of the Virgin Mary and of our good Lord, I am a
man very much feared! When I announce that I am going
to write a booklet relating the shady deals of this or that
congressman . . . oh, my boy, the old so-and-so looks me
up immediately in order to soften my verses. (*With his
fingers he makes a sign indicating money.*) If I were to
announce on this sign that I was going to write "The Story
of Joe Burro," you can be sure that the priest would open
the door right away and he himself take the cross in.

Joe looks at him with distrust.

ROSA: What do you need to be able to do that?

RIMER: Well, his consent, in the first place. And in the second
place, you know . . . the price of paper is sky-high, the
printers eat you out of house and fortune . . .

ROSA: Oh, we have to pay . . .

RIMER: Oh, about fifty dollars to help out. (*He goes over to
Joe.*) But I guarantee results.

JOE (*vigorously*): I don't want you to do anything.

RIMER: All right, you'll be sorry. I guarantee that all I have to do is to announce it and the priest will take it all back . . .

JOE (*interrupting him, angry*): I don't want you to do it. I told you that!

RIMER: OK then. You're the one that loses. You and our nation's poetry.

Master Coca struts down the hill, and stops at the café. He is a tall, muscular, and agile mulatto. He is wearing bell-bottom white trousers and a knit shirt.

COCA: *Buenas tardes.*

GALICIAN: Wow!

RIMER: Good afternoon, Master Coca.

COCA: The old Rimer himself . . . I've got a little business for you, my friend . . . (*To the Galician.*) Give me a shot.

The Galician pours out the brandy. A far-off rumble is heard.

St. Barbara's Day . . . just got to have some heavy rumbling.

RIMER: Already left your stevedore job, Master Coca?

COCA: Yeah. I worked until one o'clock unloading a Dutch freighter and then I took off. Today, Yansan's day, is no day to load; it's a day to have fun.

RIMER: Are we going to have a *capoeira* match today?

COCA: A little later on. In a while we'll have a real good time. I'm going to be in a match with Manny. (*He notices Joe Burro.*) They tell me there's a man here who wants to go into the church with a cross and the priest won't let him.

GALICIAN: That's him over there.

COCA: But doesn't a cross belong in a church?

RIMER: It does, but it seems that the cross is for Yansan, and the priest didn't like the idea.

COCA: And he closed the door?

RIMER: That's not hard to understand. Didn't he try the other day to keep me from selling my books here at the church entrance?

COCA: Why?

RIMER: He said that "The Story of the Mulatta Esmeralda" was obscene. He said it in a sermon. And from that day whenever those religious women pass by, they turn their heads as if I were the Devil himself.

GALICIAN: I don't like *los padres*. But this one is doing us *un buen servicio*. On account of him my business has increased and my picture was even taken.

RIMER: If he really wanted me to, I could make the priest open the door in two shakes.

GALICIAN: No, *hombre*. Let the fellow stay here. The longer he stays, *mejor*, so much the better . . .

RIMER: I'm going to hop over to the St. Barbara market.

COCA: Oh, today's celebration has already begun there. *Capoeira*, samba line . . . it's a good thing it's banned.

RIMER: A lot of tourists?

COCA: I saw some outsiders.

RIMER: I'll go over there. (*He goes up the hill with his booklets under his arm.*)

ROSA (*to her husband*): Do you know what time it is? Three o'clock. Aren't you hungry?

JOE: No. Go over to that stand and buy yourself something to eat. (*He takes a bill from his pocket.*)

Rosa takes the bill and goes over to Auntie.

AUNTIE: What do you want, dearie?

ROSA: Something to satisfy my hunger.

AUNTIE: You need something. You've been here all day.

ROSA: Since early this morning.

AUNTIE (*looking at Joe Burro sympathetically and incredulously*): And he seems to be such a good man . . .

POLICE AGENT (*typical, classic secret police agent. His hat down over his eyes, his hands in his pockets, he inspires more fear than respect. At first sight, he seems as much a fugitive of the law as he does its representative. He enters from the right and crosses the stage slowly, as he goes toward the café. On passing by Joe Burro, he looks at him at length with bold curiosity*): A double shot. (*He looks around him, seeking someone, and then looks at his watch.*)

During the Agent's entrance, Rosa has been picking out some tidbits from the Bahiana's stand. She takes them now, wrapped in a banana leaf, from the Negress. She pays.

AUNTIE: Tell him not to get discouraged; Yansan is very powerful!

Rosa laughs, takes the tidbits over to Joe Burro. He refuses them with a gesture. The Policeman comes in from the right with a newspaper in his hand.

POLICEMAN: Look! On the front page with a photograph and everything! (*He shows the newspaper to Rosa, who runs toward him anxiously.*)

ROSA: My picture?

POLICEMAN: I'm in it, too.

ROSA (*looking at the picture*): Well . . . you came out very good . . . a very good likeness!

POLICEMAN (*smiling, proud*): Yeah . . . I think I came out good . . . I'm going to take it to my wife.

ROSA: I didn't come out very good though . . . (*Indicates displeasure.*) Terrible.

POLICEMAN: Don't let it bother you. That's the way photographs are in the paper.

JOE (*his attitude now toward Rosa is one of restrained, quiet aversion. Although he does not yet seem to be sure of her infidelity, instinctively he begins to feel that she is on the other side, on the side of those who for one reason or another do not understand him, or pretend they don't understand him*): So what does it say there?

POLICEMAN (*as if he had just thought of reading the article*): Oh, yes . . . (*He reads.*) "The new Messiah preaches revolution."

JOE (*surprised*): Revolution? . . . (*He stretches out his neck to read over the Policeman's shoulder.*)

POLICEMAN: That's right, revolution. It's right here. (*He continues.*) "Twenty-five miles carrying a cross for agrarian reform and against the exploitation of man by man." (*They look at each other, not understanding.*)

JOE: I thought that fellow was a little touched in the head . . .

POLICEMAN (*continuing to read*): "As far as the priest of St. Barbara's Parish is concerned, he is the Devil in disguise. Who is this Joe Burro? A mystic or an agitator? The people look at him with admiration and respect, everywhere he goes with his cross. But the priest drives him out of the temple. In the meantime, Joe Burro is ready to fight

to the end!" I don't believe the young man understood
your situation very well. (*He looks at him with some distrust.*) Or maybe I didn't. (*He gives the newspaper to Joe
Burro.*) You can read it. But don't throw it away. (*Beginning to leave.*) I want to take it home. (*He leaves.*)

ROSA: Joe, I don't like this.

JOE: Neither do I.

ROSA: I didn't understand too well what they put in the
newspaper, but something tells me that it's not good.

JOE (*not hiding the resentment that he feels toward her*):
Maria de Yansan put it quite well. The promise had to be
a big one . . . No doubt, St. Barbara believed that what I
promised was not enough and she is collecting for the rest.
(*He looks at Rosa.*) Or she is punishing me because I
promised so little.

ROSA: Then I too am being punished . . .

JOE: Or maybe she is making me go through all this to test
me. To see if I give up the vow. St. Barbara is testing me
. . . and a little while ago I almost fell for it.

ROSA: When?

JOE: When that female character said all that. The blood rose
to my head and, if I had allowed myself to be tempted, I
would have killed a man or a woman . . . I would have
gone to jail . . . and I would not have been able to keep
my promise. I thought of that, at the time, and I suffered
everything in silence. It was a test. All of this is a test.

ROSA (*seeking a justification for her own conduct*): That must
be it. Of course. It's the only explanation for everything
that has happened. St. Barbara used me to test you.

JOE: But St. Barbara would not have done it if she didn't
know you better than I do . . .

ROSA (*vehemently*): I felt, Joe . . . I felt that there was a will
stronger than mine which was driving me over there . . .
And you helping. You're also to blame. I didn't want to
go and you insisted. I'm not trying to excuse myself, but if
all of this is the work of St. Barbara, what could I do
about it?

JOE: You could resist temptation, as I have done.

ROSA: It was different. It wasn't me she was putting to the
test. It was you. And if she is a saint, if she can bring about
a miracle, she can make me do what I don't want to do,
like she did. She can put the devil inside me, like she did.

But that won't happen again. I even feel that it didn't happen. Since, if it was a divine test . . .

JOE (*not very convinced*): We'll take care of that matter later, on our return. (*He reads the newspaper.*)

Pretty Boy enters from the right and goes directly to the café. He goes over to the Agent. He has a newspaper under his arm.

PRETTY BOY (*in a low voice, secretly*): You came right away. (*To the Galician.*) A shot.

The Galician serves him.

POLICE AGENT (*in the same manner*): What do you want to talk to me about? If it's about your return to the police force . . .

PRETTY BOY (*interrupts, smiling*): No, nothing like that. I don't even think about going back. I'm enjoying life too much.

POLICE AGENT: Well, be careful. Your files are being kept up-to-date.

PRETTY BOY (*laughing*): I don't believe it. You people don't even know what's going on. Look over there . . . (*He nods in the direction of Joe Burro.*) In my day, that guy would already be in the "cooler." (*In another tone.*) And you fellows drove me out . . .

POLICE AGENT: Who is he?

PRETTY BOY (*pointing to the newspaper*): Take it, read it . . . You don't even read the newspaper and you want to be up-to-date.

The Agent begins to read the paper closely, from time to time looking at Joe Burro, as if to verify what is in the article. Pretty Boy throws a bill on the counter.

POLICE AGENT: Have you already talked to him?

PRETTY BOY: Yeah. The man's dangerous. He'd have us believe he's a saint, but that priest fellow over there knew what he was doing when he closed the church and swore he wouldn't let him in.

POLICE AGENT: But that's kind of strange.

PRETTY BOY: If I were you, I'd "put him away" for a few days . . .

POLICE AGENT: But it can't be done that way. I've got to investigate, then report to the Commissioner.

PRETTY BOY: Come now, you people don't know your job. You catch him in the act.

POLICE AGENT: In the act of what? He's not doing anything . . .

PRETTY BOY: Oh, no? Social agitation!

POLICE AGENT: Come with me.

PRETTY BOY (*beginning to walk out*): He'll tell you the story of a burro, but don't fall for that stuff.

GALICIAN (*to Master Coca*): The police . . . want to arrest *el hombre*!

COCA: But they can't do that. To make a promise is not a crime.

Joe Burro receives Pretty Boy and the Agent with suspicion. Rosa indicates a certain uneasiness in the presence of Pretty Boy. The latter introduces the Agent.

PRETTY BOY: A friend. He wants to talk to you. He wants to help.

POLICE AGENT: Hi there!

JOE (*a revolt of unexpected magnitude begins to grow within him*): To help . . . Everybody wants to help . . . (*He snatches the newspaper from Rosa's hand and tears it up.*)

ROSA (*astonished*): Don't do that, man! It belongs to the policeman! He asked us to keep it for him.

JOE: The policeman also wants to help. (*He repeats like an obsession.*) Everybody wants to help . . . (*His look, which now begins to be that of a cornered beast, falls on Pretty Boy.*) Everybody . . .

POLICE AGENT: Do you know that your ideas are very dangerous?

JOE: Dangerous?

POLICE AGENT: You shouldn't say those things in the paper. And much less here, in the public square. This could cause you a lot of trouble.

JOE: More than I've already had?

POLICE AGENT: I've seen people go to jail for much less.

ROSA: To jail?

POLICE AGENT: I'm advising you as a friend.

JOE: As a friend. I see that I'm surrounded by friends. Everywhere I look there are friends . . . Each one wanting to help more than the next.

POLICE AGENT: You're a rebel.

JOE: I wasn't one, no I wasn't. But I'm beginning to be one.

POLICE AGENT: Is that why you're here since early this morning?

JOE: It is. (*Becoming angry.*) And I won't leave here until everybody understands me. Everybody.

POLICE AGENT: How do you expect to do that?

JOE: How? . . . I don't know . . . But there must be a way . . . there must be a way . . . (*Desperately.*) I'd like to throw a bomb . . . (*He makes a gesture, as if he were throwing a bomb against the church, but his arm becomes immobilized in the air. He realizes the heresy he was about to commit, and he lets his arm drop and looks upward.*) May God forgive me!

The Agent and Pretty Boy exchange significant glances.

(*Joe Burro advances two or three steps in the direction of the church, goes away from the group and shouts as loud as he can.*) Father! Father!

Ray-the-Rimer comes down the hill and witnesses the scene, curious.

Father, I walked twenty-five miles to get here! God is my witness! I haven't eaten yet today . . . and I'm not going to eat until you open the door! One day, two . . . a month . . . I'll die of hunger at the door of your church, Father!

The Galician comes out of his café and walks to the middle of the square, at the same time that two men, with Jew's harps in their hands, come down the hill. They stand next to Master Coca and witness the scene.

(*Shouting, as if possessed.*) Father, you must hear me, Father!

Suddenly the door of the church opens and the priest comes out. The Sexton is behind him, very much afraid. A deep silence. The Priest walks to the top of the steps.

PRIEST: What are you trying to do with all that shouting? To show a lack of respect for this house, the house of God?

JOE: No, Father, just to remind you that I am still here with my cross.

PRIEST: So I see. And that insistence on heresy shows how
much you have strayed from the Church.

JOE: Very well, Father. If that's so, God will punish me and
you'll not be to blame.

PRIEST: Yes, I will. I am a priest. I must concern myself
with the glory of the Lord and the happiness of men.

JOE: But you are making me so unhappy, Father.

PRIEST (*sincerely convinced*): No! I am defending your happiness, keeping you from losing yourself in the darkness of
witchcraft.

JOE: Father, I have nothing to do with the Devil, only with
St. Barbara.

PRIEST (*now addressing all those in the square*): I spent the
whole day studying this case. I referred to books, sacred
texts. The explanation for everything is in that burro. It is
the Devil! Only the Devil could lead someone to ridicule
the sacrifice made by Jesus.

ROSA: No, Father, no.

PRIEST: Why not?

ROSA: Because I know him. He's a good man. Until today
he's done only good.

PRIEST: Lucifer was also an angel.

ROSA: He's even too good. He's never done wrong to anybody,
not even to a little bird. He's a person who'll share what
he has with others. Who'll even stop eating . . . to be able
to feed a burro. He's a good man. I'll guarantee that.

PRIEST: How can you guarantee it?

ROSA: I'm his wife. I live with him. I sleep in the same bed.
I eat at the same table.

PRIEST: That doesn't mean anything.

ROSA (*more vehemently*): Why doesn't it?!

*The Policeman comes in from the right and stops in the
middle of the square.*

PRIEST: Lucifer deceived the Lord until the last moment. (*He
raises a warning finger.*) But I recognize his followers!
Even when they disguise themselves in sheep's clothing!
Even when they hide behind Christ's cross! The very same
cross they mean to destroy! But they will not destroy it.
They will not destroy it!

*At this moment the Monsignor enters. The Priest is at the
height of his anger. On seeing the Monsignor his arm*

becomes immobilized in the air as if confronted with a supernatural apparition.

Monsignor!

SEXTON: Monsignor Otaviano!

PRIEST (*shouting toward the square*): Make way for our Monsignor!

All make way and bow respectfully. The Monsignor advances toward the church. As he passes Joe Burro, the latter falls at his feet and kisses his hand.

MONSIGNOR (*paternally, very kind*): I know. I'm considering your case. (*He goes into the church, followed by the seminarist, the Priest, and the Sexton. The door closes.*)

POLICEMAN: It's Monsignor Otaviano! He must have come under orders from the Archbishop.

ROSA: And the priest was in holy terror when he saw him, didn't you notice?

RIMER: No doubt the Archbishop told him to pin the priest's ears back.

AUNTIE: Good going!

GALICIAN: Good going, my eye. If they let *el hombre* in, it'll ruin our business.

JOE (*hopefully*): Could it be? . . . Could it be that the Archbishop found out about it?

POLICEMAN: Come now, the whole city already knows about it! It was on the radio.

COCA: High and low all over the city, nobody talks about anything else!

JOE: And for him to come here just on account of this . . .

ROSA: It's because he brought an order. And an order from the Archbishop!

RIMER: He told the priest to stop acting like a fool.

COCA: He told him to open the door.

AUNTIE: I told you so: Yansan is very powerful! Now he's going to get in! He's going to get in!

JOE: I knew that St. Barbara wouldn't forsake me!

The door of the church opens. The Monsignor and the Priest come out, followed by the Sexton. There is a deep silence of expectation.

MONSIGNOR: I come here at the request of Monsignor the Archbishop. His Excellency is very worried about the importance that this incident is taking on and he charged me, personally, to settle the question. In order to give an example of the tolerance the Church has for those who stray from its sacred canons . . .

JOE (*interrupting*): Father, I'm a Catholic. There are a lot of things they say that I don't understand, but I want you to know that I'm a Catholic. I may have done wrong, but I'm a Catholic.

MONSIGNOR: Very well. We are going to give you an opportunity. If you are a Catholic, renounce all the acts you practiced through the Devil's inspiration and return to the fold of Holy Mother Church.

JOE (*not understanding*): How, Father?

MONSIGNOR: Renounce the promise you made, recognize that it was made to the Devil, cast that cross aside and come alone, to ask God's pardon.

JOE (*seized by a terrible conflict of conscience*): Do you really think I should do that?!

MONSIGNOR: It is the only way in which you can save yourself. The Catholic Church grants us, the priests, the right to exchange one promise for another.

ROSA (*urging him to yield*): Joe . . . perhaps it would be better . . .

JOE (*in anguish*): But Rosa . . . if I do this, I'm failing to keep my promise . . . be it Yansan, or St. Barbara . . . I'm failing to keep it . . .

MONSIGNOR: Under the authority with which I am invested, I free you from that promise, as I said. Come make another . . .

PRIEST: Monsignor is giving a proof of Christian tolerance. It now remains for you to choose between the Church's tolerance and your own stubbornness.

JOE (*pausing*): You free me . . . but it was not to you I made the promise. It was to St. Barbara. And who'll guarantee me that, as a punishment, when I go back to my farm I won't find my burro dead?

MONSIGNOR: Decide! Do you renounce it or don't you renounce it?

AUNTIE: Mercy! Help him, Saintly Mother!

COCA: May the spirits help him!

JOE: No! I can't do it! I can't risk my burro's life!

PRIEST: Then it is because you believe more in the power of the Devil than in the power of God! It is because everything you did was indeed done through the Devil's inspiration!

MONSIGNOR: Then I can do no more. (*He crosses the square and leaves.*)

JOE (*he runs after the Monsignor*): Monsignor! Let me explain! (*At the height of desperation.*) Let me explain!

PRIEST: Let no one now accuse us of being intolerant. And may all remember the words of Christ: "For there shall arise false Christs and false prophets, and shall show great signs and wonders, insomuch as to deceive, if possible, even the elect."

JOE: Father, I don't want to deceive anybody.

PRIEST: Yes, you would deceive many and many would follow you when you left here.

JOE: I don't want anybody to follow me.

PRIEST: But they would follow you as they have already followed you, not knowing that they were following Satan!

JOE (*suddenly beside himself, he runs over to the cross, lifts it like a battering ram and shouts*): Father! For St. Barbara, or for Satan, I'm going to put this cross in the church, cost what it may!

PRIEST (*receding in fear, before the firm decision he sees in Joe Burro's face*): There you have the proof: a Catholic does not threaten to invade the house of God! Officer! Arrest that man!

And, confronted by Joe Burro's advance, as the latter goes toward the church, he runs, followed by the Sexton, and closes the door at the very moment that Joe goes up the steps. The latter, rebellious and defeated, heaves the cross against the door. The cross falls, noisily, on the steps. Joe Burro sits on one of the steps and buries his face in his hands.

COCA (*to the two men with the Jew's harps*): Stay here. I'm going to call the others . . . (*He goes up the hill.*)

PRETTY BOY (*to the Police Agent*): What are you waiting for? . . . Aren't you convinced yet? . . .

POLICE AGENT (*nods affirmatively*): Wait . . . (*He goes out to the right.*)

ROSA (*who has noticed the exchange between the Police Agent and Pretty Boy*): Wait for what? Who's he?

PRETTY BOY: A Secret Police Agent.

ROSA (*beginning to understand*): The police! You . . . ?! You
    informed on him . . . ?!

PRETTY BOY: In a little while, you'll be free of that fool.

ROSA (*in horror at the idea of betrayal*): You shouldn't have
    done that! You shouldn't have!

PRETTY BOY: It's for your own good. For our own good.

ROSA (*in anguish over the conflict of conscience that is de-
    veloping in her*): No . . . not like that, no! I didn't want
    that! . . .

PRETTY BOY: Well, . . . it's done now.

*Rosa struggles with her conflict: on one side, her feeling
of loyalty generating a natural repugnance to this denuncia-
tion. On the other, all her suppressed sexual desire, her
longing for liberation, indeed for self-realization as a
woman, which Pretty Boy has awakened in her. Mean-
while, Joe Burro, seated on the church steps, is suffering
great torment. He sobs convulsively. The two players begin
to play their Jew's harps.*

And slowly, as the lights go down, the curtain falls.

ACT III

*It is late afternoon. The square is full of people. Joe Burro
and Rosa are on the church steps. The Galician is in his café.
In front of the café, a capoeira group has formed. Two of
them playing Jews' harps, one a tambourine and another the
reco-reco (a scraping instrument), are seated on a bench, and
the "comrades" form a circle, in the center of which, squat-
ting, in front of the musicians, are Master Coca and Manny.
Ray-the-Rimer is in the group but Auntie is not on the scene.
The Jews' harps wail and Rosa, overcome by curiosity, walks
over to the group.*

LEADER OF THE CHORUS (*singing*):
                Missy, what you sellin' there?
                In this land of Solomon
                I sell rice from Maranion.
                Boss told me to sell it all

By end of day, when night will fall.
It's the best I've had,
Co-ma-rade.

CHORUS:
Yeah, yeah,
Best I've had,
Co-ma-rade.

LEADER:
Rooster crow.

CHORUS:
Yeah, yeah,
Co-ma-rade.

LEADER:
Cock-a-doodle-doo.

CHORUS:
Yeah, yeah,
Co-ma-rade.

LEADER:
Noonday snack.

CHORUS:
Yeah, yeah,
Noonday snack,
Co-ma-rade.

LEADER:
Knife to kill.

CHORUS:
Yeah, yeah,
Knife to kill,
Co-ma-rade.

LEADER:
Knife that's sharp.

CHORUS:
Yeah, yeah,
Knife that's sharp,
Co-ma-rade.

LEADER:
Day is done.

CHORUS:
Yeah, yeah,
Day is done,
Co-ma-rade.

LEADER:
Gotta go away.

CHORUS:
> Yeah, yeah,
> Gotta go away,
> Co-ma-rade.

LEADER:
> To see the world.

CHORUS:
> Yeah, yeah,
> To see the world,
> Co-ma-rade.

And the match begins. Master Coca and Manny, balancing and twisting their bodies on their hands, circle within the group and begin their match—a kind of dance-struggle, its choreography carried out to the beat of the Jews' harps.

RIMER (*shouting*): I want to see a cross-buck, Master Coca!
A VOICE: Manny, giv' im a good one, you know where!
ANOTHER VOICE: I'd like to see this in a real match.

LEADER OF THE CHORUS:
> Who taught you that witchcraft stuff?
> Was my missy's black boy, Joe,
> Boy that cost a bit o' dough;
> Dough you need to win, you know,
> Co-ma-rade.

CHORUS:
> Come, come, Catherine,
> Full of evil, see Eileen.

LEADER:
> Tomorrow is a holy day,
> The Lord's body on display.
> Those with clothes will go to pray;
> Those without will have to stay.

CHORUS:
> Come, come, Catherine,
> Full of evil, see Eileen.

LEADER:
> Boy, what was your teacher's name?
> Who showed you how to play that game?
> Was Uncle Moe, that was my master,
> None there was, was ever faster.
> Was from him that I did learn

> To twist and kick and wheel and turn,
> Co-ma-rade.

CHORUS:

> Come, come, Catherine,
> Full of evil, see Eileen.

*Rosa, apprehensive, nervous, loses interest in the group.
She goes over to the hill, looks up anxiously, as if waiting
for someone, then goes back to where her husband is. The
rhythm of the match now changes.*

LEADER OF THE CHORUS:

> Pick up the orange, heh, heh,
> If my baby goes, I don't stay.

CHORUS:

> Pick up the orange, heh, heh.

LEADER:

> My shirt is of the finest lace.

CHORUS:

> Pick up the orange, heh, heh.

LEADER:

> If my baby goes, I don't stay.

*And the match changes again, becoming fast now, with
the two players exchanging blows with astonishing agility,
to the rhythm of the music, which is continuously accele-
rated.*

LEADER OF THE CHORUS:

> St. Barbara, flash away.
> St. Barbara, light the day.

CHORUS:

> St. Barbara, flash away.
> St. Barbara, light the day.

LEADER:

> I'm going to ask the saint
> To give heed to my complaint.

CHORUS:

> St. Barbara, flash away.
> St. Barbara, light the day.[5]

---

[5] The match should not last over two minutes, so as not to interfere
with the dramatic continuity of the play.

This refrain is repeated several times, each time in a faster rhythm until Auntie appears at the top of the hill and cries out in a resounding chant.

AUNTIE:
> Listen here! I've got fresh *ca-ru-ru!*
> With herbs, and oil, and spices too.

The singing and the accompaniment stop suddenly. The players stop their match.

It's St. Barbara's *caruru*, my friends!

The group breaks up, gaily. They all gather around Auntie, who sets up her stand in the usual place with the assistance of members of the group. The musicians stay on their benches and Master Coca goes over to the café. Rosa stays by her husband, indicating her nervous state and growing anxiety.

RIMER: The first *caruru* is for me, Auntie.

Auntie fills a plate and sets it aside, on the ground.

Who's that for?

AUNTIE: It's for the saint. (*Fills another plate, gives it to Rimer.*) Now you can have some.

Rimer takes the plate and goes over to the café.

COCA (*takes a bill from his pocket and puts it on the counter*): I'll bet a hundred.

GALICIAN (*puts a bill on Master Coca's bill*): Covered.

COCA: And who'll hold it? (*Rimer approaches.*) Ray-the-Rimer.

RIMER: I want to get into this bet, too.

COCA: The Galician says that priest fellow won't let the man in. I say he's going to get in today, cross and all.

GALICIAN: He won't get in. I know that *padre*. Girls with low-cut dresses don't get into that church. *Yo* myself saw him stop Mass until a *turista americana* wearing slacks got out . . .

RIMER: And I tell you the man will get in, but not today, tomorrow. The priest wants to humiliate him first, but later he'll be afraid the guy will complain to St. Barbara, and he's going to open the door.

GALICIAN: But, *señores, ustedes* don't understand. He didn't make the promise to St. Barbara. It was to Yansan, in a voodoo session.

COCA: And what's that got to do with it?

GALICIAN: Well, it's that voodoo is voodoo and a church is a church.

COCA: And ain't the saint the same one?

RIMER: No, the Galician is right. The saint can be the same one, but the priest is afraid of competition. He wants to protect his business.

COCA: It won't do him no good. Yansan is powerful. The man will get in.

GALICIAN: Neither Yansan nor all the voodoo idols can get him in.

RIMER: He'll get in, all right. Tomorrow he'll get in. (*In a mysterious tone.*) And don't be surprised if I'm the one that gets him in . . .

GALICIAN: *Usted?*

RIMER: Yes, me, Ray-the-Rimer.

COCA: And how?

RIMER: Ah, that's a professional secret . . .

COCA: Then, if he goes in today, I win. If he goes in tomorrow, you win. If he doesn't get in, the Galician wins.

RIMER: Agreed.

COCA: Put up a hundred. (*Reaching out.*)

RIMER (*holding on to the plate with one hand, he goes through his pockets with the other*): I don't have it right now, but I'll give it to you tonight.

COCA (*not trusting him*): So that's the way it is, eh? (*He gives the money to the Galician.*) Since there's some doubt, you keep the money, Galician.

MANNY (*advancing toward Master Coca*): You cut quite a figure in a *capoeira* match, Master Coca.

COCA: Thanks. Thanks a lot.

MANNY: I'd gone to the market, thinking the celebration would be there. They told me there that everybody had come over here.

COCA: On account of the man with the cross.

MANNY: He says he wants to carry out his promise to Yansan . . .

ONE OF THE GROUP: He wants to put that cross in the church.

ANOTHER OF THE GROUP: And they even wanted to arrest him.

MANNY: Just for that?

ONE OF THE GROUP: Just for that.

MANNY: They can't do that!

COCA: No, they can't, and they ain't going to. The man ain't done nothing.

RIMER (*going over to Joe Burro*): Tomorrow . . . tomorrow you'll get in, my friend. I guarantee it. I'm going home today to write that priest's story, I know a few things about him . . . and if I have to, I'll make up some. Tomorrow I'll be here with a sign: "Coming! The Priest Who Closed the House of God!" You'll see whether or not he opens the door. He'll either open it or he'll have to give me a tidy sum not to publish my verses. (*He winks and leaves.*)

AUNTIE (*to Rosa*): Don't you want some too, dearie?

ROSA: No.

AUNTIE: It's St. Barbara's *caruru*. We used to make it and give it away free. But today, with things the way they are, we have to charge.

GALICIAN (*crosses the square with a plate of sandwiches in his hand and goes to Joe Burro*): But *yo*, I don't charge *usted* anything. (*Offering them to him.*) It's on the house.

JOE: For me?

GALICIAN: *Sí, para usted*. Hot dogs. Later I'll bring some *café*.

JOE: No, thank you.

GALICIAN: *Usted* take it with no strings attached. We could make a little deal. If *usted* promise not to move from here, I'll provide, at no charge, food and drink *para ustedes*, both of you.

JOE: No, I'm not hungry.

GALICIAN (*very worried*): But *usted* won't be able to hold out that way!

JOE: It doesn't matter.

GALICIAN (*offering it to Rosa*): *Usted*, don't you want some? . . .

ROSA: Not right now.

GALICIAN (*shrugs his shoulders, resigned*): Well . . . (*He returns to his café.*)

JOE (*he notices an obvious uneasiness on the part of Rosa, who looks constantly, in fear, toward the hill or toward the street, expecting to see the police come into view*): What's wrong with you?

ROSA: Nothing. I'd like to get out of here.

JOE: By yourself?

ROSA: No, with you.

JOE (*purposefully*): I thought you were tired of me.

ROSA (*nervously*): I'm tired of this farce. We're here like a couple of fools. All these people are laughing at us, Joe! And those that aren't laughing are trying to take advantage of us! They're bad people who think only of doing evil. (*She takes him by the shoulders and shakes him as if trying to call him back to reality.*) Leave the cross there where it is, Joe, and let's go back to our farm, before it's too late!

JOE: What are you afraid of?

ROSA: Of everything.

JOE: Isn't it just of yourself?

ROSA: That too! But it's no longer me who is in danger, it's you.

JOE: What danger?

ROSA: Don't you see? Don't you feel it? Don't you breathe it? It's in the air! . . . And each minute that passes the danger increases. (*She looks around like a cornered animal.*) This square keeps getting smaller and smaller . . . as if they were closing all the exits. (*She turns to him vehemently.*) Let's go away, Joe, while we still have time!

JOE (*suspicious*): What's happened to you all of a sudden?

ROSA: It's not all of a sudden. Ever since we arrived I've been wanting to go back. You were the one that insisted on staying. If it had been up to me, you would have left that cross there and gone back right away. (*Deliberately.*) By now, you would have been out on the road, far from here, and nothing would have happened . . .

JOE: Do you think that after coming twenty-five miles I was going to return without keeping my vow?

ROSA: You've already kept that vow, Joe. It's not your fault if there are some people always ready to see devils everywhere, even in those who are on their side and who also hate the Devil. They are people who will end up making out the figure of the Devil in their own shadow.

The door of the church opens a little and the head of the Sexton is seen in the opening. On seeing Joe Burro, he goes inside again and closes the door.

ROSA: You see? The priest told him to look and see if you were still here. He's not going to open the door until we leave. Let's go, Joe!

JOE (*he reacts with anger, trying to fight an inner desire to give in*): No, I've already told you I won't do it. I won't take a step away from here until I've carried the cross into the church.

The Secret Police Agent enters from the right and crosses the square toward the café, looking furtively at Joe Burro. On seeing him, Rosa cannot conceal her uneasiness. Her look of fright follows him until he reaches the café.

AGENT (*to the Galician*): A brandy with honey.

The Galician serves him the drink.

JOE (*noting Rosa's apprehension*): What's wrong?
ROSA: That guy's not on our side.
JOE: What's that got to do with it?
ROSA: I've heard that he's from the police.
JOE: I'm no criminal. I haven't done wrong to anybody.
ROSA: That's why I'm afraid, because you don't know how to do wrong . . . and they do!

Master Coca and Manny go to the café, and take places at the counter next to the Agent.

GALICIAN: What are they going to do with *el hombre*?
AGENT: Let me take care of this.
COCA: But he ain't done nothing . . .
AGENT (*casting an intimidating look at Master Coca*): And it's better not to stick your nose into somebody else's business.

The Agent drinks the brandy with one swallow, puts a coin on the counter, and again crosses the scene, with a mysterious air, leaving by the street on the right. Master Coca and Manny exchange a look of solidarity.

ROSA: He just came by to see if we were still here . . . Let's get going before he returns.
JOE: Don't talk foolishness. I'm not a child to jump and take off just because things might get hot. (*He begins to cut tobacco with a small knife.*)

Marli enters from the right, she crosses the stage slowly, with a provocative walk.

RIMER (*referring to Marli*): Good-looking girl . . . too bad she's married to humanity . . .

Master Coca laughs.

MARLI (*at the café, to the Galician*): Did you see Pretty Boy?

GALICIAN: He's already been here several times today.

MARLI (*referring to Rosa*): I know . . . and I also know why.

GALICIAN: Yansan's festival? . . .

MARLI: No, it's not Yansan, it's some other idol . . .

ROSA (*to Joe Burro*): I'm going over there. I've got to talk to that woman.

JOE: And what've you still got to talk to her about? Isn't the shame she made you suffer enough?

ROSA: But I've got to, Joe! I've got to. (*She goes to the café. Joe Burro follows her with a look of deep disillusionment.*) I've got to talk to you.

MARLI (*hostile, surprised*): To me?

ROSA: Or rather to him, to Pretty Boy. Where is he?

MARLI: You shameless bitch. You go to bed with my man and then you've got the guts to come and ask me where he is! Isn't yours enough for you? Do you need mine to be satisfied?

ROSA: I don't need your man for anything. I only want to talk to him, to prevent a calamity.

MARLI (*in a threatening tone*): If you want to avoid a calamity, you'd better let him alone.

ROSA: But I've got to talk to him. I swear it's very serious.

MARLI: You can fool that idiot of a husband of yours, but you can't fool me.

ROSA: Where does he live?

MARLI: He lives with me.

ROSA: That's a lie. I know he lives in a hotel.

MARLI: Well then, go there after him and see what happens to you.

ROSA (*countering*): Cut all that. I'm not afraid of you.

MARLI: Nor me of you.

The two look at each other menacingly, almost at the point of fighting. Joe Burro, who has heard the discussion, approaches.

JOE: Rosa, have you lost your head? Don't you know your place? Arguing out in the street with a . . . (*He completes the sentence with a gesture of contempt.*)

MARLI: With a what, you pious old fool? Sanctimonious, my eye! His wife going to bed with my man, and him over there holding on to that cross! Is that also part of the promise?

ROSA: Shut your mouth! Leave him alone. He's got nothing to do with this!

MARLI: He doesn't! Isn't he your husband?

ROSA: He is, but he won't stoop to argue with you.

MARLI (*looks him over with even more scorn*): You spineless cuckold! (*Turns her back toward him sharply, and goes up the hill.*)

The Galician laughs out loud, but stops suddenly, before the threatening look of Joe Burro. The latter, with an instinctive move, raises the knife he had been using to cut tobacco.

ROSA: Joe!

GALICIAN (*afraid*): I'm sorry, *señor*, . . . *usted* can't believe those women . . .

JOE (*to Rosa, in a tone that reveals his disillusionment, his revolt, and his decision not to be deceived anymore*): To-night we'll go away.

ROSA: And why not now?

JOE: We'll let St. Barbara's day pass.

ROSA: Tonight may be too late . . .

JOE: Too late for what?

ROSA: To return!

JOE: And what did you still want to talk to that character about?

ROSA: To ask him to leave you alone.

JOE: Me?

ROSA: He informed on you to the police.

JOE: But I'm an honest man. I've never had anything to do with the police.

ROSA: I know. But they twist things. They confuse everything. (*In anguish.*) Joe! Listen to what I'm telling you. We've got to get out on the road right now. This very minute.

The Reporter and the photographer come in from the right, in time to hear Rosa's last speech.

REPORTER: What's that? You're already thinking about leaving?!

JOE (*hostile*): I'll go when I feel like it. I don't have to report that to anybody. (*He turns his back on the Reporter conspicuously, and goes over to the cross on the church steps.*)

The photographer talks a little with the members of the capoeira *group and then leaves followed by Master Coca and three or four others.)*

REPORTER: Now you're not serious, are you? . . . Because I expect you to do what you promised. My newspaper is doing its part. I've already arranged it so your stay here until Monday will be as pleasant as possible.

ROSA: How's that?

At this moment, the members of the capoeira *group enter, bringing in first a tent, already assembled, and then a spring mattress. On the tent there is a sign: Gift of the Canvas House. On the mattress there is another: Courtesy of the Blue Dream Shop. To the great astonishment of Joe Burro and Rosa they put the tent in the middle of the square and the mattress inside the tent.*

REPORTER: We went to our advertisers and they immediately agreed to collaborate with us.

The photographer enters bringing in a small table and a portable radio which he also puts in the tent.

JOE (*surprised*): You brought those things . . . for us?

REPORTER: Well . . . we thought that a little comfort during these days wouldn't minimize in any way the value of your promise. Besides, Monday, after your triumphal entrance into the church, you'll ride all over the city in an open car, with an escort, over a route extending from here to the editorial offices of our newspaper. From there, you'll go to the Governor's Palace, where you'll be received by the Governor.

Joe tries to say something but is interrupted.

I know: you're going to say that if the priest at St. Barbara's doesn't let you in his church, the Governor will also shut the door in your face. Don't worry. We're taking care of all the details. And if you can just say a word or two on behalf of the official candidate for the next elections, everything will be arranged.

ROSA: Please, get all that stuff out of here. We're leaving.

REPORTER: Leaving? You can't do that . . . That would be a disaster for me . . . The paper has already incurred many expenses . . . we've bought fireworks, and arranged for a band for your return . . .

ROSA: We're going back today.

REPORTER: Today?! But it doesn't give us enough time! . . . Nothing is ready . . . What do you think, madam? That it's a simple matter to organize a promotional campaign? It's very easy to take hold of a cross, put it on one's back, and walk twenty-five miles. But a newspaper is a very complex thing. To mobilize all the departments in order to provide proper coverage . . . and then, I already told you, tomorrow is Sunday and there's no paper!

ROSA (*becoming angry*): And what difference does that make to me?! To hell with your paper! I want to get out of here! Joe's right, you all want to help, to help . . . you help all right, to ruin people's lives.

REPORTER: Do you need any . . . specific help?

ROSA: Yes, I do. The police are patrolling the square.

REPORTER: The police?

ROSA: A Secret Police Agent. They want to arrest him.

REPORTER: Why?

ROSA (*she thinks a little*): Perhaps because he's too good . . . And because the others are such terrible people.

REPORTER: Well . . . I thought there was something else behind this story of a burro and a vow . . . a secret intent and a political objective. The police, naturally, also thought so . . .

ROSA: But he has no other purpose, only to keep his promise!

REPORTER (*he smiles in disbelief*): Naturally, you're not going to give it away. Nor he either. But you can count on me and on my newspaper. If he's arrested, we'll give the matter full coverage. We'll have headlines on the front page. It'll be wonderful for him!

ROSA: Wonderful! Wonderful to be arrested?!

REPORTER: Every leader has to be arrested at least once!

ROSA: Leader . . . I think you're a little crazy. You, that priest, the police, all of you. And me too. If I don't watch out, I'll end up that way too. (*She looks, anxiously, toward the top of the hill.*)

REPORTER (*calls the photographer aside*): Get ready, for any moment we can have a real brawl here . . .

Rosa, in anguish, goes back to where her husband is.

ROSA: Give up, Joe, give up.

JOE: Why don't you sit down here and wait until it's time to go?

ROSA (*sits on one of the steps*): OK. We'll wait . . .

RIMER (*goes up to them with his booklets*): And while you're waiting, here's a chance to add to your intellectual development. "The Story of the Mulatta Esmeralda," all modesty aside, is a true gem of Brazilian literature. For only five cents you can read the most inspired verses ever inspired by a mulatta.

Joe Burro shakes his head. Ray-the-Rimer goes over to Auntie.

RIMER: Poetry isn't holding up too well, Auntie. But your *caruru* is certainly tops. (*Goes over to the* capoeira *group.*)

Joe Burro goes up one or two steps, stares, rebellious, at the closed door.

AUNTIE (*to Joe Burro*): Don't get discouraged, young man. Today is Yansan's day, wife of Xangô, god of thunder and lightning. Soon, in the voodoo sessions, she'll come down on her horses. Go talk to her, lad, go ask for Yansan's protection, for every door will be opened.

Rumbles are heard, louder than before.

Listen! . . . (*She points to the sky.*) Yansan is speaking! . . . (*She bends down, touches the ground with her fingertips, then her forehead, and salutes Yansan.*) Mercy, Saintly Mother!

At this moment, Pretty Boy appears on the hill. Rosa gets up, as if moved by a spring. Joe Burro, with his eyes fixed on the door of the church, does not see him. He does not see that Rosa's and Pretty Boy's glances cross from one end of the square to the other. From the hill, he makes a sign to her, inviting her to accompany him. Rosa hesitates, undergoing a great conflict. She looks at Joe Burro, at Pretty Boy. The latter waits for her, certain that she will end up by going to meet him. Auntie, the Galician, and Ray-the-Rimer notice what is going on and watch attentively. Seeing that she does not come to a decision, Pretty Boy shrugs his shoulders, smiles, and beckons with a short farewell gesture. He starts up the hill, but he stops after taking two or three steps, outside the visual angles of Rosa and Joe Burro. She, as if drawn by a magnet, begins to walk in his direction, when Joe Burro turns around.

JOE: Where are you going, Rosa?

ROSA (*stopping*): I'm going over there. I'll be right back.

JOE: Where over there?

ROSA: To the hotel where I slept. I remember now I left my handkerchief there. (*She advances in the direction of the hill.*)

JOE: Rosa!

ROSA (*she stops, having reached the hill, and sees Pretty Boy waiting for her*): What do you want?

JOE (*with an appeal and a warning that is almost a supplication*): Leave that handkerchief there!

ROSA (*still hesitating a little*): I can't, Joe. I need it!

JOE: I'll buy you another one, Rosa!

ROSA: Joe, why spend money foolishly? . . . I want that one! (*She goes up the hill.*)

Pretty Boy puts his arm around her waist and they both go up the hill. The Galician and Ray-the-Rimer exchange significant looks.

RIMER (*singing*):
> He who cuts and shapes the wood,
> Who makes it shine, now don't you doubt it,
> Takes on himself all the work
> And then ends up without it . . .

The church bells begin to ring the Angelus. The Religious Woman appears at the top of the hill, in a hurry. On passing by the capoeira *group, which comes to life again, she puts on an air of repulsion and indignation.*

RELIGIOUS WOMAN: What a lack of respect! Right in front of the church! What is this world coming to?!

AUNTIE (*offering some to her*): Caruru, dearie?

RELIGIOUS WOMAN (*stopping near her*): What?

AUNTIE: Yansan's caruru . . .

RELIGIOUS WOMAN (*as if she had heard the name of the Devil*): Yansan?! Don't speak to me of Madam Yansan! I am an apostolic Roman Catholic and I don't believe in witchcraft!

AUNTIE: 'Scuse me, dearie, but aren't Yansan and St. Barbara the same thing?

RELIGIOUS WOMAN: Indeed they are not, madam! St. Barbara

is a saint and Yansan is . . . is part of that *candomblé*, voodoo, may God forgive me! . . . (*Crosses herself several times and leaves.*)

CHORUS (*singing*):

> He who cuts and shapes the wood,
> Who makes it shine, now don't you doubt it,
> Takes on himself all the work
> And then ends up without it.

Master Coca enters running.

COCA (*to Joe Burro*): Comrade, get out of here! They're planning to frame you!

JOE: What's that?

COCA: A police car has just arrived. They're with the priest in the sacristy.

AUNTIE: Did they come for him?

COCA: Of course!

JOE: But I didn't steal anything, I didn't kill anybody!

RIMER: Do you want a piece of advice? From my own experience: with the police, it's better to run than to argue.

COCA: Get out of here quick. We'll hold them back until you get away!

JOE: No, I'm not going to run like an ordinary criminal if my conscience is clear.

RIMER: He won't leave that cross.

COCA: We'll hide the cross.

AUNTIE: And at night he can take it to Yansan.

COCA: We'll all take it! All us *capoeira* folk of Bahia!

AUNTIE: It's the same thing, my son! Yansan is St. Barbara. There, in our *candomblé* sanctuary, I'll show you the statue of the saint.

COCA: You've got to decide, my friend! Before it's too late.

JOE (*shaking his head, feeling himself lost and abandoned*): St. Barbara has abandoned me! Why, I don't know . . . I don't know!

ROSA (*she comes running down the hill*): Joe! It's no use . . . It's no use anymore . . . I talked to him, but it's no use. The police are already here! They're coming to surround the square.

COCA: Didn't I tell you?

RIMER: You've got to hurry, brother!

AUNTIE: Get out of here, my son!

ROSA: Let's go, Joe.

JOE: St. Barbara has abandoned me, Rosa!

ROSA: If she's abandoned you, then you abandon your promise. Who knows, she herself may not want you to keep your vow.

JOE: No . . . even if she does abandon me . . . I must go to the end . . . even if no longer for her . . . so that I can be at peace with myself.

Suddenly, the door of the church opens and the Commissioner, the Secret Police Agent, the Policeman, the Priest, and the Sexton come out.

AGENT (*pointing at Joe Burro*): It's that fellow over there. (*He advances toward Joe Burro, followed by the Commissioner and the Policeman.*)

POLICEMAN (*as if excusing himself*): I wore myself out asking him to get out of here, Commissioner, but it didn't do any good . . .

COMMISSIONER (*makes the Policeman stop talking with an authoritative gesture*): Your papers.

JOE (*surprised*): My papers? . . .

COMMISSIONER: Your identification card.

JOE: I don't have any . . .

COMMISSIONER: Some other card, some other identification.

JOE: Young man, I just came here to keep a promise. The saint knows me, I didn't have to bring any identification card.

COMMISSIONER (*he smiles ironically*): To keep a promise . . . you seem to think that we're a bunch of fools.

AGENT: In a minute he'll tell you the story of the burro . . .

COMMISSIONER: He'll tell all these stories all right, but in the station house. Come along, come with me.

JOE (*he looks at the Commissioner, at the Secret Police Agent, and at the Policeman, without understanding what is going on*): With you . . . what for?

COMMISSIONER: You'll find out later. I am the Commissioner of this District. Obey.

JOE: I can't. I can't go away from here.

COMMISSIONER: Why can't you?

COCA: A promise, Commissioner. He's a believer.

COMMISSIONER: The priest said that he threatened to invade the church. He asked for protection.

AGENT: I myself heard him say that he was going to throw a bomb. Everybody here heard him.

COMMISSIONER: A bomb, eh? . . . Let's go to the station house . . . I want you to tell me exactly what this is all about.

AGENT: Let's go. (*He takes Joe Burro by the arm, but the latter breaks loose from him.*) What's this? Are you going to resist?

POLICEMAN (*calming him*): I think it's better you obey . . .

COMMISSIONER: If he resists, so much the worse for him. I'm not here to waste my time and I know that kind, too. The only way they give up is with bullets.

ROSA: No!

JOE: You must be mistaken. You must be confusing me with somebody else. I'm a peaceful man. I only came here to keep a promise I made to St. Barbara. (*He points to the Priest.*) The priest can tell you whether I'm lying or not.

PRIEST: It is a lie, yes it is! And not only a lie, but a sacrilege!

JOE: Father, you can't say it's a lie; that I didn't make that promise!

PRIEST: Yes, perhaps you did make it, inspired by Satan! Some say that we are no longer in an age of belief in witches. Yet they still exist! Perhaps they have changed form just as Satan has changed methods. It is more difficult to combat them now, because their disguises are many. But the objective of all of them continues to be just one: the destruction of Holy Mother Church!

COMMISSIONER: Father, this man . . .

PRIEST: This man had every opportunity to repent. God is my witness that I did everything possible to save him. But he doesn't want to be saved. So much the worse for him.

COMMISSIONER (*having come to a decision after the Priest's sermon*): Yes, so much the worse for him. (*He takes a step toward Joe Burro who draws back, cornered against the wall.*)

JOE (*having decided to resist*): No! Nobody is going to arrest me! I didn't do anything to be arrested for!

COMMISSIONER: If you didn't do anything, you have nothing to fear. You will be released later. Let's go to the police station.

ROSA: No, Joe, don't go!

POLICEMAN: It's better . . . at the police station you can explain everything.

RIMER: Don't fall for that, my friend.

JOE: I've just decided: only dead will they take me from here. I swear it by St. Barbara, only dead.

AGENT (*sees the knife in Joe Burro's hand*): Watch out, chief, he's armed! (*He notices the hostile attitude of the* capoeira *group.*) And those people are on his side!

COCA: That's right. And you ain't going to arrest nobody here.

COMMISSIONER: And why aren't we?

MANNY: Because it ain't right!

COMMISSIONER: Are you trying to start trouble?

COCA: That's up to you . . .

COMMISSIONER: Stay out of it, or you'll be sorry!

AGENT: And they better get out of the way.

ROSA: Joe!

JOE: Go away, Rosa! Don't come over here!

Joe Burro, a knife in his hand, recedes in the direction of the church. He goes up one or two steps backwards. The Priest comes behind him, strikes him on the arm, and the knife falls in the middle of the square. Joe Burro runs and bends down to pick it up. The police take advantage of the situation to fall on him, to subjugate him. And the capoeira *group falls on the police to defend him. Joe Burro disappears in this human mass. A shot is heard. The crowd disperses as if before a stampede of cattle. Just Joe Burro remains in the middle of the square, his hands on his stomach. He takes one more step in the direction of the church and falls dead.*

ROSA (*crying out*): Joe! (*She runs to him.*)

PRIEST (*beginning to realize his guilt*): Blessed Mother!

COMMISSIONER (*to the Agent*): We'll go get some reinforcements. (*He leaves, followed by the Agent and the Policeman.*)

The Priest goes down the church steps, walking toward Joe Burro's body.

ROSA (*with hate*): Don't come near here!

PRIEST: I wanted to commend his soul . . .

ROSA: Commend it to who? To the Devil?

The Priest lowers his head and returns to the top of the steps. Pretty Boy appears on the hill. Master Coca looks at his friends, inquisitively. They all understand his intention and respond affirmatively by nodding their heads. Master Coca bends over in front of Joe Burro, takes him by the arms; the other men also come over and help him carry the body. They put it on the cross, facing upward, with the arms extended, like a person crucified. They carry him in this way, as if on a stretcher, and advance toward the church. Pretty Boy grasps Rosa by the arm, trying to take her away. But Rosa repels him with a jerk and follows the group. Pretty Boy shrugs his shoulders and goes up the hill. Afraid, the Priest and the Sexton draw back, the Religious Woman flees, and the capoeira *group goes into the church with the cross with Joe Burro's body on it. The Galician, Ray-the-Rimer, and Rosa bring up the rear of the procession. Only Auntie remains on the scene. A tremendous roar of thunder breaks out over the square.*

AUNTIE (*cringing in fear, with the tips of her fingers she touches the ground and then her forehead*): Mercy on us, Saintly Mother!

AND THE CURTAIN FALLS SLOWLY

AND THEY TOLD US WE WERE IMMORTAL

OSVALDO DRAGÚN

Translated by Alden James Green

Osvaldo Dragún was born in San Salvador, Entre Ríos, Argentina, in 1929. After pursuing a career in law, he abandoned his university studies in favor of a career in dramaturgy. Committed to a philosophy of denouncing social injustices, he has consistently censured the materialism and hypocrisy of the modern world, which dehumanizes man and deprives him of his freedom and dignity. In his earliest play, *La peste viene de Melos* (1956), the conflict of a traditional class struggle pits greed and economic value against love of liberty and honor in an ancient Greek setting. A later historical play, *Tupac Amarú* (1957), based on the episode of a colonial Incan leader, shows an existentialist attitude of self-determination and the importance of the individual, which allows the Incan to win a moral victory in death over the perverted values of the oppressive Spanish society. After these adaptations of historical reality in symbolic form, Dragún turned in subsequent plays to an immediate present in Buenos Aires. In addition to his condemnation of an insensitive society that demands mass conformity, he exposes the social and economic pressures that create erratic behavior, class discrimination, and even sexual frustration. In 1957 Dragún wrote the *Historias para ser contadas* (*Stories to be Told*), which brought him an international reputation. These vignettes with disproportionately long, self-explanatory titles in the *commedia dell'arte* tradition reveal sterile human relationships, the power of money, and the sacrifices of human dignity necessary for physical survival in the contemporary world. Brief emotional pieces with few characters on a stylized or empty stage, they have proved so popular that Dragún has written later works in a similar format. He captures the authentic atmosphere of Buenos Aires in his works through the social milieu, characterization, the linguistic forms, and the popular media of dance, poetry, and songs.

The title of *And They Told Us We Were Immortal* (*Y nos dijeron que éramos inmortales*, 1963) comes from a poem included within the play. In this penetrating examination of the alienation of youth, the title stands as a succinct thematic statement about the false illusions that parents and society had created for them. After a brief but bitter military

120

experience, Jorge, the central character, returns to a society that has exploited him and his friends but is now oblivious to their needs. An overprotective mother, an alcoholic father, and the general unhappiness of his household had poorly conditioned him to face the realities of the world. He realizes that parental value systems (if any) are no solution to his problems, tensions, and insecurities. More important than the conflict between generations, however, is the emphasis on changing values that require constant reexamination. The concepts of justice, loyalty, duty, allegiance, family, marriage, and sex can only be handled through a realistic appraisal of one's capabilities, and the existential determination to be oneself.

Although Dragún's most recent works show a regrettable tendency toward a highly politicized drama, which has clouded his aesthetic sensibilities, he remains the most success- ful and stimulating Argentine dramatist of his generation.

Characters

GEORGE, 21 years old
BERT, 21 years old
MARTHA, mother of George
STEPHEN, George's older brother, 32 years old
FRANCIS, George's father
LAURA, George's sister, 28 years old
JOAQUIN, Laura's husband
ADA, George's fiancée, 20 years old
RAMON, Ada's father
CLARA, Ada's mother
THE OLD MAN
SAMUEL, Aaron's father
AARON
THE WOMAN
THREE YOUNG MEN
TWO WAITERS

ACT I

Scene 1

A middle-class house in a borough of Buenos Aires. Somewhat modest. Arranged with cleanliness, but without taste. To the right of the spectator, the dining room, which generally functions as a family room. A table, chairs, two armchairs, a sideboard, and a clock on the wall. On the back wall, a window that looks onto the street. Next to the window, a street door, on a platform slightly above the level of the stage. To the left of the spectator, and on another level of the stage, a room with two beds, a dresser, a library, and a small desk. On the left side of the set, two doors, one to George's parents' bedroom, and the other to the kitchen. Neither of these rooms is visible to the audience.

The stage is empty when the curtains open. There is little light, as the afternoon is dying. The wall clock shows almost seven; a few minutes before, its bells ring. Outside the shouts of the children of the borough are heard, and a mother calls her child to come and "do his homework." A minute afterward, George appears behind the panes of the window. He looks into the room. Bert appears next to him. Pause. Both disappear. Pause. The doorbell rings. No one answers. The bell rings again. Pause. Behind the door, George and Bert are heard murmuring. A key is introduced into the lock. The door opens, George enters, followed by Bert. George shuts the door behind him. Both young men have crew cuts and carry big duffel bags on their shoulders. George leaves his leaning against the street door. Bert keeps his on his shoulders. Bert limps, and walks with the help of a cane.

GEORGE: They always leave the key under the windowsill. I told you so.
BERT: Ahuh.

George goes to the doors and yells in front of each one.

GEORGE: Mamma! Stephen! Mamma!

No one answers. Pause.

No one's home.
BERT: But the telegram?

GEORGE: I don't know. Put down the bag. You look like
   Santa Claus.
BERT: No. It's late. If your family should come . . .
GEORGE: Go on! Put down the bag.

*It is seven o'clock. The clock bells begin to ring. At the
same time, the bells of a nearby church begin to ring. Bert,
his duffel bag still on his shoulder, goes to the window and
looks out.*

BERT: You have a church nearby?

George goes to the window.

GEORGE: Yes.
BERT: Did you used to go?
GEORGE: Yes, when I was a kid. (*Turns to Bert.*) Put down
   the bag. Now you look like a camel.
BERT: Seriously, no. It's late, and if your family comes . . .
GEORGE: Shut up, Limpie. (*George takes away the duffel bag
   and puts it next to his, also leaning against the wall. He
   returns to Bert.*) Well, this is my house.
BERT (*scans it, smiling*): I know. You described it like this,
   that night.
GEORGE: Yes, as if I had worn it, or carried it in my pocket.
   Bert, do you think Aaron would have liked it?
BERT: I like it.
GEORGE: And Aaron?
BERT: Sure, with a little smell of fish . . .

George smiles, barely.

GEORGE: Sure. (*Looks around.*) How odd. Nothing's changed.
BERT: When was the last time you were here?
GEORGE: My last leave was at Christmas.
BERT: And why should things have changed in three months?
GEORGE: I don't know. But it seems strange. (*George goes to
   the sideboard and opens a door.*) What do you want to
   drink?
BERT (*shouts, like an oft-repeated battlecry*): Grapa, you
   fool!
GEORGE (*gets to his feet brandishing a bottle of grapa, and
   shouts like a hymn of response, opening his arms*): Grapa,
   Limpie! (*He goes toward the table with the bottle and two
   glasses.*) The old man uses it as an appetizer.

BERT: Yeah? My uncle uses it as breakfast, lunch, and dinner.

George fills the glasses to the rims.

Hey, I took a bath before leaving Cordoba!

George gives him the glass. Bert looks at it reflectively.

My uncle . . . My aunt . . . I hope that damned old man
hasn't sold the house with my aunt inside of it.

GEORGE (*laughs*): What's your house like, Limpie?

BERT: Amusing. You see that in your house the furniture's on
the floor? Well, in my house the floor is on top of the
furniture. Everything's upside down. (*Pause. Then, hol-
lowly.*) Amusing . . .

GEORGE (*laughs, then lifts his glass*): To Aaron, OK?

BERT: Sure, to that Jew: skinny, lazy, *swell*, and . . . dead!

*They look at each other, Drink their drinks in one swallow.
George remains looking down.*

GEORGE: I saw him this morning. I didn't want to say anything.

BERT (*looks at him apprehensively*): Who?

GEORGE: Aaron. On the train. We were inside, and he was
sitting outside. He was telling us about his father, like that
night, and that he was going to get married, and . . . He
stayed on the road, sitting on a pole, like a bird.

BERT: Cut it, George. Aaron's dead. They killed him that
night, just like they might have killed us. Cut it.

George looks at him, nods, and refills the two glasses.

GEORGE: I know he's dead. (*He drinks, and Bert follows
suit.*) This is my house, Limpie! (*He leaves his glass on
the table and goes toward the left.*) I'm going to show you
the album.

BERT: What album?

GEORGE: What d'you mean, "What album?"? My album. (*He
looks in the sideboard.*) Where could it be?

BERT: You have an album? Of what?

GEORGE (*hunting*): What d'you mean "of what?"? Of me . . .
Sure, it's in . . . (*He has already crossed the stage and
stops in front of the left room.*) It's in my room. (*He
enters the left room. Bert follows.*) Strange . . . I'd forgotten that I had my own room.

BERT: You forgot because you have it. I sleep in the dining
room.

GEORGE (*strikes one bed with his hand*): This is my brother's
bed. (*Hits the other bed.*) This is MY OWN bed! (*Goes
toward the wardrobe.*) This is MY OWN side of the wardrobe! (*He opens the wardrobe door.*) These are MY suits.
You like them?

BERT: Yeah . . . They're dark . . .

GEORGE: If you like them, I'll give you two or three.

BERT: Lookit, I'd look like a canned sardine in them.

GEORGE: There you are! Needling me again because you're
bigger than me.

BERT: It's a good thing I am bigger so that I could take care
of you when they shouted "Georgette" at you in boot
camp.

GEORGE (*pensively, but not sadly*): Yes, at first they called
me Georgette, and I used to bite like a woman.

BERT: No, you bit to defend yourself. Anything goes!

GEORGE: Yes, but Limpie, you remember that night, all of us
were scared to death, Georgettes, or not . . . (*He takes
the album out of the wardrobe.*) Here it is. And your glass?

BERT: I left it in the dining room.

GEORGE: Come on. We've just started, haven't we? (*He looks
at his room with a puzzled gaze.*) Even my room doesn't
seem to be my room. (*George goes toward the dining
room.*)

*Bert stays in the room and runs his hand over George's
bed. He speaks toward the dining room.*

BERT: It's because you have it. (*He goes toward the dining
room where George is refilling the glasses.*)

GEORGE: What'd'you say?

BERT: It's because you have it. You can afford not to recognize it.

GEORGE (*drinks*): I give it to you, Limpie.

BERT (*drinks and looks at him*): Are you potted, idiot?

GEORGE: Drunk? No, I'm hardly . . . (*Shrugs.*) . . . sad. (*He
starts turning the pages of the album.*) Look at this photo,
Limpie: "Georgette in fourth grade!"

Bert looks at the picture and laughs.

And here's "Georgette's birthday party."

Bert keeps laughing. George lifts his head and looks at him fixedly.

I'm sad, Limpie. Perhaps we'll never see each other again.
BERT: Don't be silly.

George again turns the pages of the album.

GEORGE: And here's Georgette reciting the *Ode to the Flag*, at a school party.
BERT: Reciting what?
GEORGE: The *Ode to the Flag*. Don't you know the *Ode to the Flag*? By Belisario Roldan?
BERT: No.

George drinks and begins to recite, glass in hand.

GEORGE:
> Hail, Immortal Standard,
> Lady of the country of races,
> Mother of three sovereignties . . .

(*Breaks out laughing.*) And all the rest! I remember the flag we wrapped Aaron in when they killed him! It looked like a sausage! Immortal standard! And all the rest of it! (*Stops laughing and looks at the album.*) Now that I think about it, this is a comic album.
BERT: Who's this?
GEORGE: My girl. Ada.
BERT: She's nice.
GEORGE: I'll give her to you.
BERT: OK. (*He takes the glass George hands him.*) You weren't serious about us not seeing each other anymore, were you?
GEORGE: No, Limpie, I wasn't serious. (*They drink.*) If they heard us talking, would they understand us, Limpie?
BERT: Why, what are we saying?
GEORGE: We seem crazy.
BERT: It's the fifth drink.
GEORGE: The fifth! How are we going to be after the tenth?
BERT: We're not. I'm not having any more.
GEORGE: You know what, Limpie? We can spend the whole night drinking and singing. How about it?
BERT: Are you crazy? You're at home, and your old man and old lady are going to come home . . .

GEORGE: Let's go, Limpie. Let's go downtown. I want to see
   if Buenos Aires has changed.
BERT: You're plowed, Georgette. Why should it have changed?
GEORGE: Because Aaron's dead. That's why, Limpie! And
   because they buried him like a sausage in the Immortal
   Standard, Lady of three . . . (*He becomes silent. Barely
   laughs.*) I'm drunk. (*He looks at Bert. He is not drunk.
   Pause.*) I like you a lot, Bert.
BERT: I do, too, George. You were great to me. Damn it all,
   I wish to God that you were my uncle instead of that
   damned old man! (*They both laugh.*)
GEORGE: What are you going to do, Limpie?
BERT: I don't know . . . I can't box anymore . . . unless
   they'd let me use my stick.
GEORGE: You know, Limpie, we should become partners: You
   fake him out, and I'll hit him.
BERT: You couldn't do it. You might be able to bite him.
   (*They laugh.*) And you . . . what are you going to do?
GEORGE: I don't know . . . be a telephone pole, I guess, so
   as to have my head in the wind. I don't know . . . Before
   I was drafted I was going to college. Now I don't know.

Bert goes on looking at the album.

BERT: And who's this?
GEORGE: Me, imitating Al Jolson. (*He kneels, opens his arms
   and intones the first two strophes of "Mammy" in the Al
   Jolson style.*)

Bert laughs, astonished.

BERT: You used to do that?
GEORGE: Yeah! I put on makeup and everything. I was very
   amusing. Mamma was proud of Georgette.

*The street door begins to open. Bert and George look
toward it. As the duffel bags are leaning against the door,
the person trying to open it has to push hard. Finally the
bags fall over and the door opens. Martha, George's mother,
enters. Surprised, she looks at the duffel bags and understands. She turns on the lights and looks toward George
and Bert. She can hardly murmur.*

MARTHA: Georgie? . . . Baby!
GEORGE (*softly*): Hi, mamma.

MARTHA (*looks at him*): Baby! Baby! Baby, what luck! You're the same as ever.

GEORGE: Mamma, this is Bert, an army buddy of mine.

Martha turns to him as if she had just noticed him.

BERT (*timidly*): Pleased to meet you, ma'am . . .

MARTHA: A pleasure, young man . . . (*But she has already turned back to her son.*) Baby! Why didn't you let us know you were coming?

GEORGE: I did. I sent a telegram.

MARTHA: We didn't get anything. That rotten service. If you have the receipt papa can go lodge a complaint . . .

GEORGE: It doesn't matter. I'm here.

MARTHA: Yes. You're here. Fortunately I cleaned the house and waxed the floors this morning . . .

GEORGE: Yeah, it smells clean. And papa? And Stephen?

MARTHA: They're auditing at the bank, and you know that when they audit, papa . . . and Stephen was taking an exam. Why didn't you let us know by phone that you were coming today?

GEORGE: I didn't think of it. I sent a telegram. I thought that was enough.

MARTHA: That blasted telegraph service. To get here alone . . . with no one home . . .

GEORGE (*hard*): It doesn't matter. I came with Limpie.

MARTHA (*looks at him, surprised*): Limpie?

GEORGE: Bert.

Martha looks at Bert and realizes that he uses a cane.

He was crippled the night they killed Aaron.

Martha nods, and feels herself won by compassion. She moves toward Bert.

MARTHA: Won't you sit down, young man?

But George cuts her off, brusquely, and disillusionedly.

GEORGE: Leave him alone. You're going to spoil him. He sits on his cane. Right, Limpie?

Bert smiles broadly.

BERT: Right, Georgette.

*George laughs, but his mother appears very surprised at
hearing her son called Georgette. George understands the
confusion of his mother, but doesn't try to allay it. Just
the opposite.*

GEORGE: That's what they called me there! Georgette! And
I used to bite, like a woman! But Limpie stood up for me
. . . He was a champion boxer . . . what class, Limpie?
BERT: Middleweight.

*Martha keeps looking at the boys, not understanding their
strange language.*

MARTHA: Uh . . . would you like something to drink? Coffee,
tea . . .?
GEORGE: We don't need any, mamma. We stole papa's bottle
of grapa.

*Martha looks at the nearly empty bottle and then looks
at her son.*

Don't worry. At camp we drank a gallon a night between
Limpie and me.

Martha is totally confused. Bert realizes it, and says softly.

BERT: Don't pay any attention to him, ma'am. It's a joke.
MARTHA (*not very convinced*): Yes . . . I realize. (*She would
like to go on talking with her son, but she feels that the
presence of Bert alienates her from him.*) Would you like
to stay and have dinner with us? My husband will be home
soon and he'd like to meet you . . . A friend of Georgie's
. . . Although I'm sure that your family must be waiting
for you . . . I mean, as I was for Georgie . . .

Limpie understands perfectly.

BERT: Yes, yes! My family is waiting for me. (*Bert goes to
his duffel bag, throws it over his shoulder.*)

George rapidly crosses the room toward his friend . . .

GEORGE: Stay, Limpie.
BERT: No, seriously, George, they are waiting for me.
GEORGE: Another grapa, then!
BERT: No, George. I'd see the street car numbers double.

GEORGE: Another . . . (*Looks at him. Pause.*) Don't leave me alone, Limpie.

BERT: Are you crazy? You're at home . . .

GEORGE: Won't I see you again?

BERT: Sure. Whenever you feel like it. I'm not going to do anything for a while. Call me.

GEORGE: Seriously, don't you want me to give you anything?

Bert smiles.

A suit . . . my bed . . . my girl? . . .

BERT: So long, Georgette. (*Bert goes out.*)

George stays near the door. Pause. He takes his duffel bag over his shoulder and crosses the stage toward his room.

GEORGE: I'll put this in my room. (*George goes into his room.*)

Martha runs to the telephone and dials a number.

George sets down the duffel bag and strokes his bed. Suddenly he throws himself on it, face downward.

MARTHA (*into the telephone*): Laura? . . . Georgie arrived! Yes, Georgie! Just now . . . He says he sent a telegram, but you know that service . . . Yes, he's very well! Good . . . Come to dinner! (*Martha hangs up.*)

George has gotten up and returned to the dining room.

When Martha turns around, she sees him in the doorway.

I talked to your sister. She and Joaquin are going to come for dinner.

George nods, and she takes the bottle to the sideboard as she continues talking, trying to do it in such a way that George won't notice.

Laura's going to have a baby.

GEORGE: Why did you throw him out?

MARTHA: Who?

GEORGE: Bert.

MARTHA: But I wanted him to . . .

GEORGE: No, you didn't want him to. That's why he went.

MARTHA: I didn't realize. I wanted so much to be alone with you. (*Smiles.*) I'm happy that papa and Stephen get home later. Baby! My baby! We missed you so! I brushed your

suits twice a week . . . Papa started to write letters to you
and then tore them up! . . . He never could write letters!
And Ada and I just waited for your return and took care
of your books . . .

GEORGE: Everything's like it was . . .

MARTHA: Now, yes. You've returned, and everything's the
same as it was.

*George looks around, goes to a wall where one of those
typical proverbs that announce the decalogue of family
life hangs. He unhangs the frame and reads.*

GEORGE: I thought about this a lot: "This house is the whole
world."

MARTHA: It's been there since you were born.

GEORGE: Yes, that must be why I thought about it a lot. Because it's been there since I was born. (*Rehangs the motto.
Returns to his mother.*) Like you. I missed you a lot, too,
mamma. I needed to come back, to be with you again,
to feel protected, like before.

MARTHA: My dear baby. It's all over.

GEORGE: Yes, it's all over. There's only a scar smaller than
the one from my appendicitis left from my wound. And I'm
home again. It's all over. (*Pause.*) So Laura's going to be a
mother?

MARTHA: She wants a girl, Joaquin a boy . . . (*She smiles.*)
Always the same.

GEORGE: And papa . . . is he well?

MARTHA: Well enough. When he doesn't smoke or drink, his
ulcer doesn't bother him, but he always . . .

George, smiling, finishes the sentence.

GEORGE: but he always smokes and drinks! I know: always
the same.

MARTHA: Seriously, did you drink so much there?

GEORGE: Sometimes more, sometimes less.

MARTHA: Georgie!!

GEORGE: What, mamma?

MARTHA: You didn't drink here . . .

GEORGE: No, mamma. (*Pause.*) And how's Ada?

MARTHA: Very well. She started studying pharmacy. I was
at her house today. Did she write that her father bought a
car?

GEORGE: Oh, yeah? No, she didn't write anything about the car.

MARTHA: You should call her up . . .

GEORGE: Later. Now I want to be with you. (*Sits down.*)

They remain silent. His mother looks at him. Takes a step toward him.

MARTHA: Georgie . . .

GEORGE (*interrupting*): Mamma, please don't fuss. You've got to let me get readjusted.

MARTHA: Of course . . . But I'd like to help you . . .

GEORGE: If you can't help me, who could?

MARTHA: Georgie, were you a good friend of that boy . . . of Aaron?

GEORGE: More or less. Not before, but that night, yes. That night we became good friends. Aaron, Limpie, and me . . . friends to the death . . . I mean . . . well, that's the way it was for Aaron.

MARTHA (*approaches George*): When I went to Cordoba, to the hospital . . . I wanted to help you . . . But you didn't even see me! You were there, in bed, looking at the ceiling. And I wanted to help you, Georgie! . . .

GEORGE: I know, mamma. But you asked me, "How are you, Georgie? How are you, Georgie? How are you, Georgie?" And I . . . And how was I to know how I was! (*He goes to the window and looks out. Pause.*) Yesterday was the first day of fall . . .

Martha looks at him. She begins to cry, with soft sobs.

Then George hears her, he turns around, surprised.

Why are you crying, mamma? I'm not insane. The bullet hit me in the shoulder, not in the head. My head's working very well. Mamma, I'm not insane. Stop crying!

MARTHA (*stops crying, and looks at him, confused*): I don't understand . . . you're different . . . and I don't understand.

GEORGE (*softly*): Give me time. Now I'm here again, with all of you . . . with my room . . . my suits . . . my books . . .

MARTHA: All that is yours, baby! Everything in this house! And we'll do everything possible to help you start feeling good again.

GEORGE: I know, mamma.

The street door starts opening. Martha turns her head, and calls.

MARTHA: Dear?

Stephen enters, talking as he shuts the door. He hasn't seen George.

STEPHEN: No, it's Stephen. Papa stayed at the cigar stand . . . (*Turning around, and seeing George, he is amazed.*)
MARTHA: He sent a telegram, but it didn't arrive.
GEORGE: Hi, Stephen.
STEPHEN: Hi, George. (*Pause.*) You look well . . . if . . . You look well.
GEORGE (*somewhat confused, lowers his gaze, and then looks at Stephen again*): How was the exam?
STEPHEN: I didn't take it. They put it off until tomorrow.
GEORGE: You look well, too.
STEPHEN: No, I'm a cellar rat. Always yellow. You're nice and tanned.
GEORGE: Yes, they made me rest in the sun.

The door opens violently, and the father enters, very excited.

FRANCIS: The man at the cigar stand told me he saw! . . . Georgie!
GEORGE: Papa . . .
FRANCIS: Why didn't you let us know?
MARTHA: He sent a telegram, . . . and it didn't arrive.
FRANCIS: Telegram! You should have let us know by phone. Always the same . . . No, I'm not scolding you. I'm overjoyed to see you, and so I scold. Just today I was talking about you to the auditor at the bank. We invited him to your eighteenth birthday party, remember?
GEORGE: Yes, I remember.

His father looks at him, pats his arms.

FRANCIS: Is your wound well?
GEORGE: Yes, papa. Nothing more than a scar.
FRANCIS: Good, good. You're home at last. It's all over. I'm not very religious, but I can say: "It's all over, thanks be to God." (*To Martha.*) Did you talk to Laura?
MARTHA: Yes. They're coming to dinner.

FRANCIS: Tonight we celebrate. All together once again, like before. (*Looks at George, smiling.*) How do you find him, dear?

MARTHA: My baby, the same as ever.

GEORGE (*softly*): I'm not a baby anymore, mamma.

FRANCIS: Of course not. When I returned from the service I had to hang a sign on the door of my house. It said, "I forbid anyone to call me baby or Franny . . ."

GEORGE: You're the same as ever, papa.

FRANCIS: Except for my ulcer when I have to eat some of your mother's stews.

MARTHA: It's not my stews. It's the cigarettes and your blessed gin.

FRANCIS: Speaking of gin, and even though you don't drink, a glass would go well now, wouldn't it, George?

MARTHA: He drinks now. When I arrived I found him with a friend and they'd drunk almost your whole bottle.

Francis looks at George, surprised, but without losing his smile.

FRANCIS: Oh yeah? Well, there are more bottles at the store. They taught me how to smoke in the service. It's got to be good for something, hasn't it? (*While he was talking, Francis took the bottle of grapa out of the sideboard.*)

Stephen doesn't stop looking at George, and the latter occasionally surprises the inquisitive gaze of his brother. The father, surprised, contemplates the empty bottle.

FRANCIS: You sure did drink, eh?

MARTHA: Don't give him any more, dear.

George, unable to contain himself further, shouts.

GEORGE: I'm not a baby anymore, mamma!

Everyone looks at him, surprised at his unexpected outburst.

MARTHA: What did I say?

GEORGE: Excuse me. I'm tired . . . Suddenly I feel very tired. I'm going to lie down for a while . . . tonight people are coming, and . . . excuse me, mamma. (*George exits slowly toward his room.*)

Everyone watches him, still not recovered from surprise and consternation. Stephen goes toward the room and stands there, looking at George. Francis and Martha look at each other.

MARTHA: What did I say?
FRANCIS: I don't know . . . nothing, I guess . . . He'll get over it. I speak from experience.

George, seated on his bed, looks at his room. He takes a pencil from the desk and writes something on the wall. Stephen watches. He enters the room . . . The doorbell rings. Martha goes to answer it.

STEPHEN: What're you doing?
GEORGE: Nothing. I'm just writing, "the mother whore who dropped him."

Martha returns to Francis. She carries a telegram and reads.

MARTHA: "Will arrive tomorrow. George." (*Pause. She looks at her husband.*)

The light dims. Slow curtain. Limpie crosses the stage in front of the curtain. He walks slowly, leaning on his cane, and is alone.

Scene 2

After Limpie has crossed the stage, the curtain slowly begins to open . . . the stage remains dark . . . and then, suddenly, all the lights go on at once, and conversations begin. Ramon and Clara, Ada's parents, are on their feet, saying good-bye near the door. Ada and George, forward on the left side, dance to music from a record player. Francis, Martha, and Laura are saying good-bye to those who are leaving. Joaquin is seated in an easy chair, giving the impression that alcohol has irrevocably thrown him there. In his room, barely illuminated by a night light, Stephen is studying.

RAMON: Don't be too late, Ada.

Ada keeps on dancing, without looking away from George.

ADA: I won't, papa.

RAMON: Well, good night. I wish that everyone could have such nights. People would be better for it.

CLARA: Let's go, dear. Good night! . . . (*Kisses Martha and Laura.*) Ady, put on your coat when you go out. It's cold.

ADA: Yes, mamma.

FRANCIS: We'll walk you a ways.

RAMON: Don't trouble yourselves. The car's at the corner.

FRANCIS: That's all right.

RAMON: Say good-bye to Stephen for us.

Clara, Ramon, Martha, and Francis go out.

LAURA (*to Joaquin*): Let's go.

JOAQUIN: Impossible. Nothing in the world would move me from here.

LAURA: Then I'll stay. You're capable of committing any atrocity.

JOAQUIN: It would be worse if I did it in front of my child. I read a real good joke today; about whether the son is the father's, and you know . . . One guy asks another . . .

LAURA: Don't be inane.

JOAQUIN: OK. It's your loss. (*With an effort, he gets to his feet.*) God save me, my head feels like a pumpkin.

LAURA: You're going to be sick. It always makes you sick, but you insist on drinking.

JOAQUIN (*to George and Ada, who continue dancing, close together, and very slowly*): Hot, eh?

LAURA: Shut up.

Joaquin looks at George and Ada. He laughs. He goes toward the door of the room where Stephen is studying.

JOAQUIN: Hey, Doctor!

Stephen lifts his head and looks at Joaquin.

Good evening!

LAURA (*goes toward Joaquin*): Leave him alone. He has an exam tomorrow.

JOAQUIN: Study, study! I sell 'em insurance and you keep 'em healthy for me. We're the two pillars of society.

STEPHEN (*smiling*): Almost.

JOAQUIN: But if you want to graduate some day, why are you

always getting into arguments? What if the Congo, what if
Cuba, what if all the world? . . .

LAURA: Let him study. (*She takes Joaquin by the arm.*)

*The latter thinks about what he has said, shrugs, and turns
his head toward Stephen.*

JOAQUIN: What if the Congo . . . What if Cuba . . . Wait,
when you get married like me . . . you'll stay home and
fight with your wife, nothing else . . . What if the Congo
. . . what if? . . .

LAURA: Shut up! You're acting like a child.

JOAQUIN (*points to George*): He doesn't talk. George, did
you dance with any girl like that one in Cordoba?

George doesn't answer. Pause.

ADA (*to George*): Did you dance with any girls like this
one in Cordoba?

GEORGE (*looks at her. Pause*): No.

JOAQUIN: He spoke!

The noise of a car passing is heard.

There go Ada's parents. Nice engine.

LAURA: What do you know about engines?

JOAQUIN: I know all I need to know for when I have my own
car. (*Suddenly, pitifully.*) Laura, honey, I feel sick . . .

LAURA: I told you so. Come on and lie down in my parents'
bed. (*Takes him by the arm.*)

JOAQUIN: I think I mixed too much. I feel awful.

LAURA: Ada, bring me some coffee, will you? (*Takes Joaquin
to her parents' bedroom.*)

George tries to hold Ada, but she softly frees herself.

ADA: I'll be right back. (*Exits to the kitchen.*)

*George is alone. He turns off the music. Stephen is almost
asleep over a book. George goes toward his room. He stops
at the doorway. He watches Stephen. The latter lifts his
head, and sees George.*

STEPHEN: I fell asleep. And the others?

GEORGE (*shrugs his shoulders*): They're around.

STEPHEN: Excuse my shutting myself in to study, but that
exam's driving me crazy . . .

GEORGE: Sure.

STEPHEN: It'll be the third time I've taken it. The professor has a grudge against me, and he always finds a way of getting back . . .

GEORGE: Bust him one.

STEPHEN: What? (*laughs.*) No, I can't give him any provocation. But I'm tired . . .

GEORGE: Are you still working at the office?

STEPHEN: Yes. What else can I do? (*Passes his hand over his eyes.*) I'm falling asleep.

Ada comes out of the kitchen with a cup of coffee, goes toward George.

ADA: I'll be right back. Put on the music. (*Exits to the bedroom.*)

STEPHEN: Have you been having a good time?

GEORGE: Yes.

STEPHEN (*watching him*): After I take this exam, I'd like to talk to you.

GEORGE: About what?

STEPHEN: About everything. About what you plan to do now . . .

GEORGE: Nothing.

STEPHEN: Nothing?

GEORGE: Nothing.

STEPHEN: Why?

GEORGE: Because that's how it is. Study, I don't want to disturb you.

STEPHEN: You're not disturbing me!

GEORGE: Are you trying to treat me like a war hero, too? I have the impression that all of you want to keep me in a little cushioned box. (*Goes toward his bed.*) Did mamma pad the mattress? No, she didn't . . . How strange.

STEPHEN: What's the matter? Did Joaquin's inanities bother you? You used to like them . . .

GEORGE: Did I?

STEPHEN: Yes . . . Well, he was always an "amusing character" . . .

GEORGE: Yes. (*Pause.*) Stephen, why couldn't we ever be friends?

Stephen looks at him, surprised. Ada arrives.

ADA: You didn't put on the music. (*She leads George away by the arm.*)

Stephen gets to his feet.

STEPHEN: Listen, Georgie . . .

George stops, looks at his brother; Stephen looks at George, but finally turns his gaze to the book, forced by the imminence of the exam.

GEORGE: I know . . . You have to study.

George and Ada go into the dining room. Stephen remains indecisive, but finally sits down to continue studying. Ada puts on the music. They begin to dance. George squeezes her against him, but she softly pulls away and barely kisses him. Then George kisses her violently. She struggles and manages to turn her head. The door opens, and Francis and Martha enter.

FRANCIS: The devil, it's cold out there.
MARTHA: Where are Laura and Joaquin?
GEORGE: In the bedroom. Joaquin got sick.
MARTHA: It's always the same when he drinks. Take him your drops, dear.
FRANCIS (*going toward the sideboard as he talks*): Let's hope they work quickly and they leave me my bed. I have to get up early. (*He takes a bottle and a glass out of the sideboard. Takes them to the bedroom.*)
MARTHA: Don't say anything to him or he'll feel worse.
FRANCIS: I'm not an idiot, am I? (*Enters the bedroom.*)

Martha turns to George.

MARTHA: The neighbors told me that they'd like to see you. You should have gone by to say hello.
GEORGE: I forgot. I'll stop by tomorrow.
MARTHA: Did you see the boys at the café? They always used to ask about you.
GEORGE: Yes, I saw them. They said, "Hi, how are you?" and I said, "bad," and they were startled because they would have had to ask me, "Why bad?" and I would have had to tell them, and then they would have had the responsibility of knowing why bad. So they were startled . . .
MARTHA (*startled, she interrupts him*): Georgie!

GEORGE (*looks at her*): It was a joke. I said fine, and nothing happened.

ADA (*laughing*): I don't understand it, but it makes me laugh because it's so silly.

The telephone rings. Martha answers it.

MARTHA: Hello. Yes . . . Yes, he's here . . . Who? . . . Oh, how are you, young man? . . . Yes, his mother. Just a minute. (*To George.*) Your friend Bert.

George runs to the phone and grabs it.

GEORGE (*shouting happily*): Limpie! What do you say, Limpie? . . . (*Laughs loudly and continues shouting.*) Where you got guard duty? (*Laughs again.*) Don't let anyone through even if he's a colonel! When they see someone aiming at them they shit, just like a recruit. (*He laughs.*)

Stephen and Francis have stuck their heads out of the doors. Martha and Ada, astonished, look at George, while the latter continues shouting.

Where are you, Limpie? . . . Where? . . . OK, I'll be right there.

MARTHA: Georgie!

George looks at her as if he had just realized that the others existed.

Ada's here . . . and us . . . Ada's here . . .

George looks at them. Nods in silence. Talks to Limpie again, but the tone is hollow.

GEORGE: Listen, Limpie . . . I won't be able to today . . . some other day . . . yes, the family . . . we're all here, you know? . . . Yeah, Limpie, I'll call you . . . So long, Limpie . . . (*Shouts.*) And don't let anyone through, even if he's a colonel. (*Laughs loudly.*)

Limpie has hung up. George's laugh dies as he looks at the receiver. He stops laughing and hangs up the receiver. Pause.

GEORGE: Let's go, Ada, I'll take you home.

MARTHA: But it's early, baby . . .

GEORGE: I want to walk a bit. (*To Ada.*) Don't you want to walk with me for a while?

ADA: Sure. Let's go. (*Puts on her coat.*)

GEORGE (*looking at everyone*): Excuse me for what I said . . . that word . . . I didn't realize . . . And it was Limpie!

MARTHA (*as if she didn't care*): That's all right, baby. Don't be late. You're very tired.

ADA (*to everyone*): Good night. It was lovely. (*She kisses Martha.*)

Ada and George exit. Short pause. Laura comes out of the bedroom.

LAURA: Well, he's getting better. Your drops did him good.

MARTHA: Baby, how does Georgie seem to you?

LAURA (*almost indifferent; she has her own problems*): Well, the same as ever. Quieter. (*Sighs.*) I couldn't pay much attention. I had to keep Joaquin from starting to tell jokes in front of Ada's parents.

FRANCIS: Martha, you can't make a drama out of one word . . .

MARTHA: It's not because of one word. It's everything . . . I feel as if he were far away.

STEPHEN: He is far away, mamma. He's "there."

FRANCIS: But it's only natural. He happened to be in the middle of a revolution, they wounded him, they killed his friend . . . but he'll get over it. You shouldn't exaggerate, either. Leave him alone, Martha. Don't meddle!

STEPHEN: Papa, George needs help.

FRANCIS: He has help here! He has a house, and he can study! Now we've got to leave him alone.

MARTHA: I can't leave him alone when I feel that he's going away from me. You weren't here today, that's why you talk like that. He and his friend, the one he calls Limpie . . . talked in such a strange way. Nobody could have understood them!

FRANCIS: It's always been like that, Martha, and the world never ended. Leave him alone.

LAURA: Papa's right, mamma. (*Looks into the bedroom.*) Let's go, Joaquin, try to get up. (*Returns to the others.*) When I wanted to be a teacher, no one told me that it would or wouldn't make me happy. I became a teacher, and now the kids give me headaches and make me want to kill them. And when I wanted to get married, no one told me that it would or wouldn't make me happy. And I got married, I'm going to have a kid, and in time I'll get used to my husband's jokes. George'll adjust, too, mom. Why pretend that our life's a drama? Sometimes it just makes me die of laughter.

Joaquin enters from the bedroom. Shamefaced and almost staggering.

JOAQUIN: How stupid of me . . . Pardon me . . . and I wanted to feel good tonight.

LAURA: Everyone forgives you. Put on your coat. (*Helps him.*)

FRANCIS: Take the drops with you. (*He goes to the bedroom to get them.*)

Laura kisses her mother.

LAURA: Good night, mom.

MARTHA: Good night, baby. (*Kisses her.*)

Laura kisses her father, who has returned with the drops.

LAURA: Good night.

FRANCIS: Good night. Take the drops. (*Gives her the bottle.*)

She keeps it and kisses Stephen.

LAURA (*to Stephen*): Good night. Good luck on the exam.

STEPHEN: I never knew you felt . . .

LAURA (*cutting him off*): You never asked me. (*Goes to Joaquin.*) Come on, dear!

JOAQUIN (*unsteady*): Good night . . . and pardon me . . .

Laura takes him by the arm.

FRANCIS: I'll go with you.

LAURA: No, daddy. You don't need to.

Francis goes with them. Exit. Martha watches them leave and returns to Stephen.

MARTHA: You're the oldest, Stephen. I don't understand much of what you do, but you're the oldest. I always wanted to do things the best way possible . . . for you, not for me! I agreed to anything . . . I went hungry in order to buy you clothes when you were small . . . then to buy school books

. . . And now that we're better off, with more comforts, my children don't seem very happy.

STEPHEN: It's not your fault, mamma.

MARTHA: But I've always lived for you, for this home. And at times I had to guard it with my teeth, because your father . . . And now I see Georgie . . . I don't know what's the matter; he has everything: he's healthy, and . . . I want to help him, Stephen.

STEPHEN: Don't get mad, mamma, but maybe you won't be able to anymore.

MARTHA: Why shouldn't I be able to: He's my son!! (*Looks at him. Pause.*) Oh, now I see that that isn't all! . . . The same thing happened with you. One day you started to go away from me, and now we don't understand each other very much . . . We hardly talk!

STEPHEN: I'm studying, working . . . and I have other things to do. It's not my fault.

MARTHA: It's not very comfortable to blame ourselves, is it?

He doesn't answer.

OK, but you live in this house, and if I can't help Georgie, you have to.

STEPHEN: Me? Look, today he asked me, "Why weren't we ever friends, Stephen?" And it's the truth. There're not ten years difference between us: it seems like fifty. Once I saw him in the movie house, with his friends, cheering the German generals in an American movie.

MARTHA: What's that got to do with it?

STEPHEN: Try to understand. Apart from Belgrano and San Martin, we had different heroes.

MARTHA: What I understand is that you can't go out in the street to help others and leave your brother alone when he needs you!

Stephen, surprised, looks at her. Francis enters from the street.

FRANCIS: The devil, it's cold out there. Let's go to bed, dear.

STEPHEN: Is there more coffee in the kitchen?

MARTHA: I think so.

Stephen exits to the kitchen.

FRANCIS: I have heartburn.

MARTHA: You drank and smoked a lot.

FRANCIS: I did yesterday, too, and I didn't have heartburn. But today, with your stew . . .

Martha and Francis enter the bedroom. Stephen comes from the kitchen with a cup of coffee, and goes to his room, sits, drinks, and goes on studying. Francis comes out of the bedroom with a shirt on.

When are you going to learn that your stew gives me heartburn? (*Takes a glass and a bottle out of the sideboard and returns to the bedroom.*)

The lights of the house dim as a shaft of light illuminates George and Ada, tightly embraced on one side of the stage.

GEORGE: Let me come in.

ADA: No, papa and mamma would hear us.

GEORGE: Let's go to your room.

ADA: Don't be a fool. (*Laughs.*)

GEORGE: I'm serious. I need to talk, Ada.

ADA: Come see me at school tomorrow.

GEORGE (*kisses her*): Let me come in, Ada.

ADA: You don't want to talk. No, George, I don't want to. I'd best go.

GEORGE (*holding her*): Ada!

Pause.

ADA: No, George, afterward you wouldn't marry me.

GEORGE (*surprised*): Why not?

ADA: It's always the same . . . and I don't want it to happen to me. Mamma would suffer so much.

GEORGE: Oh, what an idiot!

ADA: Maybe I am an idiot, but it's awful easy for you to say so. George, papa wants to help us. He told me so today. Why don't you go back to school, and within a year we'd be able to get married.

GEORGE: You're acting like a good usurer, Ada.

ADA: I want to marry you, George. Papa will help us.

GEORGE (*after a pause*): All right, Ada.

ADA: Will you talk to him?

GEORGE: Yes.

She kisses him. He caresses her violently.

Let me come in, Ada . . .

ADA: They can hear us, honey . . .

GEORGE: Will you let me come in, or not?

ADA (*pause*): Yes . . .

GEORGE (*looks at her*): See you tomorrow, Ada. (*Begins to leave.*)

ADA: George!

GEORGE (*comes back*): See you tomorrow, Ada.

ADA: See you tomorrow, George . . .

Exits on one side. George comes forward. In front of him, Bert advances with his cane. George sees him.

GEORGE: Limpie! How'd you know where I was?

Aaron appears from the other side in his army uniform.

AARON: Hi, George.

GEORGE: Aaron? (*Turns to Bert.*) Then this isn't real, Limpie.

BERT: No, Georgette, it's not real.

GEORGE: Then what do we do now?

AARON: Dance, as always.

They begin to sing "The Song of Day and Night," dancing . . . Limpie uses his cane as one of the typical elements of the music hall.

ALL:
> Oh, when I was born
> My family declared war on death
> And voted in the ballot box of Mamma's womb:
> The future is yours!

AARON: Mine?

BERT (*to George*): Yours.

GEORGE (*to Bert*): Yours.

AARON: But I am dead.

BERT: I am crippled. (*Taps with his cane.*)

GEORGE: And I am alone.

They resume singing.

ALL:
> Oh, when I was born
> In my ear they whispered "The Song of Day and Night"
> And I grew with my arms to the pole,
> And my feet to the center of the earth.

(*Very softly.*)

Bert looks at him and smiles faintly as he nods. Goes toward the drink stand.

BERT: Two of gin.

The Woman gives him two large glasses of gin. Bert returns to George and gives him a glass. They look at each other and drink without saying anything.

Well . . . How are things going for you? I haven't seen you since the day we got back . . . I didn't call you because . . .

GEORGE (*uncomfortable*): Good . . . I went back to college . . . That's why I couldn't call you in all this time.

BERT: Oh, sure. You *were* studying. And what were you studying?

GEORGE: Law.

BERT: Look! (*He aims and fires.*) How's your mother?

GEORGE: Fine, fine. (*Pause.*) I'm getting adjusted . . .

Bert takes the glasses and goes toward the drink stand. The Woman fills them and he returns with them. George takes his and drinks.

Laugh! I'm going to get married. Tonight, at the birthday party, I'm going to talk with my father-in-law.

BERT: Look!

GEORGE (*looks at the Old Man who is reading*): What's he reading?

BERT: What're you reading, sir?

OLD MAN: World history.

BERT: And what does it say?

OLD MAN: Well . . . (*Shrugs his shoulders and goes on reading.*)

GEORGE: How are things with you, Limpie?

BERT: Fine, too. My uncle and aunt are getting used to the cane . . . My older brother's going to find me work . . .

GEORGE: Things are going well, then. (*Pause.*) Did you call me for something in particular?

BERT: To see you. (*Pause.*) That's a lie. Aaron's father is going to come. I brought him the pictures we took the day before . . . those pictures, remember?

GEORGE: Yes, I remember.

Bert aims the rifle. Before firing he looks at George.

BERT: You want to try?

GEORGE: No. I'd never hit anything.

BERT: I do. They taught me well. I never miss. Tell me to miss, or I'll leave the old man without any prizes.

The three youths in black boots have returned to the Woman of the drink stand.

FIRST YOUTH (*to Second*): Well?

SECOND YOUTH: Wait.

THIRD YOUTH (*to First*): Go on playing until he decides.

The Second and Third Youths go back to the games, while the First Youth stares at the Woman. She looks up and returns to her book, not conceding him any importance.

BERT (*to George*): So you're getting married, eh?

GEORGE: Yes.

BERT: A pretty girl. I'd say so from the photo album . . .

GEORGE: Yes. When you're away, you don't realize . . . And you, Limpie, when?

BERT: Me? (*Laughs.*) I'd have to marry a one-eyed girl who walks slow!

GEORGE (*laughs*): No! The cane makes you look like an aristocrat.

BERT: Sure. That's what my uncle told me. My uncle's very amusing, you know. (*Imitates his uncle.*) I'm going to sue the army! Since they sent me home crippled and with a cane, they're going to have to pay me a big indemnity! (*Fires the rifle. Pause.*) Your glass is empty, Georgette. (*Goes to the drink stand.*)

GEORGE: No, Limpie, it's Ada's birthday.

BERT (*from the drink stand*): So much the better. To Ada, then. (*To the Woman.*) Two of gin.

WOMAN (*watches him as she pours*): Do you feel bad, Limpie?

BERT: No, Ada, I feel very well.

WOMAN: I'm not Ada, Limpie.

BERT: Tonight all women are Ada. (*Goes to George with the glasses.*) To Ada, Georgette!

GEORGE: To Ada, Limpie . . . Why don't you come with me to the birthday party?

BERT: Are you crazy?

GEORGE: Come, Limpie.

BERT: Looking like this? I can see your father-in-law's face now!

GEORGE (*offended*): He's a good guy.

BERT (*looks at him, aims, and fires*): Bull's-eye! (*Looks at George.*) I called you for something else, too. I'm going to stick up a fellow at midnight tonight. Will you come with me?

GEORGE: Come off it!

BERT: Seriously. In the port, near my house, they're selling a boat. We could buy it, and go off somewhere until things blow over . . .

Samuel, Aaron's father, enters, carrying a package under his arm, looking around for someone with his myopic eyes.

GEORGE: Come off it, Limpie.

Bert looks at him, takes the rifle, and approaches the Old Man and aims at him.

BERT: Stick 'em up.

The Old Man looks at him astonished. Bert continues, his voice cruel.

If you don't give me the cash, I'll blast you.

The Old Man, alarmed, looks at him and begins to raise his hands . . . Bert breaks out in a horselaugh and returns to George, still laughing.

Georgette, I swear, you've never in your life seen a boat like that one. It can sail the seas, and there's no storm that could sink it. Imagine, you and me up in the rigging, hailing the ocean liners.

GEORGE: You're insane, Limpie.

BERT: Yes, Georgette, I'm insane. Why don't you take me to Vieyetes and get the fifty bills reward. (*Aims and fires.*) Bull's-eye.

The kids have put on jazz music. They elbow the Second Youth who approaches the drink stand and leans on it with his elbows.

SECOND YOUTH (*to the Woman*): Do you dance?

The Woman lifts her head, looks at him, and goes back to writing, without saying anything. The kid goes back to the others, angry. Samuel, still standing in the middle of

*the stage, looks for someone. He looks like the picture of
uprootedness and homelessness.*

GEORGE: So you're going to work?

BERT: And you're going to get married . . . and become a
lawyer? Look, it'll be a time to remember thirty years
from now. Huh, Georgette?

GEORGE: Yes. Can you imagine . . . thirty years from now?
(*Begins to sing.*)

    Oh, when thirty years have gone by,
    And what I don't know no longer matters to me;
    Before I die, I can call a priest
    And haggle over
    The hereafter.

    But why
    Did they teach me how to shoot?

*Bert throws him the gun. He aims at the audience, and
shoots.*

OLD MAN (*reading*): In 1789 the French Revolution put an
end to the aristocracy.

BERT (*singing*):

    Oh, when thirty years have gone by,
    And I'm not the only cripple;
    Before I die, I can call a priest:
    Father, it was only youth
    Absolve me!
    And then we'll haggle over
    The hereafter.

    But why
    Did they teach me how to shoot?

*George throws him the rifle, he aims at the audience, and
shoots.*

OLD MAN (*reading*): In 1810 the Revolution of May put an
end to Spanish domination.

GEORGE:

    Oh, when thirty years have gone by,
    And a double belt
    Holds up my trousers,
    Before I die, I can call a priest,

And haggle over
The hereafter.

But why
Did they teach me how to shoot?

Bert throws him the rifle, etc.

OLD MAN (*reading*): In 1917 the Russian Revolution put an
end to Tsarist tyranny.
BERT (*sings*):
    In thirty years,
    When I'm as blind as lame,
    Walking backward
    And looking in a mirror,
    Before I die, I can call a priest,
    And haggle over the hereafter.
(*Pause.*)
    But why
    Did they teach me how to shoot?

George throws him the rifle, etc.

OLD MAN: In 1958 the Cuban Revolution freed the people
from imperialism.
BERT *and* GEORGE (*singing a duo*):
    Oh, when thirty years have gone by,
    I can say to my picture
    "Snotty nosed,"
    And before I die, I can call a priest,
    And haggle over
    The hereafter.
(*Pause. Speaking.*)
    The only problem is . . .
(*Singing.*)
    Why
    Did they teach me
    How to shoot?
OLD MAN (*reading*): In 1970 because of an eclipse of the
sun, the soldiers turned their guns and fired against their
generals.

*Pause. Bert aims and fires. The kids have seen Samuel.
They laugh. The Second Youth goes toward him and runs
into him as if he hadn't been watching where he was going.
The package falls to the ground.*

SECOND YOUTH: Excuse me, eh? I didn't mean to.

Tramples Samuel's package. Samuel is on his knees to pick it up: a smoked fish comes unwrapped.

Great God! Some contraband fish just arrived from Palestine!

The kid returns to his friends who are guffawing. The Woman of the drink stand approaches Samuel to help him.

SAMUEL: You don't need to . . . You don't need to . . . Thank you very much . . . Ma'am, I'm looking for a young man named Bert . . . You don't happen to . . .

WOMAN: That's him. The one with the cane. (*Helps Samuel up.*)

SAMUEL: Thank you very much . . . Thank you very much . . .

The Woman returns to the stand; Samuel goes toward Bert.

Are you Bert?

Bert turns to him. George keeps looking at the audience.

I'm Aaron's father.

George doesn't turn, but tension is seen on his face.

BERT (*confused*): Ah . . . How are you, sir?

Bert looks at George, hoping he will turn around, but the latter stares frozenly ahead.

SAMUEL: Better, thank you . . . Little by little we're getting adjusted. His mother still . . . but we're getting adjusted. (*Samuel stays silent an instant, his gaze lost, then smiles gently at Bert.*) So you're Bert. You and Aaron were good friends, weren't you?

BERT: Yes, he and . . . (*Looks at George, who doesn't turn.*) He and I were good friends.

SAMUEL: I'm glad, I'm glad . . . I mean that you're well. (*He looks around with a vague little lost smile.*) A lot of young people come here, don't they? Just now, a kid pushed me . . . After all, they're young . . . (*Looks at Bert.*) His mother wanted to come. I didn't bring her . . . She cries.

Bert clumsily pulls an envelope out of his coat.

BERT: These are the pictures.

Samuel starts to pull them out of the envelope, hesitates, and puts them back in. Always his little smile on his face.

SAMUEL: It's best I look at them at home . . . with his mother. (*Points to the envelope.*) Did they come out well?

BERT: I think so, although there wasn't enough light.

SAMUEL (*after a pause*): He wasn't handsome, but we never thought that he could die . . . Not even after they notified us. Afterward, you adjust . . . Eh?

BERT: Sir, after they notified you, didn't you go out and set something afire?

SAMUEL: What would I have gained by setting something afire? Would Aaron have come back to life . . . I'm used to waiting.

BERT: Waiting for what?

SAMUEL: Waiting.

BERT (*shouts*): But waiting for what?

OLD MAN (*hits the counter with his hand*): Play, play! Don't make a scene. This is an amusement park. (*Goes on reading.*)

SAMUEL: You're young, I'm old, and you ask me? Aaron was young. If he were alive, I could answer, because Aaron knew . . .

BERT: Aaron knew?

SAMUEL: Yes, he knew. That's why we never thought he could die. Did you know that he was studying engineering?

BERT: No, he never said so. There wasn't much time . . .

SAMUEL: He was studying engineering. He wanted to build. (*Takes a paper from his pocket.*) This was Aaron's . . . . Since you were his friend and remembered us, I brought it to you. (*Gives him the paper, and takes a watch from his pocket.*) Oh, how late it's gotten. His mother must be waiting for the pictures. We never go to bed so late.

Takes Bert by his hands. Bert doesn't answer. Samuel begins to leave. Suddenly stops and returns to Bert.

Do you like fish? I'd like to have you come to lunch someday . . .

BERT: Yes, sir . . . someday . . .

Samuel nods and exits. The three kids have put on music and are dancing. George stays looking ahead. Bert goes to the drink stand. The Woman fills his glass and he returns. Looks at George, and suddenly hits the counter violently.

You can turn around now. The old man's gone. You can
turn around, and get married, and all the rest!

GEORGE (*without turning*): Shut up, Limpie.

BERT: I never knew what went on in the world. Not before,
or now. Before, when I was boxing, no one told me anything, and it didn't bother me. Now no one tells me anything, but I know why, Georgette! They wash their hands
of it! Aaron died in vain! Seriously, Georgette . . . look at
us! You, you're adjusting . . . his father's adjusting . . .
I'm adjusting . . . He died in vain, Georgette. Tsk, tsk, and
there goes a worm carrying him off.

GEORGE: What'd the old man give you?

BERT (*reads the paper, becomes surprised*): A poem.

GEORGE (*takes the paper*): Aaron's? He never told us he
wrote poetry . . .

*Aaron appears in front of the curtain in his army uniform.
He comes forward and sits on the proscenium, looking at
the audience. He begins to talk to it. Conversation.*

AARON:
And they told us we were immortal,
But that was only the first step.
To be born is as easy
As to find a stone, a tree, or a fly.
And they told us we were immortal.
Those who told us died,
And were forgotten,
Because it is as easy to be born
As to find a stone, a tree, or a fly:
The only miracle is the life of a man.
Stars exist
And the sun and the moon exist:
The only miracle is the life of a man,
Because it has to be made.
And then, perhaps we are immortal.
Neither God nor death are problems for me:
They neither cure my liver nor make me laugh.
The only miracle is the life of a man,
Because it has to be made.
And then, perhaps we are immortal.
My twenty years:
A bow and arrow,
Hurled forward.

My twenty years:
A catapult charged
With twenty tons of questions:
That's the miracle.
And then, perhaps I am immortal.

OLD MAN (*gets to his feet and shouts like an officer giving orders*): Attention, soldiers!! Forward, March! A revolution has broken out, and you are charged with defending the country, the flag, the national anthem, and the honor of the army. Forward! March!

On the last "March," Aaron falls into the pit as if he had been shot. He disappears. The Old Man goes back to his reading.

BERT: He died in vain, Georgette . . . We all wash our hands . . . he died in vain.

GEORGE (*long pause*): I have to go . . . They're waiting for me.

BERT: Will you come with me tonight? At midnight at the . . .

GEORGE: No, Limpie.

BERT: We were more alike, that night, faced with death, eh, Georgette? Now we've got to go on, and each one chose a different route . . .

GEORGE: Yes, Limpie . . . So long. (*George exits.*)

Bert aims and fires. The Second Youth approaches the Woman at the drink counter.

SECOND YOUTH: What time do you get off, so I can wait for you?

WOMAN (*maternally*): Go on, baby. Why don't you go study instead of wasting time here?

The Second Youth looks at her angrily and explodes.

SECOND YOUTH: WHORE!!! (*He grabs the money box from the counter, and exits running, followed by his friends.*)

WOMAN: Hey, my money box! . . .

The shout had been more of surprise than of anger. Bert continues firing. The curtain falls violently. George appears in front of the curtain, crosses the stage, and exits on the other side. From the same side, the Old Man appears.

OLD MAN (*to the audience*): Tonight, at twelve o'clock, a lame young man, twenty-one years of age, entered a dry goods store. In one hand he carried a revolver, and in the other, nailed to the handle of his cane, a small Argentine flag.

The Old Man exits. As he exits, the curtain opens. A shaft of light illuminates George, his back to the audience. He is in the middle of the stage. Laughter, shouting, and music are heard. George leaves the shaft of light and slowly disappears in the shadows. The stage is empty. The noises slowly decrease. All the stage lights go up violently in the total silence.

Scene 2

When the stage is lighted, we see a large room in Ada's house. The chairs and easy chairs are against the walls to make room for the people. All the lights are on. A waiter passes and puts out one section of lights. He exits. Laura enters from the right side. She slowly crosses the stage and lets herself fall in a chair on the left side. Her advanced state of pregnancy causes her to be very tired. Martha enters from the right side. Goes toward her daughter. A muffled noise of voices and laughter reaches the room. Martha sits in a chair next to Laura.

MARTHA: At last. Almost everyone's gone.

LAURA: Have you seen Joaquin?

MARTHA: He went to say good-bye to people. Why does he drink so much?

LAURA: Maybe it makes him feel good.

MARTHA: It doesn't do anyone any good. He'll be sorry when it's too late.

LAURA (*vengeful*): Georgie got here drunk.

MARTHA: That's not true. He met that friend and . . . (*Pause.*) Yes. He drank a lot. Marriage is going to do him good. I want to see my children happy. (*Distant guffaws are heard.*) Ada's family is amusing, don't you think so?

LAURA: Yes.

Martha watches her.

MARTHA: Are you tired, baby? It's the first one. The second is . . .

LAURA: I don't know if we'll have another. Things aren't going very well for Joaquin, and I'll have to quit my job at the school to take care of the baby.

MARTHA: You can bring him over to the house so you won't have to quit teaching.

LAURA: No. It'll be better for me to quit. I can't stand those brats anymore . . .

Clara, Joaquin, Francis, and Ramon enter from the right.

LAURA: I'm thirsty . . . (*Pause.*) Joaquin, bring me some pop.

Joaquin goes to a table, gets a glass, and brings it to Laura.

RAMON (*to Francis*): Come on. I want to show you the site I'm planning to build on for the kids. (*To Martha.*) You come, too, ma'am. It's the best place in the house. Come on, Clara. I want to show them the site where I'm planning to build for the kids.

Ramon, Clara, Francis, and Martha go toward the back door. Francis returns to Laura.

FRANCIS: Are you coming?

MARTHA: Leave her here. She's tired.

The four exit. Joaquin goes to the table and pours himself another glass. Laura doesn't turn to look, but guesses it.

LAURA: Don't drink anymore.

JOAQUIN: It's good whiskey. If I don't take advantage of it now . . . (*Goes toward Laura and sits beside her.*) I'm whipped. And tomorrow I have to persuade that fat penny pincher to buy insurance. How can you persuade a two-hundred-and-forty-pound butcher that he could get sick and die? I talk and talk, and the fat man laughs. He's sure he can never die. (*He drinks.*) But after all, it's 3,000 pesos.

A waiter enters and approaches Joaquin. The latter leaves his empty glass on the tray, and takes a full one from it. He watches the waiter, who leaves whistling.

They have so much money they don't know what to do with it. George is lucky. (*Drinks.*)

LAURA: It's going to make you sick.

JOAQUIN: Listen, Laury. Why don't you quit riding me? You

sit up there with the airs of a queen, and look down on
me as if I were a . . .

LAURA: The only thing I'm asking is that you don't drink.

JOAQUIN: Why? Because I'll stick my foot in it?

LAURA: No. Because it makes you sick.

JOAQUIN: Not *this* whiskey. What makes me sick is that grapa
your father buys.

LAURA: You don't have to drink it.

JOAQUIN: Here we go away. Are you mad at me, Laura?

LAURA: I'm only asking you not to drink anymore.

JOAQUIN (*almost furious*): Come off it, for once. (*He re-
pents.*) Everything's going to change, Laura honey. Tomorrow I'm going to persuade the fat man that he's on the
point of death, and then I'll hunt up an army of fat men,
and break the world record for life insurance sales to fat
men.

LAURA (*looks at him*): Give me a kiss, Joaquin.

JOAQUIN (*happy*): But of course, Madame. (*Bends down and
kisses her. Puts his hand on her stomach.*) This one's mine.
Who can take away my past prowess?

LAURA: You smell like alcohol.

*Joaquin looks at her and stiffens. Angrily, and in one gulp,
he drains his glass.*

JOAQUIN: Your marriage wasn't much of a success, was it?
Every time we go to a party and they talk about marriage,
I can't help but think that you didn't have much luck with
your marriage . . .

LAURA: Joaquin! . . .

JOAQUIN: Seriously, Laury. I can't stop thinking it. Well, I
didn't have much luck either . . . George, yes. In three
months he's getting married, and he's getting a boxcar full
of money along with his wife.

LAURA: Did you want a dowry?

JOAQUIN: There it is: you're riding me again! (*Looks at her.*)
What have you got against me, Laury?

LAURA: I haven't got anything against you.

JOAQUIN: Yes, you've got something against me. I'm stupid,
but I'm not an idiot. (*Pause.*) I wasn't talking about a
dowry . . . But a little money would have done us good.
I never had money, and I don't know what I'd be capable
of doing if I did. George was lucky. (*Sits facing Laura.*)

Do you remember the blond kid I introduced you to at the movies? The one who worked with me at the company?

LAURA: Yes.

JOAQUIN: Well, I told you he married the daughter of one of the partners. And you know what the boys nicknamed him at the farewell party? Just think: "goldballs."

LAURA: Don't even think of saying that in front of George.

JOAQUIN: I wasn't saying it about him, Laury, seriously. I was just talking for the sake of talking. George is different, I know . . . but money is going to do him good. You feel better . . . you . . . you know. Those 3,000 pesos are going to come in handy for the doctor bills.

LAURA: I can stay in the ward, Joaquin . . .

JOAQUIN: In the ward? You're crazy. And be mixing with God knows what sort of people?

George and Ada enter from the right, arm in arm. They go through the room from left to right as if they were taking a stroll.

ADA: You know what my cousin told me when she was saying good-bye?

GEORGE: Which one?

ADA: The tall blonde. You know what she said to me?

GEORGE: No.

ADA: That you're very handsome. It's a good thing she's married. (*Pause.*) You really are handsome.

GEORGE: Ada, are you happy you're marrying me?

ADA (*looks at him*): Why? (*Startled.*) Aren't you?

GEORGE: I'm asking you.

ADA: Certainly, I'm happy.

GEORGE: Why?

ADA: What do you mean "why"? (*Confused.*) Because I love you . . . I was thinking today . . . What would you think if I quit studying pharmacy and started studying law. We could study together.

GEORGE: And it's all the same to you?

ADA: And to you?

GEORGE: Ada, are you afraid of saying what you mean?

ADA: I want to do what you want, nothing else.

GEORGE: It's your major.

ADA: What's that got to do with it? I want to do what you want, nothing more.

GEORGE: Don't be foolish.

ADA: You got mad. I thought you'd be pleased. Let's not argue, George. I don't want us to argue tonight. (*Sees Laura and Joaquin.*) Hi. (*Takes George by the arm and goes toward Laura and Joaquin.*) You're getting awfully bored, aren't you?

LAURA: Your family's amusing. You already know ours. That's the way we are.

JOAQUIN: They even changed me. Before I got married I knew some magic tricks. Afterward . . . I got married.

ADA: And you ran out of magic?

JOAQUIN: More or less, yeah, more or less. (*Takes out a handkerchief.*) It's a bit dirty, but it doesn't matter. (*Puts it over Laura's abdomen.*) Nothing here . . . Nothing there. (*Joaquin takes back the handkerchief and passes his hand over his wife's stomach.*) But wait three months and see what I pull out. (*He laughs. Ada does, too.*)

ADA: What a ham.

JOAQUIN: George, why don't you do your imitation of Al Jolson?

GEORGE: I don't feel like it.

JOAQUIN: I remember the last time I saw you do it at the club!

ADA: It was great!

JOAQUIN: I always thought that you were going into the theatre. The money you could have made doing that imitation.

GEORGE: I don't even remember how it went anymore . . .

ADA: Sure you do, George! How could you forget it? Are you going to do it for us later?

GEORGE: Maybe . . . I don't know . . .

JOAQUIN (*patting him on the back*): Look at how he is because they caught him.

LAURA: Joaquin, you know your jokes can lead to . . .

JOAQUIN: Sticking my foot in it, eh? I know, Laury, I know . . .

GEORGE: In reality they didn't catch me. I caught her: her, her father, her mother, and the apartment they're going to build for us.

Ada gets nervous and tries to give the conversation a joking tone.

ADA: No, George. Don't start in again! He's been the same all night. It seems as if he wants to get even with me for the way he blushed when he talked with papa. Or perhaps he wants to send our marriage to the devil!

JOAQUIN: No! Is he crazy? (*Smells his breath.*) You drank a whale of a lot of whiskey.

GEORGE: I didn't drink whiskey. I drank grapa, with Limpie.

JOAQUIN (*surprised*): With whom??

GEORGE: You don't know him. He walks like this (*Limps.*) and he has a machine gun hidden in his cane that goes rat-ta-ta-ta. (*As he makes the noise of the machine gun, he mimics a person holding a machine gun firing on them. Laughs. Embraces Ada.*) I caught her, or she caught me: how should I know? And after we get married the papers are going to say: "The smiling young couple is traveling to Brazil, Europe, Africa, and Asia. Thanks to their smile, no company was willing to charge for their passage."

Joaquin laughs.

LAURA: Joaquin, take him to the bathroom and put a hand-kerchief soaked in cold water on his head.

JOAQUIN (*surprised*): But Laury, he's having a good time!

LAURA: Take him along, Joaquin, before the others come back.

George goes toward Laura.

GEORGE: Laury, Laury! Do you remember when I was a kid you used to read me *Treasure Island*? Can you tell me where the hell it was? Everyday I remember less.

LAURA: Georgie, we're not kids anymore.

GEORGE: Sure. And we've got to adjust . . .

Laura looks at him and doesn't answer. Then she looks at Joaquin.

LAURA: Take him along, Joaquin.

George goes toward Joaquin.

GEORGE: Take me along, Joaquin. (*To Laura.*) But I'm not drunk, Laury! (*Passing Ada, he touches her chin.*) For you, yes . . . For you, yes.

JOAQUIN (*laughs while taking him by the arm*): They mixed marijuana with your gin.

George and Joaquin go off right. Ada watches them leave. Laura watches Ada.

LAURA: You shouldn't pay much attention to him. After he's seen that army buddy . . .

ADA: I know. He thinks I don't understand. But I don't want to argue now. In three months, it's going to be different.

LAURA: Living with your parents is going to do him good.

ADA: I think so. At first I thought we ought to be independent, but later I realized that George isn't ready yet. He needs someone near him to serve as an example . . . (*Breaks off.*) I didn't mean to say that your father . . .

LAURA: I understand. My father isn't a very good example.

ADA: I don't know whether mine is, Laura, but I always thought that my marriage should be like his and mother's.

LAURA (*looks at her, surprised*): I guess I didn't know you very well. Perhaps because at age twenty, I . . .

ADA: Times change, don't they? And a girl has to protect herself. George thinks that I'm a bit of a fool, but right now I don't want to argue with him. After we get married, everything's going to be different. I want him to graduate, to study . . . Papa's going to help him. And George is very intelligent, Laura.

LAURA: Yes. He always was. And you, what are you going to do?

ADA: I don't know . . . Maybe I'll quit studying. My courses don't mean much to me. And people go to school more to cause trouble than study. Stephen says something like "That's only youth." Papa says they're communists . . . I don't understand much about it. You know something, Laura? Lately, the place where I've been most comfortable is at home. And I think that George is going to feel comfortable here, too.

LAURA: Ada, I'm not sure that George is looking for comfort right now.

ADA: He really doesn't know what he wants. He thinks he does, but he really doesn't know.

LAURA: And you, do you know what he wants? What I'm going to tell you is something very few people know: I'm not happy, and it's my fault for not having known enough to accept Joaquin as he is.

ADA: I know exactly how George is. (*Pause.*) I've been his woman for a month, and a woman gets to know her man very well. (*Looks at Laura.*) Does what I said bother you?

LAURA: No . . . It surprised me a little.

ADA: He was the first, and only one. Besides that, he'd already decided to talk with papa.

LAURA: Ah . . . You used that to bind him closer to you?

ADA: I don't know . . . It could be. He wanted it so much . . .

LAURA: Don't talk anymore, Ada. (*Pause.*) You're lucky. If it were I who was twenty years old, I'd take George by the arm and run away with him.

ADA (*looks at her defiantly*): Why do you think I said what I said? I don't want you all to go on thinking I'm a fool. Besides, Laura, where would you run away with him to?

LAURA: That's right . . . to where? . . . I never knew . . .

ADA: Don't get angry with me. I can make him happy.

LAURA: I'm not angry. What right do I have to be, after all? I never did anything for him.

ADA: I can make him happy, Laura!

LAURA (*looks at her*): The smiling couple . . .

ADA: What's wrong with it?

Francis, Ramon, Clara, and Martha enter.

RAMON: . . . and it's a big lot. When George graduates we can build a study there where the factory warehouse is now.

FRANCIS: Maybe I'll be able to help with something then.

RAMON: Don't worry about it. What are we working for, if not for our children?

Waiters enter and take out glasses and bottles during the following scene. Clara and Martha go toward Laura and Ada. The four women sit down. Ramon and Francis go toward the other end of the room and also sit down. It is the typical division into women and men.

MARTHA: Where's Georgie?

LAURA: He went out for a while with Joaquin.

RAMON (*to Francis, at the other end of the room*): What I like best about parties is when they're over and only the family's left.

FRANCIS: It's the same with me. I spend so much time on my feet in the bank, that I dream of sitting down.

CLARA (*to Martha, at the other end of the room*): Don't be angry with me, but I'm very happy that the children are going to live with us. We've never had our baby away from us.

MARTHA: Why should I get angry. I understand you perfectly!

ADA: Mamma, I'm not planning to let you butt into our life.

CLARA (*smiling*): Of course not. You're going to ask us yourself.

Joaquin enters from the right, goes to Laura, crossing the stage.

JOAQUIN: Your little brother's a straitjacket case. That bullet must have hit his head. You know, he wasn't drunk. Seriously. He got into the bathroom and said he wanted to be alone. Alone in the bathroom . . . to think!

MARTHA (*surprised*): What's the matter with Georgie?

LAURA: Nothing, Mamma. He didn't feel very well.

CLARA: Did he drink a lot? Ady, why did you let him?

ADA: He didn't drink at the party. He met an army buddy earlier. He'll be all right.

JOAQUIN: Who is Aaron?

MARTHA: Why? The friend who was killed in Cordoba. Why?

JOAQUIN: Ah . . . him. He kept repeating his name.

LAURA: Go along. Don't leave him alone.

Joaquin goes out again.

FRANCIS (*to Martha, from his armchair*): What's going on, Martha?

MARTHA: Nothing. Georgie didn't feel well.

FRANCIS: Why don't you call Stephen?

MARTHA: No. He'll be all right, and Stephen has to study.

FRANCIS: For all the good it'll do him! If he keeps getting into trouble at school, how can he expect them to pass him? Oh, well, he'll learn by himself.

ADA (*crosses the stage toward her father*): Papa, for our wedding, are you going to give us a party or a present?

RAMON: Which would you prefer?

ADA: A present.

RAMON: A present! Fine. What?

ADA: A trip to Europe.

RAMON: Not a bad idea. We'll think about it. You could visit your grandmother in Barcelona. (*Turns to Francis.*) You know, my mother's 100 years old and still living. Of course, her life's very different from ours.

FRANCIS: Yes, this life wears you out. Sometimes I dream of going to the country, but I don't know . . . The city hasn't treated me very well.

Ada goes toward the women, and says to Clara.

ADA: You were right. Papa will give us the trip to Europe if we go to visit grandma.

CLARA (*to Martha*): My mother-in-law is 100 years old. At first she wouldn't forgive Ramon for not marrying a Spaniard, but when we sent her a picture of the baby, the old lady melted. It'll be a good thing for the kids to go. Ramon would like to, but he's estranged from his brothers . . . by politics, you know.

RAMON (*to Francis*): In 1936, when the Civil War started, I had a little shop and was raising money for the Republicans. My brothers were Republicans, and I very nearly went out to fight. Now they won't forgive me for the fact that my partner is pro-Franco. As if I were a different person—a criminal, or something of the sort! . . .

FRANCIS: Ah, when business and politics get mixed up! You read the papers and every day you understand less. Finally you throw them away. I swear I'd like to go to the country.

The telephone rings. It is on a little table on the left side. Very far forward. Ada answers.

ADA: Hello? . . . Hi, how are you? . . . Yes, wait a second . . . (*To Martha.*) Ma'am, Stephen. For you.

Martha looks at her surprised. Goes to the phone.

MARTHA: What is it, baby? . . . Yes . . . When? . . . What a thing! . . . What . . . No! . . . No, Stephen, I'm not going to tell him anything! Don't tell me what I have to do! I know very well! I'm not going to say a word to him! He needs to have peace and quiet! (*Hangs up and remains standing near the phone.*)

FRANCIS: What is it, Martha?

MARTHA: Stephen. Someone called for Georgie. It's not important.

Martha remains in the same place. She and Laura look at each other. The two waiters enter, and approach Ramon.

WAITER: We're through, sir.

RAMON: Oh, yes. (*Gets to his feet and gives them a tip.*)

WAITER: Thank you very much, sir. Good night.

RAMON: Good night.

Exit waiters.

Good. Ada, you can bring the cake now.

ADA: Yes, papa. And all of you start thinking of a wish! (*Exit Ada.*)

CLARA: I'm going to bring the champagne. (*Exit Clara.*)

LAURA (*to Martha*): What did Stephen tell you?

MARTHA: Nothing.

George and Joaquin enter from the right.

(*To George.*) Do you feel better?

GEORGE: Yes.

JOAQUIN: Leave him alone, he's almost over it. (*Laughs and goes toward Laura.*)

MARTHA: What's the matter, baby?

GEORGE (*pause*): I saw Aaron's father today . . . Mamma, am I doing the right thing?

MARTHA: But Georgie! . . .

GEORGE: Seriously, mamma! Am I doing the right thing? When I came back with Limpie, we thought that Aaron's death was something terrible and absurd, and that we should do something. Today I saw Aaron's father . . . And I felt that we hadn't done anything.

MARTHA: What can you do? I didn't know Aaron, but I was just as sorry about his death as I was about your wound. You can't stay tied to it, Georgie. A lot of people die, but nonetheless you've got to go on living. You're young, and you have your whole future ahead of you. Aaron's father would tell you the same thing. You've got to forget . . .

GEORGE: I knew you'd tell me that. And I am forgetting. But am I doing the right thing in forgetting?

MARTHA: Of course you're doing the right thing. It's not for nothing that you're forgetting. You returned home, to your family, to your studies . . . and you're going to make your own home. It's not for nothing that you're forgetting.

GEORGE: Then why am I not comfortable in forgetting?

MARTHA: Give yourself time. But you have to help. You can't let things get out of proportion. Your mother, who knows it by experience, tells you so.

Ramon yells toward the interior.

RAMON: Where's that cake?

FRANCIS (*goes toward George*): Are you OK now, Georgie?

GEORGE: Yes, papa . . .

FRANCIS: It wasn't a very good idea to drink before you came was it, Georgie?

MARTHA: It doesn't matter anymore. No one noticed.

FRANCIS: No, but he might have made a fool of himself. Don't defend him: he doesn't need it. I said it for his own good, nothing more. He wouldn't like Ada's family to get a bad impression of him, would he?

LAURA (*to Joaquin, who is at her side*): I'd like to go soon, Joaquin . . . I don't feel well . . . I'm tired.

JOAQUIN: Sure, Laury, right away . . . When the music and the dancing are over, parties are a drag. (*Pause. Looks at her.*) Forgive me for what I said today. We shouldn't spend our lives fighting . . .

LAURA: No, you're the one who has to forgive me.

JOAQUIN: When the baby's born, everything's going to be different. You'll see, Laury. Kids unite . . .

LAURA: Yes, Joaquin.

Enter Clara and Ada. Ada carries a cake with twenty lighted candles, and Clara carries a tray with a bottle of champagne and glasses.

ADA (*entering*): Did you each make a wish?

Ada and Clara leave everything on the table. The characters surround the table, facing the audience.

CLARA: This cake is for the family, and no one else. I had to hide it.

Ada laughs and approaches George.

ADA: Do you feel better?

George nods, smiling.

You know what? We're getting out of a wedding party. Papa's giving us a trip to Europe. (*To Ramon.*) Isn't that right, papa? You're giving us a trip to Europe.

RAMON: I said I'd think about it.

ADA: Then you're giving us a trip to Europe. (*Laughs.*)

JOAQUIN: George, are you going to do your imitation of Al Jolson?

GEORGE: Yes. In Europe.

ADA (*laughs*): First we're going to eat the cake, and afterward, yes, George.

GEORGE: I don't even remember it, Ada . . . .

ADA: But I do: "Mammy, oh, Mammy!" You remember? (*To the rest.*) We've got to turn off the lights.

Ada puts out one section and Ramon another. Only a dim, diffused light and the light from the twenty candles remain.

Good. Now everyone make a wish. But please don't tell it, or you'll ruin everything!

JOAQUIN: Make 'em big ones since they don't cost anything!

There is a pause; then the wishes begin to be heard, each one told in a monotone.

CLARA: I want my baby to be happy, and us to live a long time to help them, and then to give us grandchildren.

FRANCIS: A wish . . . hurried like this, you can't . . . a wish . . . perhaps to go to the country . . . a wish . . . Oh, I'm going to start thinking now . . .

MARTHA: I want my children to be happy. If I wasn't really happy and I had to sacrifice myself: don't I deserve to have my children happy?

JOAQUIN: Can I sell the fat man? . . . There's not much time left until the baby's born and we need a refrigerator and a washing machine, and . . . oh, I have to make a wish. I wish I had a million pesos.

ADA: I want to live like mother and father, but differently.

LAURA: Let it be a boy! Let it be a boy! It's horrible to be a woman!

GEORGE: A wish. The same as on that night, when the star fell. And we didn't ask for anything, because we didn't know that everything would end so soon. Perhaps my only wish was to shout. Ada, will we be able to shout together sometime? Ada!

ADA (*strongly and laughing*): Good. And may they all come true.

She blows out the candles. Laughter and applause. Ramon and Joaquin turn the lights back on. Ada and Clara start cutting the cake, and Ramon opens the bottle of champagne. Stephen enters slowly from the right. Ada sees him.

ADA: You got here just in time.

STEPHEN: Mamma, did you tell him?

MARTHA: No. There'll be time tomorrow.

FRANCIS: Did you tell him what?

MARTHA: It's not important.

STEPHEN: Then I'll tell him. George . . .

MARTHA: Stephen, I forbid you . . .

STEPHEN: He's not a baby anymore, mamma, at least I don't think so.

GEORGE (*surprised*): It's about me? (*To Martha.*) Did you tell me what?

Martha doesn't answer.

What do you have to tell me?

STEPHEN: They called from the police station . . . Limpie tried to rob a haberdasher, and they caught him. He fell making his getaway. He asked them to call you. He needs to see you.

RAMON: Limpie? Who's he? Where did you meet robbers?

ADA: They were army buddies.

STEPHEN: Well, that's all. I thought I should tell you.

GEORGE: Thanks, Stephen. (*To the others.*) You'll pardon me if I don't stay to eat cake. (*Goes toward the right exit.*)

ADA: George! Where are you going?

GEORGE (*surprised*): What? He needs to see me. I'll be back later.

FRANCIS: But Georgie! Why should you go to the police station because a stickup man wants to see you. Maybe he told them you were partners, and that's why they called you.

RAMON: Listen to me, George, your father may be right. And even if he's not, it's not a good idea to go alone. Wait until tomorrow, and I'll go with you, with a lawyer.

GEORGE: But he needs me today! Now! (*Goes to his mother.*) You knew and you kept quiet and soothed me . . . but . . . but what if it had been me, mamma?

MARTHA: He's not my son.

GEORGE (*looks at her and nods*): Sure. "This house is the whole world." Sure. (*Looks around.*) And this is my world. And you're its inhabitants. Sure.

ADA: George, why didn't he call you before holding anyone up? Afterward is just dandy!

GEORGE: It's not dandy for him. You don't know him. And he doesn't have anyone. Let's go together, Ada!

ADA: You told me he lived with an aunt and uncle.

GEORGE: Let's go together, Ada.

ADA: But does he live with an aunt and uncle or not?

STEPHEN (*to George*): What are you planning to do?

JOAQUIN (*to George*): Listen to me, George, I was drafted, too, but when I got out, I went to work. I realized that the fling was over. Just because you go into the army doesn't mean you have to become a stickup man!

STEPHEN (*to George*): What are you planning to do?

GEORGE (*pause. Turns to Stephen*): Nothing. This is my world, isn't it? Bert's a Martian. I'm not. Enough trouble, then! Here I live, and I have to have as good a time as possible. Right now, we have to start having fun. Until now you were bored, and you were afraid because I made you nervous. Well, it's finished: Let's have fun. Joaquin, tell us one of your stories.

MARTHA: Georgie . . .

GEORGE: Come on, Joaquin. A good one. I'll be the Master of Ceremonies like at the club. (*He shouts.*) I give you the GREAT JOAQUIN!

Pause. Joaquin looks at everyone, shrugs, and starts talking. The expressions of the others change gradually from surprise to amusement.

JOAQUIN: Well, when I go like this (*Snaps his fingers.*) the ladies should plug their ears . . . An English salesman returned home ahead of schedule and when he entered his bedroom, he found his wife in bed with his best friend. The salesman approached, and said to his friend, "Oh, John, you, my best friend, the man I kept from dying of hunger, for whom I risked my life in the war, the one I gave all my pipes to . . . John! At least don't be rude: Get off of my wife and listen to me!"

Everyone laughs.

Oh! I forgot to go like this. (*Snaps his fingers.*)

Laughter. George applauds.

GEORGE: Now it's your turn, Don Ramon! No one leave the room! We've just begun. Don Ramon!

Ramon hesitates.

JOAQUIN (*to Ramon*): Go on, it's just the family!

Ramon looks at everyone.

RAMON: All right. Mine will be a story about my country. An old gypsy who lived in the caves of a mountain felt that he was about to die. He called his sons and said to them: "My sons, my last wish is that if I die in the upper cave, you bury me in the lower cave, and if I die in the lower cave, you bury me in the upper cave." The sons looked at each other, very surprised. "So be it, Father. But can you tell us why?" "To screw you up, my sons, to screw you up."

Everyone laughs. Stephen starts to exit. George sees him.

GEORGE: Don't tell me you're getting bored, Stephen. And we just started. It's my turn now.

Stephen remains standing on the right.

Sit down. Mine's a long one!

He pulls up two chairs, the others each pull up one, except for Stephen who remains standing. They form a little frieze with their backs to the audience, facing the table. George takes the cake.

This is yours, Ada. (*Puts it on her lap, and climbs up on the table, which forms a little stage.*) I'm going to tell you a Jew-joke. Come on! Who doesn't know a Jew-joke? Come on, Don Ramon, how many Jew-jokes have you told at the expense of some customer of your factory? But don't worry: even Moses allows them. Do you know why Moses took the Jews through the desert? No? Because he was ashamed to take them through the streets!

Applauds like an emcee. The rest do too although they are surprised and looking at each other. George signals for them to quit clapping. Silence.

The Jew of my story had a Jewish name, naturally. He was named Aaron. And in the army when the corporal didn't know his last name, he didn't say "Aaron what?" but, "Erring, Herring?" and it was funny. It was so funny that one day when he was on guard with the machine gun, we all went and asked him: "How much'll you sell it for?" All of us: I, Limpie . . . ! Ah, you don't know Limpie . . . Limpie's the famous stickup man who walks like this. (*Imi-*

tates an exaggerated limp on the table.) And he has a
cane with a machine gun in the tip. Ratatatata! (*Pause.
Looks at them. Starts to intone.*)

> Limpie wanted
> To rob a haberdashery.
> He got tangled in some lace, and fell.
> Oh, sad day!
> Fallen Limpie looked at the stars,
> And then he cried.
> Like me,
> Like me.
> Limpie and his shadow look like a rug
> In the haberdashers.
> Oh, what a sad day!
> He found work,
> Like me,
> Like me.

(*George taps with his feet on the table. Pause. Looks at
them.*) And Herring was silent and looking ahead, and
after the wake, we found out that he was studying engineering because he wanted to build; and we found out that he
used to write poetry . . .:

> "And they told us we were immortal,
> Those who told us, died, and were forgotten."

. . . But that didn't matter to us. We were so alive, and
behind us was our home, our family, the café, the billiards,
and "The future is yours." Like you told me, papa, when
I was twelve years old and you used to take me to the
parades in Palermo and we saw the soldiers pass: The poor
little soldiers and the generals. "The future is yours,
Georgie." And the country, and the flag, and "anyone can
be president." Well, you were never president, papa. But
you might have been a corporal, or a lieutenant, or a captain. Because the corporal, the lieutenant, and the captain
told us the same thing that night: "The future is yours,
soldiers! And the country, and the flag, and anyone can be
president!" Well, it made us laugh thinking about people
who clean up horse crap being presidents of the country,
the future, and the flag! Forward, march! Sure, Joaquin!
You were in the army, too, and you know just what it's
like to go in a jeep with Limpie, and the little Jew, Aaron
Herring, and a corporal, and a lieutenant, and a captain,

and a machine gun that winks its eye at you like a joke. "Aaron Herring, how much'll you take for the machine gun?" And Herring looked: ahead. And for the first time we realized that the stars existed, and that we were twenty-one years old, and that despite, "The future is yours," your hands can't break a machine gun. "Papa," I shouted, "I want to go home!" "The country, soldiers, and the flag, and the honor of the army! Forward, march!" the corporal-papa, and the lieutenant-papa, and the captain-papa told me. "Papa, I want to go home!" And then the stars came down on top of us: as if the sky had been throwing hot cigar butts at us. And the corporal, and the lieutenant, and the captain wept as they dragged themselves along the ground. "The country, soldiers, Forward, march!" and they cried and cried. What? My country never told me that my country was a laxative. And they cried, and cried, and Limpie, the famous stickup man was boxing with the pasture. And he was crying. And only the little Jew Aaron Herring remains to be told about: lying down, looking upward and ahead. "Aaron, we're big boys now, and this isn't a parade." We've got to go home, Aaron, and put ourselves in the safe, because I'm twenty-one years old, and this I don't understand. Papa'll tell us. Papa'll tell us all, Aaron. And then I realized that Aaron Herring was dead and would never again be able to build or write verses. "Get up, Aaron! Anyone can be president!" But Aaron Herring was dead, and would never again be able to build or write poetry. Then I lay down, and looked at the stars, and I cried! "I want to go home, papa." And I cried, because I was twenty-one years old, and they'd told me, "The future is yours," and something that wasn't me ripped my flesh and bones, and I didn't understand anything.

(*Pause.*)

Ladies and Gentlemen: My joke is entitled: "The Story of Aaron Herring, the Jew: dead, buried, and forgotten." That's what you wanted me to tell you, mamma, there in Cordoba, when you kept asking me: "What's the matter, Georgie? What's the matter, Georgie? What's the matter, Georgie?" Did you want me to tell you that? And Ada, and the cake with twenty little candles, and the smiling couple who travels to Europe . . . (*He shouts.*) THAT'S WHAT YOU WANTED, ISN'T IT?

Everyone stands. He spreads his arms.

Wait, you still haven't seen the best part!

Everyone looks at each other and slowly sits down. George kneels on the table and spreads his arms in the typical Al Jolson style. More than singing, he says.

> Daddy!
> What bitchy life did you make for me?

ADA (*stands*): George!

GEORGE: Wait, I'll tell you. You still haven't seen the best part!

(*Pause.*)

> Mommy!
> Your daughter's going to give birth,
> And you,
> All you
> Ghosts from a museum,
> Are you going to leave the new
> Brand-new
> Child,
> Rosy and
> Snotty,
> The same world you left for me?
> Listen!
> Do you know what a question is?
> Listen to the wind
> And the airplane!
> And you all
> Dead-papa-dead
> Dead-mamma-dead
> Ay! Ada-so-dead!
> Who can I ask?

(*Talks softly.*)

> "This House Is the Whole World" is a bad joke.
> It's the worst joke I've ever been told . . .
> Listen! Life can be a song!
> It can be a tic-tac
> And it can be a tic-toc
> And a run and a walk.
> But all this, where is it?

Who can I ask?
Listen, I want to live!
(*Almost crying.*)
Daddy, what bitchy life did you make for me?

George stays kneeling with his arms spread, crying. Pause.
Stephen advances toward George, moved by his new vision
of his brother.

STEPHEN: George . . . dear Georgie.

He says it softly, in contrast to the offended voice of Ada,
who stands.

ADA: George! But George!

George looks at her.

GEORGE: Oh . . . you! (*He jumps off the table and goes down*
the center to in front of the proscenium.)
STEPHEN: George!

George reaches the center of the proscenium. Stephen
comes behind. The curtain falls rapidly behind them.
George and Stephen are illuminated by a shaft of light.

Where're you going?
GEORGE: To see Limpie.
STEPHEN: To tell him what?
GEORGE: How should I know?
STEPHEN: You can't tell him "How should I know what."
GEORGE: Leave me alone, Stephen. What do you know?
STEPHEN: Ah, yes . . . What do I know! The only one who
has the right to be furious is you. Not I . . . I've been
studying medicine for ten years, and I've been working for
fifteen, and maybe I'm going to have to study for another
ten . . . and a moth-eaten old man flunks me because I
happen to think things should change . . . But you're the
only one who has a right to be furious and bitch about
things.
GEORGE: Limpie's waiting for me. And we, even though we're
brothers, we don't have anything in common.
STEPHEN: I know it. And it's my fault. I left you alone too
long. I thought you were a stupid brat who was going to
spend his life playing billiards, but when you came back . . .

GEORGE: You had to study! And I couldn't come into the room so as not to bother you!

STEPHEN: I was wrong! But we can still talk . . .

GEORGE: Talk . . . about what? Are you going to tell me too, that Aaron's dead, and that I have to adjust and live like them?

STEPHEN: No. You can't live like them! Neither you nor I can live like them. But don't blame them for everything. The old man and old lady had arms as long as yours, and they wanted a world as big as the one you want. It kept getting smaller . . . and now they don't count anymore. You and I are going to live another way. But to live another way doesn't mean writing on the wall, "The mother whore who dropped him."

GEORGE: Stephen, now don't you tell me, "The future is yours!"

STEPHEN: Laugh, but I'll tell it to you. It's yours and mine.

GEORGE: What's the future, Stephen?

STEPHEN: It's a lot of things, I believe.

George breaks out crying.

Why are you crying?

GEORGE: Because when it gets here, I'll be dead!

STEPHEN (*hugs him, and shakes him hard*): Georgie, listen to me! Georgie! Death exists, and is waiting, but it's not a problem. Our only problem is how to live. Do you hear me, Georgie? Do you hear me? That's what Limpie's waiting for you to tell him. Do you hear me, Georgie? Do you hear me?

The light goes out on them suddenly, and another spotlight comes up on the left, where the Old Man appears with a top hat and a cane.

OLD MAN (*sings and dances*):
      Hey, you:
      Throw this old man a coin!
      This old, old world
      About to spawn.
(*Talks to the audience.*)
      I had everything in my top hat:
      Pharaohs, kings, democracy . . .
(*Sings again.*)

Hey, you:
Throw this old man a coin,
This old, old stevedore
Old stories are finished:
I'm about to spawn
Hey, you: throw this old man a coin,
This old whorehouse bellhop.
I am about to spawn, I tell you.
I'm not sorry.
It was the time to live
The old clowns are through:
They bored me!
They screwed me.
And now I'm about to spawn.
Hey, you:
Throw this old man a coin,
To buy a cradle,
And a rifle!

Lights up on George and Stephen. Down on the Old Man.

STEPHEN (*shaking George by the shoulders*): Listen, Georgie.
Listen. You have to hear me! You have to listen to me!

THE END

THE PLACE WHERE
THE MAMMALS DIE

JORGE DÍAZ

Translated by Naomi Nelson

Jorge Díaz, a naturalized Chilean, was born in Argentina in 1930. A professional architect, he entered the theatre through his work as a scene designer for a local theatre group in Santiago. Díaz's dramaturgy expresses a preoccupation with the problems of communication and commitment, of individual relations and social institutions. For the most part, he deals not so much with the process as with the result of a pervasive dehumanization of a conventional world into a particularly grotesque reality. He constantly challenges us, through exaggerations beyond the point of caricature, to envision a deformed world in which violence and inhumanity have become accepted dimensions. His very popular *Cepillo de dientes* (1961) plays on noncommunication and character transposition within the framework of a grotesque game. Later, feeling his effectiveness mitigated by the rampant black humor of his earlier plays, Díaz adopted a more hard-line approach to the problems of social reform, as in the brilliant *Topografía de un desnudo* (1966). The experiment with new forms of expression has led to a new play in completely invented language, *La orgástula* (1970), which relies on phonetic connotations to achieve an erotic tone and effect.

The Place Where the Mammals Die (*El lugar donde mueren los mamíferos*, 1963) is a supremely ironic presentation of the artificiality of charitable institutions, of organizations that exist to perpetuate themselves and to absolve their participants' collective conscience of any valid social responsibilities. It matters little, or not at all, that the recipient of the benefactors' generosity is debased and eventually destroyed. Rusty (Chatarra), the symbol of poverty, is overcome by his patrons' protective interests, but even in death, as a monument to their eternal solipsism, he continues to serve.

Although Díaz shows the influence of other European and North American writers of the Absurd, the final product is uniquely his own. Speaking of his own direction, he says: "My possibilities for expressing a Latin American reality are related to the contrasts between an absurd reality and the certainty that an internal logic of events exists which is rejected by this absurd reality. These contrasts, for me, attain

182

such an extreme violence that they produce distortion and the absurd in dramatic form."[1] Although living in voluntary exile in Madrid, Díaz remains Chile's leading contemporary dramatist.

[1] Jorge Díaz, *Teatro* (Madrid: Taurus Ediciones, 1967), p. 65. (My translation)

Characters

JUSTIN
ARCHIMEDES
MONICA
ANUNCIATTA
RUSTY
REPORTER
PHOTOGRAPHER

Scene

The action takes place in the Headquarters of the Ecumenical Institute of Total Assistance.

It is an enormous room that once had a sort of logical order but which now, due to the accumulation of national and international donations, is virtually overflowing. The objects that fill the room are superfluous and absurd, corresponding with the view of today's donor, i.e., that the poor are in need of bathrobes, mason jars, back numbers of magazines like *National Geographic*, etc.

On the walls are posters advertising various collection campaigns, and a plaque of the insignia of the Institute. The total effect is chaotic and incongruous.

A proscenium is formed entirely of packing boxes. Their profusion threatens to invade the set. At the beginning and end of the play, a large packing box is used for the conference table.

There is no vestige of the architectural style of this room that houses so many generous donations, but the following exits must be defined: (*a*) toward the entrance hall letting onto the street; (*b*) toward the interior of the building and other annexes; (*c*) toward the restroom.

The scant furniture to be seen is elegant and of ultramodern design.

A longish table facing the audience separates the office-warehouse from the passageway in the background.

Music

Three themes are heard:

Rusty's theme—Simple, sad, and reiterative.

The theme of the Institute—Conventionally optimistic, orchestrated.

The theme of the newspaper reporters—mostly percussion instruments—underlines their entrances.

ACT I

Justin approaches the proscenium and clears his throat.

JUSTIN: Good evening, friends! A new March of Hygiene brings us together again! Asepsis is the tie that binds. That is my motto. We shall have now a period of wholesome frankness, and shall certainly be the better informed about how to avoid contamination through carelessness, the ingestion of materials in decomposition, and the unhealthy state of our sewers. We ought to be able to combine diversion with our personal hygiene, don't you agree? Try, above all, to remember that although you are miserable wretches, you can be CLEAN miserable wretches.

Fine! We have prepared for you this evening an extensive scientific spectacular that could be entitled "The Cow and The Fly" or "The Perils of Cottage Cheese." I know of course that all of you take the precaution of carefully washing your feet before petting any animal, because a cow, despite appearances, is one. But—unfortunately not all of us remember to boil our hands before drinking milk. Nature is wise, and if you will permit me a metaphor—vegetarian. But that is no excuse for taking advantage.

The curtains open and Archimedes appears wearing a sandwich board. The front board seen at this time has the look of a line drawing such as might be seen in a laboratory, or the biology department of a school. It is an anatomical sectional view of a cow. The visceral parts each have their printed legends. The poster should have a title in Latin, and other unintelligible inscriptions.

Justin uses a schoolroom pointer to call attention to part of the picture.

JUSTIN: You can see here the delicate and complex mechanism of the pasteurization process. All perfectly dissimulated inside this animal whose photographs have become so commonplace in all our newspapers. However, the real object of this talk is not to demonstrate these picture postcards, because I know that the problems that afflict you people are much more grave. The subject for today is this: (*Justin turns Archimedes about with the pointer as though he were dealing with a trained animal. The poster seen now is of a gigantic fly. Various close studies. Unintelligible names.)*

The *Lampronia Volatile*! known as the, if you will permit me a metaphor, dung fly. The *Lampronia Volatile* hovers above us even at this moment, and is no stranger to us. This insect prefers, as do most collectors, still lifes. And there is the danger! In the suburbs where you people live, so disgracefully forgotten, the *Lampronia* has his earthly paradise.

Has anyone here held in his hand, or seen magnified a thousand times, the leg of the *Lampronia*? No? . . .

I have. It's awful! It looks like a hairy steam shovel—or the skeleton of a dinosaur—or, if you will permit me a metaphor—the leg of a fly. Yes, friends, on every lump of sugar, in each spoon of silver (and at times also of consommé) their eggs are quite visible to the naked eye of any good cooper—though not to that of a microscope. As you will have understood, we are dealing with a constant fountain of sicknesses and all kinds of stipends.

And so, when we see those tender youngsters drinking milk directly from the trough, our hygienic hearts bleed. There is nothing more noxious to the cow than cottage cheese. And what shall we say of our children, those poor indigent angels who play with flies as though they were sisters of charity? In conclusion, my poor underdeveloped friends, I shall repeat, as is customary at all these talks— The Decalogue of the Worldwide Health Organization. (*To Archimedes.*) The Decalogue!

Archimedes takes a scroll from his pocket and gives it to Justin.

(*Reading.*)
1. Do not eat your fingernails—uncooked.
2. Do not swallow saliva during difficult moments.
3. Wash your car every Saturday.
4. Do not eat duck without a doctor's prescription.
5. (This point is under restudy by the W.H.O.)
6. Don't think too much.
7. Avoid dead flies.

8. The exception proves the rule, but don't count on it.
9. If you see a fly, or a fly egg, telephone the Director General of the Public Health Department at once.
10. Pray.

All right, my friends! Memorize and comply! After all, if you must die of some kind of plague, you might as well die of an aseptic one.

We had also prepared a few words on the bacillus misanthrope, anthrax and free love—but we've thought it over and decided to conclude here.

To quote Pascal: "A small gift is a small gift." (*He makes a gesture of good-bye to the audience.*)

Archimedes applauds.

ARCHIMEDES: Turn in the corresponding coupon, and leave by the door at the back. Good night! (*Archimedes himself pulls open the stage curtain—revealing the main office of "The Ecumenical Institute of Total Assistance—Weekly Consolation for Indigents." So reads the inscription on the door. Archimedes stands applauding in the center of the stage.*)

Justin leaves the proscenium, goes to the desk and brings out a bottle of whiskey and a glass. Fills glass and drinks. Archimedes continues to applaud.

JUSTIN: It's humiliating, Archimedes. No one applauded.
ARCHIMEDES (*still applauding*): No. No one, Justin.
JUSTIN: It used to be that when we talked to the poor—the *really* poor—about their epidemics and the filth of their homes, they always applauded.
ARCHIMEDES (*still applauding*): Not these.
JUSTIN: It's that these are a prosperous middle class and they only come here to be amused. Talk to them about the dysentery in Africa, and they're bored! I don't understand it! That's enough, Archimedes. That'll do for today.
ARCHIMEDES (*stops applauding*): It was the air conditioner . . .
JUSTIN: There was a woman in the third row—hand dripping with diamonds—making obscene signs at me . . . What'd you say it was?

ARCHIMEDES: It was the air conditioner.

JUSTIN: That what?

ARCHIMEDES: That was to blame. No one can stand flies and cows in a theatre if the air conditioner isn't working.

JUSTIN: We've never had air conditioning.

ARCHIMEDES: Well . . . the truth is there wasn't anyone out there. Maybe we'll have to discontinue our talks on hygiene for indigents.

JUSTIN: It's a shame.

ARCHIMEDES: Things are getting more difficult every day. No one wants to be assisted. It's terrible.

JUSTIN: Pure egoism, Archimedes, pure egoism. The poor are using the cornmeal we provide them to make little pathways in their gardens. Even tennis courts! A textile industrialist we've been helping—a great sacrifice on our part—has been using our canned cheese to feed his fifteen Doberman pups.

ARCHIMEDES: Well, we know better than to expect any appreciation, Justin.

JUSTIN: An organization like ours just cannot be allowed to die. This just goes to show you the indifference of the authorities. The Ecumenical Institute of Total Assistance urgently needs total assistance.

ARCHIMEDES: It's not our fault if there aren't any poor people anymore.

JUSTIN: That's true. But you've got to admit that lately you haven't been as efficient as you used to be either. Two years ago you were bringing in at least six or seven poverty cases a week. Not that that was so much, but we could struggle along. But *now*, aside from that one little old lady you found at the post office eating a money order form, you don't bring in a soul.

ARCHIMEDES: What about the two we took to the International Exposition? They made our booth a sensation!

JUSTIN: Don't be such a hypocrite, Archimedes. You know perfectly well they were under contract and we paid them a good salary. One was a count and the other was a financier.

ARCHIMEDES: The newspaper said it was an impact on the social sensibilities of all thinking persons.

JUSTIN: OK. What about *since* then? Nothing. Absolutely nothing.

ARCHIMEDES: No one wants to see an abundance of hunger

and poverty more than I do! But we just don't have it! There's nothing I can do. You know that periods of crisis are transitory. One has to learn to wait.

JUSTIN: Wait! Wait for what? For them to dissolve the Institute? I've dedicated fifteen years to the poor; to studies, statistics, projects, schemes. And now this is how they repay me! One has had one single objective in life. POVERTY! And now it simply doesn't exist anymore. Well, I tell you it does exist! And if it doesn't exist it's got to be reinvented. I have to think of my vocation. That comes first! Archimedes, you are inept and I will not sacrifice a single one of my ideals to your blindness!

Archimedes approaches Justin, and as he speaks to him he blows his breath into Justin's face.

ARCHIMEDES: I have my dignity, Justin. I don't remember where it is exactly. . . . Why, you know that I . . .

JUSTIN (*drawing back*): You smell of fresh ink. You are vicious! A degenerate! I only took you on to try to help a fallen man. But I see it's been useless.

ARCHIMEDES: Everybody's got a past.

JUSTIN: Ruined by vice. You're going right on drinking ink on the sly. I haven't said anything because I wanted to avoid a scandal. But the truth is, we are using fifteen quarts of ink in this place each week!

ARCHIMEDES (*remorseful*): I can't help it, Justin. I can't.

JUSTIN: When you were given this job you were clearly warned. Not so much as a drop on the sly!—and you were to knock off chewing blotters. But no! At the very first opportunity you're licking your inky fingers. I've tried using green ink. Then red. It's all the same to you. It's the habit! You're hooked!

ARCHIMEDES (*tearfully*): Yes. It's true. I'm lost. But I'm not to blame. Twenty years in a public office was too much for me. The temptation was too great.

JUSTIN: That's enough! It's boring. I know all your misdeeds by heart. (*Searching through his papers.*) Any trace of those three indigent families we heard about?

ARCHIMEDES (*still a little weepy, consults a small notebook*): One of the families wasn't at home. They were out on their yacht. The second was in actual need of food—for some hybrid canaries they're raising. We made a deal with the third.

JUSTIN: What deal?

ARCHIMEDES: They will pass as poverty cases, fill out our application forms, and accept our gifts and cornmeal—as long as they are compensated financially.

JUSTIN: I get it. A rake-off. How much?

ARCHIMEDES: Three thousand. They need it urgently . . . to finish up their swimming pool.

JUSTIN: Are they convincing?

ARCHIMEDES: Not very. Of course I haven't seen them dirt-covered, but they're committed to give us an authentic crust, and an unbearable stench, for the day of the public presentation.

JUSTIN: Well, they'll be something to show for the week. But if you don't find something better in the next fifteen days, be thinking about what you are going to do. We're not here just to give away ink to deviant civil servants. The Ecumenical Institute has more altruistic ends in view than feeding you. I am afraid, Archimedes, that we have been mistaken in you.

ARCHIMEDES: I'll do everything possible, Justin. I swear it.

JUSTIN: Get going now. I've got a Director's meeting. Oh! Look for someone to accept all these jars. This is your last chance.

Archimedes has been staring fixedly at an inkwell on the desk. He can no longer contain himself.

ARCHIMEDES (*supplicating, indicating inkwell*): Could I . . .?

JUSTIN (*shrugging his shoulders*): Do as you please.

ARCHIMEDES: Thanks. (*Archimedes takes up the ink bottle, and with a soda straw quickly drawn from his shirt pocket, sucks noisily. Soon begins to hum a song absently, drunkenly. Exits to restroom.*)

At that moment Monica enters. She is a mature woman but very well preserved. Dresses elegantly. She is nervous and upset, but maintains her aplomb and natural distinction.

JUSTIN: Monica!

MONICA: I'm glad you're alone. This time you are going to listen to me.

Archimedes reappears putting on his jacket. He crosses the stage making for the far exit. He stops in front of Monica and humming, blows his breath in her face. He playfully

*throws up his hands, as though startled by her, turns his
back and goes out staggering a bit.*

JUSTIN: Archimedes dried up the inkwell again.

MONICA: . . . So undone, Justin. Utterly broken up . . .

JUSTIN: W-w-who . . .?

MONICA: And you're the guilty one.

JUSTIN: Who . . . was undone?

MONICA: The bridge club, of course.

JUSTIN: Why?

MONICA: In my hurry to get over here I had to leave them
with their bile in their mouths! Is it really so urgent?

JUSTIN: Yes, it is.

MONICA: Don't tell me you've found someone poor!

JUSTIN: No, Monica. No one.

MONICA: Some couple living together out of wedlock?

JUSTIN: No. They're all married . . . three or four times.

MONICA: Then I don't understand! You know perfectly well
that interrupting a hand of bridge is terribly unhealthy. It
produces neurosis.

JUSTIN: I've got to talk to you, Monica.

MONICA: How annoying! You know I can only give the
Ecumenical Institute my Saturday afternoons.

JUSTIN: And me your Saturday nights. And your husband
your Sunday naps.

MONICA: We have *got* to get organized, Justin. What would
become of me without organization!

JUSTIN: That's precisely what I want to do. Our Institute of
Weekly Consolation is dying for want of one simple thing.
. . .

MONICA: What?

JUSTIN: The disconsolate.

MONICA: Don't exaggerate. Just because we haven't found
anyone dead of starvation in six or seven years . . . is no
reason to despair!

JUSTIN: This situation has gone on too long. We're receiving
threats from Brussels. They're going to suspend all subsidy
unless we can show concrete results. The International
Organism that finances us is unhappy because we only
send in plans and brochures. They want photographs, fingerprints, tape recordings, and statistics of our social work.

MONICA: What impertinence! I'm on twelve other Boards of

Directors, and they've never tried to control me with any such rudeness.

JUSTIN: It's just policy. Nothing personal. The Brussels group is being watched by Stockholm. Stockholm is being watched by Zürich or Washington.

MONICA: It's unfair pressure.

JUSTIN: Our declaration of principles states that we needn't be expecting gratitude. . . .

MONICA (*accusingly*): Nor jubilation . . .

JUSTIN (*in the same tone*): Nor social limelight . . .

MONICA (*piqued*): Nor traffic in drugs . . .

JUSTIN (*same*): Nor international contraband . . .

MONICA: Nor can they ask us to be anonymous heroes!

JUSTIN: In this country, Monica, the only recognized heroes are firemen and cuckolds.

MONICA (*very thoughtful, with whiskey glass in hand*): Imagine it—my husband's epitaph: "The Nation to Its Heroes!"

JUSTIN (*ingenuously*): Is he a fireman?

MONICA (*ironic*): Justin . . .!

JUSTIN: Monica, this situation is very delicate.

MONICA: It does give that impression, doesn't it?

JUSTIN: Just five years ago we were making our distributions regularly. Today we have to put up rewards . . . like a trap for the unwary.

MONICA: And what about our spiritual assistance program? Our advisor on religion is so depressed I've had to send him to my beach cottage to rest. If we don't find him someone he can advise pretty soon I really believe he'll go quite mad. I'm in complete agreement with my parish priest —people have stopped being poor because of nothing in the world but lack of faith.

JUSTIN: And imagination. A few years back when I launched that Clean Latrine Campaign, the people were genuinely moved and wept, and someone, a fanatic perhaps, threw flowers at me. On the other hand, today I spoke to an empty hall—except for one millionaire who was grossly insulting to me.

MONICA: It was too good to last. (*Nostalgically.*) Those lovely Saturday afternoons in the slums! In those days Jacqueline and Grace and I visited the poor. We always took them powdered milk and insecticide. It was pathetic. The children would yell, "The ladies are here!" And right away

we'd start wiping noses and taking our census of the
couples on the outs with each other.

JUSTIN: Beautiful memories.

MONICA: . . . not to mention the little religious seeds we
would drop here and there in passing—artfully, of course.
Very susceptible, those people. We'd make novenas—and
hold obligatory Mass. One would feel so apostolic! . . .
Afterward Grace always treated us to tea and we'd gossip
about it all, laughing like loons the whole evening. . . .

JUSTIN: I never was invited.

MONICA: It was for ladies only! We fought like cats. . . .

JUSTIN: And then when I got to . . . "know you" . . . you
began to leave off the tea parties with the girls.

MONICA: I think the thing that inflamed me was that speech
of yours: "A Little Something Extra for the Working Girl."
It was so . . . complete.

JUSTIN: You were alive with a scorching proselytical fire!

MONICA: Then, you naughty boy, you told me you had a
serious problem you wanted to take up with me.

JUSTIN: I honestly had one.

MONICA: And you took it up with me. . . .

JUSTIN (with a little laugh): On a folding cot donated during
one of our campaigns.

MONICA: Your problems always came up on Saturday afternoons.

JUSTIN: They're periodic problems.

MONICA: My children were always telling me my work in
the slums would kill me.

JUSTIN: I don't believe it.

MONICA: It's sad, isn't it? Demagogism ended with the
slums, and now there are no poor. We are alone. Completely alone.

JUSTIN (taking her hand): Yes, we are alone and I have a
problem to take up with you. My problem is you. My
spiritual unrest, as always.

MONICA: But, it's not Saturday yet!

JUSTIN: I'm a little ahead. (He tries to embrace her.)

MONICA (resisting a little): Justin, you are my weekly calvary.

JUSTIN: Sacrifice yourself.

MONICA: My sensitivity will be my ruin. Where I recognize
a need, I'm capable of taking off my very clothes to cover
it.

JUSTIN (enthusiastically): Do!

MONICA: You and I are idealists, Justin. What can we do, people like us, in a time so corrupt as this?

JUSTIN (*kissing her*): We'll think of something. We could begin with kisses. . . .

MONICA: Then . . . get Wagner. It's the only thing that prepares me for that. . . .

JUSTIN (*going to record player*): Wagner! (*Justin puts on a record. A heavy, pretentious Wagnerian overture is heard. He goes back to Monica as the music plays. They kiss.*)

Enter Anunciatta, seeing the situation, she hesitates disconcerted. Becomes furious.

ANUNCIATTA (*furious*): Wagner again! Can anyone explain this?

Justin and Monica do not hear. Anunciatta approaches them and shouts.

I demand an explanation!

Only now do Justin and Monica separate. Justin coughs and walks over to the desk, opens the minutes book. Monica, utterly poised, kisses Anunciatta on both cheeks.

MONICA: Ah, it's Anunciatta—the devout! The dead fly!

ANUNCIATTA: Monica! The devourer of Justins!

MONICA: For lack of class you have a moustache.

ANUNCIATTA: For lack of shame you have money.

JUSTIN (*to both of them*): Take your seats, please.

ANUNCIATTA: The imbecile can think of nothing but seats.

Both women take seats around Justin's desk.

JUSTIN (*impassive, conducting an imaginary Board of Directors meeting*): . . . Thus we bring to order this meeting of the Board of Directors of the Ecumenical Institute. I want to welcome the members of the Directory. The order of business is the following:

MONICA (*to Anunciatta, aggressively*): Repression.

ANUNCIATTA (*to Monica*): Concupiscence.

MONICA: Metabolism.

ANUNCIATTA: Cannibalism.

JUSTIN (*continuing in his presidential tone, and jotting down notes from time to time*): The Chair will hear discussion on the first point.

MONICA (*heatedly*): It's little enough that can be said about you. This much is clear: socially resentful, virgin, to your regret, and flat-footed.

ANUNCIATTA (*heatedly*): I can only add what is already generally known—that you are analphabetic and cirrhotic.

JUSTIN (*making notes*): As we are not in agreement, the matter must be submitted to a vote.

ANUNCIATTA: I abstain.

MONICA: It shows on you.

ANUNCIATTA: And your vote?

MONICA: Secret ballot. Only the President of this assembly may know how I vote. (*Monica whispers to Justin.*)

Justin laughs as though she has told him a dirty joke.

JUSTIN: Right! Motion approved unanimously. "Charity is the basis of conviviality." We go now to the second motion. "Charity and Human Dignity."

MONICA: Owl-face.

ANUNCIATTA: Rabbit.

MONICA: Habit.

ANUNCIATTA: Fatty.

MONICA: Batty.

ANUNCIATTA: Wart.

Monica with evil gleam in eye; lets it pass. Both howl in unison like bitches in heat at full moon.

JUSTIN: We are in complete accord. At this time then, I should like to pose the essential question: Should we silence these truths that we possess, guard them secretly, or should we spread them, making of each of ourselves a veritable megaphone shouting the human ideal? . . .

MONICA: Pity, Anunciatta, that you're such small potatoes, isn't it? You're intelligent enough, sweetie, but a little out of date. You give Archimedes some looks that are strictly "going down for the third time"—makes my flesh crawl. But, of course, we have to excuse you. They say that necessity wears the face of Archimedes.

ANUNCIATTA: God forbid that I should say anything against you, Monica! You are the soul of the Institute! What dedication! It's really touching the way you lie down with every robust indigent under the age of fifty.

MONICA: I know you're an absolute tomb, so I don't mind telling you that the other day. . . . (*Murmuring.*)

ANUNCIATTA: Not a tomb. A whited sepulcher, darling. What's told to me, is dead and buried. Imagine! . . . the other night . . . (*Murmurs.*)

Both begin to chatter in such a manner that neither can be understood.

JUSTIN: Good! Your enthusiasm doesn't surprise me. And now I am going to request that the honorable Board consider the proposition of a "World Congress of Poverty," whose slogan would be: "Lend Me Your Rags!" Hungry delegates from forty countries. The final assembly to take place in the National Stadium, with the distribution of paper hats, whole cloves, and cheap editions of the telephone directory in eight languages. The subject is now open for discussion.

ANUNCIATTA: You love these conventions, don't you, maneater? You'll get to show off your new viper skin coat.

MONICA: And you, poor dried up little thing . . . you'll be the center of attention at the closing meeting wearing your bottle-bottom eyeglasses.

ANUNCIATTA: You'll be at Justin's side at every meeting, giving him little feels under the table.

MONICA: You can spread your social life over five continents —MOUSE!

JUSTIN: I am making documentary evidence in the minutes of the enthusiasm with which you have received the idea. Thank you. Thank you. Thank you. . . . Before solemnly adjourning this meeting I should like to add that I am much heartened by the human warmth that I find in the bosom of this Institute. Does anyone else have anything to add?

MONICA: Lay sister!

ANUNCIATTA: Harlot!

JUSTIN: I'll add that to the minutes. Could you repeat it for me? (*Makes note.*)

MONICA (*to Justin*): Cretin!

ANUNCIATTA (*to Justin*): Indecent.

MONICA: Insipid.

ANUNCIATTA: Greenhorn.

JUSTIN: Thank you. I declare this "regular" meeting closed, and reiterate my appreciation to these Directors, beloved in so many senses. Fall out!

*There is a brusque change of general tone now as chairs
are pushed back and the actors move about. Anunciatta
goes to the desk. Monica sits down again in one of the
better chairs.*

MONICA (*sighing*): These Director's meetings just kill me.
Anunciatta, sweetie, make us a little tea.

ANUNCIATTA: No sooner said than done, pet! We've got loads
to talk about.

MONICA: That naughty Justin was certainly playing the World
Congress close to his chest, wasn't he? He hadn't told us a
word!

ANUNCIATTA: I was nearly late getting here. Lucky I haven't
lost anything. I wouldn't have forgiven myself. (*From
behind the desk Anunciatta brings out a tray, cups, sugar
bowl, cookies, and a teapot.*)

JUSTIN: What kind of mischief were you up to, Anunciatta?

ANUNCIATTA: I was just coming back from a talk with my
pedicurist. There's no comfort like it for a poor subcon-
scious like mine.

MONICA: And speaking of poor things . . . just where are we
going to *get* some for our Congress of Poverty?

JUSTIN: Get some what?

MONICA: Poor people. It'll cost us a fortune, as always.

JUSTIN: I hadn't thought about that. . . .

ANUNCIATTA: Are they indispensable?

MONICA: Well, of course!

JUSTIN: Wouldn't the foreign delegates be enough?

MONICA: A minimum of decorum as organizers demands our
offering a few lice-ridden "folkloric" types.

ANUNCIATTA: With or without sugar?

MONICA: What?

ANUNCIATTA: The tea.

MONICA: Two lumps.

JUSTIN: I don't think we can get away with disguising anybody the way we've done before. They're sending a sociologist from Brussels.

ANUNCIATTA: Black or white?

JUSTIN: A little pedantic.

ANUNCIATTA (*serving the tea*): The way I like it. (*Anunciatta
takes the cups to the center table.*)

JUSTIN: Monica's right. It's a vital point. Well, I can't think
of *everything*. What would you advise?

ANUNCIATTA: Cookies or cake?

MONICA: Cake.

JUSTIN: Yes. That would be best.

MONICA (*serving herself*): Surely one pauper more or less won't stand in the way of our getting to know those notables in sociology. . . .

ANUNCIATTA (*with a cookie in her hand*): Aren't they a little old?

MONICA: Not at all! Young, I'd say. About our age.

ANUNCIATTA: I meant the cookies.

JUSTIN (*absently*): Young . . . old . . . what's the difference. Young *and* old, people have left off being grateful and noble.

MONICA: In summer there's a lot of that, 'specially among gas fitters. . . .

At this moment hurried footsteps are heard. Archimedes comes in running. Goes clear across the stage and out, without saying a word. All register mute expectation. He reappears, crosses the stage at a run, this time carrying a rope. He yells.

ARCHIMEDES: I've got him, . . . I've got him!

ANUNCIATTA (*alarmed*): Archie!

Archimedes comes back in pushing a large packing box showing labels such as "This Side Up," "Handle With Care," "Glass," etc. Monica and Anunciatta jump up in surprise. Justin betrays no sign of surprise.

MONICA: Archimedes, what is going on?

ANUNCIATTA: I don't think he feels well.

Archimedes collapses into a chair.

JUSTIN: No doubt he's been having a few at the stationery store on the corner.

ANUNCIATTA (*going close to Archimedes*): Archimedes! I can't believe it!

JUSTIN (*indicating the box*): Donations! Why did you do it, Archimedes? We're up to here with surplus vitamins from the United States. All you had to do was look at the labels! "This Side Up." "Keep Cool." It's vitamins!

ARCHIMEDES (*recovering his breath*): I've got . . . I've got . . .

JUSTIN (*getting to his feet*): Archimedes, what you've got, is to look for employment.

ARCHIMEDES: I've found . . . I've found . . .

JUSTIN: I don't know who's going to be willing to take you on after this, but in the meantime, get that crate out of here!

ANUNCIATTA: Poor Archie! Do you want a little cup of tea?

ARCHIMEDES: I found him! I found him. I brought him with me. He didn't want to come. . . . He didn't want to. . . .

MONICA (*condescendingly*): Calm yourself, Archimedes. Calm yourself.

ANUNCIATTA: Archie . . . please, what is it you've found?

ARCHIMEDES (*taking a deep breath*): A pauper.

JUSTIN: A what?

ARCHIMEDES: A pauper.

MONICA: You mean . . . a pauper?

ARCHIMEDES: Yes.

JUSTIN: You mean it? A real one?

ARCHIMEDES: I believe so.

JUSTIN: Where is he?

ARCHIMEDES (*waving toward the box*): In there.

JUSTIN: The United States is sending us paupers?! They've figured it right at last! If only they can send us enough to meet our needs! To fill this void. . . . You suppose he speaks Spanish?

ARCHIMEDES: I had to put him in there by force because he didn't want to come. I found him in a rubble heap.

MONICA: Then he is the real article! How exciting! (*She goes over to the box and puts an ear to it.*) He's breathing!

ANUNCIATTA (*admiringly*): You did this by yourself, Archie?

JUSTIN: I don't believe it.

ARCHIMEDES: You can see for yourself. (*Archimedes goes over to the box.*)

MONICA: I haven't seen one in fifteen years. . . .

ANUNCIATTA: Be careful, Archie! They're dangerous.

JUSTIN: I don't get this, Archimedes. About fifteen minutes ago you leave here, half-drunk. Then you come back . . . with a pauper in tow. It's not only highly improbable, it's absurd.

ARCHIMEDES: We are all weak, and I have my failings. When I staggered out of here I was feeling pretty bad, and I went over to this old tin lean-to to throw up. While I was at it, I thought I noticed something move among the cans and trash. I was dizzy and sick and it seemed to me the rust moved. But no. It was he. So I stuffed him in the box and came shoving along back here.

JUSTIN: That's about enough of fantasies! Open that box!

ARCHIMEDES: Yes, Justin.

ANUNCIATTA (*getting up onto a chair*): Don't go too close, Archie!

Archimedes opens the side of the box that faces the audience. The top falls. To the general surprise, the box is empty.

MONICA: I don't see anything. Does anyone see anything?

ANUNCIATTA: He could be somewhere in there! Was he very small, Archie?

JUSTIN: Drunken liar. Archimedes, you're fired!

ARCHIMEDES (*pleading*): You've got to believe me! He *was* here. He must have fallen out. Please! Believe me! (*Archimedes runs to the door.*) He's got to be out in the street. Come on, Justin, he's got to be out here somewhere! (*Exit Archimedes.*)

ANUNCIATTA (*gets down from chair. Goes toward the door*): Come on! Let's help him. He's got to be found alive. (*Exit Anunciatta.*)

Voices are heard offstage.

MONICA (*approaching the box*): That's strange. . . .

JUSTIN: What?

MONICA: Archimedes was telling the truth.

JUSTIN: About what?

MONICA: About the pauper.

JUSTIN: What do you mean?

MONICA: He was in here all right. He left his scent. It's unmistakable.

JUSTIN (*shrugging*): Phantoms don't have a scent, Monica.

MONICA: Let's go look for our diamond in the rough, Justin. Come on, it'll ease the boredom if nothing else.

Exit Justin and Monica. Again voices from offstage. For a moment the stage is deserted.

Slowly a hand appears from behind a packing box. A man comes into view bit by bit, an indescribably dirty and ragged soul. It is "Rusty": he is the color of his environ-

*ment. He is a man of indeterminate age, but the vivacity
of his eyes and their malice, bespeak his youthfulness.
He looks about the room with curiosity, but no particular
interest, and certainly no fear. He speaks with a Puerto
Rican accent.*

*Rusty continues his inspection. Discovers the cookies and
cake and sits down to eat them hurriedly and greedily.
The voices from offstage are closer. Enter Justin and
Monica. Then, Anunciatta and Archimedes.*

One by one they discover Rusty.

JUSTIN: Yes, I agree that we *need* him, but I *will* not go on
looking for him. His disappearance is the typical proletarian
attitude. . . . (*He sees him—is stupefied.*)
ARCHIMEDES: This is terrible. This is terrible.
ANUNCIATTA: Archie, please, don't take it so hard. (*She sees
him—is stupefied.*)

Suddenly Archimedes sees him.

ARCHIMEDES: There! There he is! It's he!
MONICA: Who?
JUSTIN: That . . .?
ANUNCIATTA (*in a shriek*): Close the doors!

All approach cautiously.

ARCHIMEDES (*triumphantly*): Anyone still in doubt?
JUSTIN: I shouldn't want to make a judgment.
MONICA: Does he speak?
ANUNCIATTA: What's his name?
ARCHIMEDES: He doesn't remember. They call him Rusty.
MONICA: Rusty? That's cute. It suits him somehow, doesn't it?
JUSTIN (*clearing his throat . . . spluttering*): Mister . . . ah
. . . mister Rusty . . .??

No response. Now in a hard, loud voice.

Rusty!
RUSTY (*eating the last crumbs of the cake*): Yes?
JUSTIN: I should like to ask you something.
MONICA: Ask indirect questions so as not to humiliate him.
With subtlety a friend is won. . . .
JUSTIN: All right. Rusty, why don't you wash? You smell
like the devil!

RUSTY: I don't smell anything, word of honor.

MONICA (*takes up a steno book to make notes. Then, in a false, condescending voice*): Would you like to request anything or ask any questions?

RUSTY: Anyone here seen my Angel?

ANUNCIATTA: My God! *Who*, did he say?

RUSTY: Came with me in the box.

JUSTIN: Who came in the box?

RUSTY: Angel. My dog. Follows me everywhere.

JUSTIN: Let's not waste time.

ANUNCIATTA: Justin . . . let me, please. (*Draws near Rusty.*) You're suffering a great deal, aren't you Rusty?

RUSTY: . . . A shoe is pinching me, miss.

MONICA (*making a note*): Shoes . . .

RUSTY: I found an old shoe in an ash can, and a bedroom slipper. Both for the left foot. Have to make out the best I can.

ANUNCIATTA (*not to be outdone*): Your loneliness is unbearable, my good man?

RUSTY: Ophelia is pretty old all right, but in the dark all cats have four feet.

ANUNCIATTA: You're . . . married?

RUSTY: . . . I'll have to ask Ophelia. She understands a lot about those things.

MONICA (*making notes*): . . . Civil . . . *and* religious ceremonies.

JUSTIN: It's not that I distrust him, but I prefer absolute certainty. We'll have to see if he has a police record. Rusty, your poverty . . . is it habitual, occasional, or congenital?

RUSTY: I'm left-handed, sir. That's why they threw me out.

JUSTIN: Threw you out? Of where?

RUSTY: I made my living with my eyes.

JUSTIN: Painter? Watch repair?

RUSTY: No. I *made* eyes. Glass eyes. I've liked them since I was a little kid. I spent hours looking at the eyes of the corpses in the neighborhood. That's how I learned. You know how it is—today practically everyone has at least one glass eye. Even people whose eyes are perfectly good and healthy. Kind of a fad. So I sold a lot. Took me about a week to make an eye—or two—whatever the order. Red eyes or yellow ones. Eyes with sweet or evil thoughts. It was a good trade till those foreign mass-produced ones began coming in.

JUSTIN: How do I know if there's any truth in all that?

RUSTY: Give me a piece of colored glass and I'll make an eye especially for you. I don't like your right eye. It's piggish and envious. As a specialist, I can tell you it's not the right note for your lecherous face.

MONICA (*scandalized, makes a note*): Get him a copy of "The Proletariat's Elementary Education" right away!

ANUNCIATTA: What about my eyes, Rusty? . . . Archie finds them timid.

RUSTY: Ordinary glass.

ARCHIMEDES (*surprised*): Oh, Anunciatta! . . . is it possible?

JUSTIN: Monica, get me that "Test for Recognizing Paupers" we had. Haven't used it in years. It's probably half eaten up by rats.

MONICA: We've got that leaflet put out by UNESCO. Same thing, more or less. I'll find one or the other. (*Exit Monica.*)

ARCHIMEDES (*interceding*): His first reaction to the food was positive, Justin.

JUSTIN: I thought it was a studied effect.

ARCHIMEDES: And . . . he has a woman and a dog. That's symptomatic.

JUSTIN: I have to be absolutely sure.

ARCHIMEDES: There are too many coincidences.

JUSTIN: Everything in due process—otherwise where would we end up?

Enter Monica.

MONICA (*giving the remains of a rat-eaten book to Justin*): This is what's left of the Test.

JUSTIN (*looking it over*): It's all right. We'll skip over the blood analysis and cranial measurement tests—and get to the essentials (*Reading.*)—*Social Psychopathology*. Chapter 15. "Free Association." Let's see now . . . Economic Resentments . . . (*Takes a large bill from his wallet and waves it under Rusty's nose.*) See this bill? Say the first thing that comes to your mind.

RUSTY: Somebody told me one time that rich people use those to wipe their behinds. Is that true, sir?

Justin makes a note in the notebook and puts away the bill.

JUSTIN (*reading from the book*): . . . Social Resentments. As a child how many persons did you sleep with in a bed?

RUSTY: Bed?

JUSTIN: Yes.

RUSTY: We slept on the floor.

Justin writes.

JUSTIN: Can you read?

RUSTY: The lines of the hand, sir.

Justin makes a note.

ARCHIMEDES (*to Anunciatta*): He is a find! Isn't he?

ANUNCIATTA: A sweet and primitive thing.

Rusty spits noisily.

RUSTY: Can I ask a question, sir?

JUSTIN: Yes.

RUSTY: Is this a jail—or a brothel? I've been everywhere, but this doesn't look like anything.

MONICA: This is the Ecumenical Institute of Weekly Consolation for Indigents. We wish to lift you from your prostration.

RUSTY: I don't understand.

MONICA: It's very simple. We want to put an end to hunger and tears.

RUSTY (*to Monica*): Has it been some time since you've wept, miss?

MONICA: Yes . . . Why?

RUSTY: You should weep more often. I tell Ophelia that weeping is good for the vision.

JUSTIN: Enough of that nonsense! We've got to finish the Test. (*Reading.*) Aspirations. What thing would you desire so that you could live more happily?

RUSTY (*thinking a long time*): A safety pin. My pants fall down.

MONICA (*making a note*): Safety pin.

JUSTIN: Nothing else?

RUSTY: A silkworm. (*Takes a matchbox out of his pocket.*) I've raised three worms just on the chance. But not one of them turned out to be a silk one. If I just had a pair. . . .

MONICA (*making a note*): Worms.

ARCHIMEDES: Ask . . . ask! This is the time for it!

RUSTY: Well . . . I believe I'll decide on some false teeth for Ophelia.

MONICA (*making a note*): Set of teeth.

ARCHIMEDES (*excited*): Ask, Rusty! Ask!

RUSTY (*becoming bolder*): If it's just a matter of asking, I would like you to make a note of another little thing, miss. I . . .

JUSTIN: That will be all. (*Closes the book.*) Although it would appear absolutely unbelievable, practically a paradox, we have here an authentic pauper.

ANUNCIATTA: Congratulations, Rusty!

MONICA (*spraying insecticide on Rusty with a fumigator*): One of our brothers has been found! Hallelujah! Hallelujah! Hallelujah! . . .

JUSTIN: And the Congress of Poverty has been saved.

ARCHIMEDES: Archimedes, your little hour of glory had to come.

ANUNCIATTA: Archie, I like seeing you so . . . reckless.

As they go on talking Rusty sits down on the floor and removes a shoe. He puts it to one side.

JUSTIN: Let's not get ahead of ourselves now. We've got to get organized down to the smallest detail. We've got to form committees and subcommittees. The very first thing is to get Rusty put away in one of the storerooms till the regular distribution day when he can be given food, clothing, and household supplies. In the meantime he can be fasting and composing himself spiritually.

ARCHIMEDES: And let's not be forgetting the press.

JUSTIN: You will head up the Press and Propaganda Committee.

ANUNCIATTA: I can take charge of the Open-Air Te Deum ceremony.

JUSTIN: It's not appropriate. We're in the middle of winter. It will be enough to stage a simple torchlight parade—after his official presentation to the public.

MONICA: We're going to have so much to do. I'll have to get myself a new dress, of course.

ARCHIMEDES: Shall I invite the Masons and the International Red Cross?

JUSTIN: Under no circumstances. We're going to keep it more or less a family affair. Something tender, full of human warmth. Simply . . . the return of the Prodigal Son.

Rusty has curled up on the floor. He covers himself with newspapers. The others, behind him, go right on talking without paying him the least attention.

MONICA: The Prodigal Son is snoring.

ANUNCIATTA: He looks like a fallen angel.

ARCHIMEDES: He has a sty.

JUSTIN: Inopportune, I must say.

ANUNCIATTA: You suppose he has a dirty conscience?

MONICA: It'll have to be disinfected.

ARCHIMEDES: I think he'll have to be locked up.

JUSTIN: No, no. When he wakes up just hang him in the closet temporarily.

The rhythm of the dialogue has picked up imperceptibly, becomes more and more rapid as the lights fade, and a single light picks up on Rusty where he lies covered with newspapers.

ANUNCIATTA: It's gotten late.

MONICA: My foot's gone to sleep.

JUSTIN: The flesh is weak, especially the buttocks.

MONICA: The gluteals can be reduced three inches by the manual method.

ARCHIMEDES: Some have much and some have little.

JUSTIN: I don't know if I have two or three double chins.

ANUNCIATTA: Sensuality is a snare.

MONICA: I don't care much for snares, but I could listen to the eardrum all day.

JUSTIN: I can't hear! What are you saying? . . .

ARCHIMEDES: Be indulgent of his bad habits.

MONICA: Today for me, tomorrow for you. . . .

JUSTIN: Ora et labora.

ARCHIMEDES: Because he is our brother.

ANUNCIATTA: Our fellow creature.

MONICA: Something like us.

JUSTIN: Us on a bus.

ARCHIMEDES: Four on one truss.

ANUNCIATTA: The friend of man.

MONICA: The umbilical cord.

ANUNCIATTA: My other self.

MONICA: Your other you.

ARCHIMEDES: Our hour.

ANUNCIATTA: Poor lamb.

MONICA: Baked ham.

JUSTIN: Wham! Bam!

*Now all four speak at once. This prattling chorus blends
with the sound of the same voices, on a tape recording,
played at a different speed.*

*The curtain falls as the distorted voices continue, and a
soft spotlight shines on the still form of the sleeping Rusty.*

END OF ACT ONE

ACT II

*As the curtains open we view the same set as in the first act,
with only a few minor changes. There is a vase of flowers on
the large table. A small pedestal on one side of the stage.
Various garlands and streamers crisscross the Ecumenical
Headquarters. Several large gift-wrapped boxes are seen on
the desk.*

*Anunciatta, obviously nervous, is arranging the flowers in the
vase. Now she goes out the door on the right. Returns with
two trays of canapés. She contemplates her handiwork. Seems
satisfied. Scares off a fly that has alighted on the canapés.
Does it a second time. Now in irritation she follows the un-
worried flight of the fly from one place to another. The fly
pauses somewhere. Anunciatta cautiously creeps up on it.
Archimedes appears on tiptoe carrying a toy horn and a box
of balloons. He is wearing a false nose. He slips up behind
Anunciatta and blows the horn.*

ANUNCIATTA (*with a shriek of surprise*): Oh!

ARCHIMEDES: Did I scare you?

ANUNCIATTA: You scared the fly. In any case, don't be walking up behind me with evil intentions. You know how
sensitive I am.

ARCHIMEDES (*showing the horn*): These are for the party.
(*Looking around at the room.*) Oh! You have really transformed this hole. Don't you think you've overdone it a
little?

ANUNCIATTA (*fixing her gaze on the fly again*): Rusty deserves it. He receives his gifts today. The newspaper photog-

raphers will be here and I don't want them to think we're chintzy.

ARCHIMEDES: You think it's necessary to blow up the balloons?

ANUNCIATTA (*as she exits through the washroom door*): Archie, it's worth any sacrifice. Nothing we can do for them is really enough.

ARCHIMEDES: For the poor?

ANUNCIATTA (*offstage*): No. I mean the reporters.

ARCHIMEDES: Ah! . . .

Anunciatta returns. She has removed her apron and is primping coquettishly. Archimedes, who has been blowing up a balloon, lets it go and looks at Anunciatta steadily.

Anunciatita . . .!

ANUNCIATTA: Don't call me that.

ARCHIMEDES: It's just an affectionate diminutive.

ANUNCIATTA: If you want a diminutive, call me Ta.

ARCHIMEDES: What?

ANUNCIATTA: Ta.

ARCHIMEDES: Ta, I'd like to tell you something you might already have suspected.

ANUNCIATTA (*concentrating solely on the flight of the fly*): I am hanging on your every word.

Archimedes, himself fascinated with the fly, begins to follow it with his gaze, moving his head about, but never changing his lyrical tone. During the following dialogue, Anunciatta and Archimedes both follow the fly's invisible flight intently. They move about with short, light steps, never once looking at each other.

ARCHIMEDES: I'm so confused, I can't find the precise words I want. . . .

ANUNCIATTA: I'll help you. Would it be any of these? Hiccoughs . . . fireworks . . . nervous tic . . .

ARCHIMEDES: Thanks. But I can't use them. It's something like . . .

ANUNCIATTA: Sandwich . . . knee . . .

ARCHIMEDES: No. Neither of those.

ANUNCIATTA: Bull . . . pheasant . . . acromegaly . . . umbilicus . . .

ARCHIMEDES: No, no, I need to tell you simply . . . (*With growing anxiety, but without ceasing to watch the fly.*)

ANUNCIATTA: Saturn . . . cancer . . . binomial . . . yogurt . . .
parsley . . . metempsychosis . . .
ARCHIMEDES (*weepy*): No, I only want . . .
ANUNCIATTA (*weepy*): Leg of lamb, bacon fat, toad . . .
ARCHIMEDES: *Toad!* That's *it!* (*He snatches the flyswatter
away from her.*) Listen now. . . . (*With emotion.*)

> A tree toad loved a she-toad
> That lived up in a tree.
> He was a two-toed tree toad
> While a three-toed toad was she.
> The he-toad tree toad tried to gain
> The she-toad's friendly nod,
> For the two-toed tree toad loved the ground
> That the three-toed tree toad trod.
> The two-toed tree toad tried in vain
> But couldn't please her whim,
> For from her tree toad bower
> With her she-toad power
> The three-toed tree toad vetoed him.

*They still have not looked at each other. Now Archimedes
beats the air with the flyswatter as he says.*

Ta, ta, ta, ta . . .

*With the last "ta" he hits Anunciatta on the backside with
the swatter. The fly falls dead and Archimedes steps on it.
Anunciatta gives a little scream.*

ANUNCIATTA: Oh! How could you have done that! How cruel,
how abominable! . . .
ARCHIMEDES: Ta, Ta, I only wanted to express my sentiments.
ANUNCIATTA (*indicating the fly on the floor*): It's horrible.
Horrible. To do this to *me*, who have given you only the
very best of myself! Don't touch me! (*Weeping, she falls
onto the sofa.*)

Enter Monica.

MONICA: What's the matter, little one? Archimedes' latest
attempt?
ANUNCIATTA: Yes.
MONICA: This could end with Anunciatta taking you seriously,
Archimedes.

Enter Justin and Rusty. Rusty is dressed exactly as in Act One, one shoe is missing. He is a little weaker from his fast.

JUSTIN (*looks about the room. Speaks to Anunciatta*): How nicely you've arranged everything! It wouldn't hurt to do a little something about yourself now. You're looking a bit dusty and deteriorated.

ARCHIMEDES: . . . I'll just go out and wait for the reporters. (*Exit Archie.*)

JUSTIN (*calling after him*): See if you can stay sober.

MONICA: Well, Rusty, this is an important day for you . . . and for us! How do you feel?

RUSTY: Hungry.

MONICA: But I gave you some tablets for that. . . .

RUSTY: They didn't do a thing for me. . . .

JUSTIN: Your privations end today, my friend. Now begins, if you will permit me a literary metaphor, a surfeit.

RUSTY: I'll have to notify Ophelia.

MONICA: Ask me for whatever you will, with absolute confidence . . . that I shall forget it immediately.

RUSTY: I lost one of my shoes, miss.

MONICA: You're an incorrigible boy! What size are you?

RUSTY: Isn't that a medical matter?

MONICA: Are there any shoes in those boxes, Anunciatta?

ANUNCIATTA: There are some special ones for water skiing.

MONICA: As you see, Rusty, we have thought of everything.

JUSTIN: Rusty, my good friend, had you ever imagined that charitable hands would one day lift you from the mire?

RUSTY: I'll tell you something, sir: I don't seem to be able to get used to it. The thing is, you aren't like the friends I have. It's different. I have to get accustomed to it. Out at the dump there's always a friend or a dog you can sleep next to to keep warm. Last night in the closet I was cold.

MONICA: Poor thing! It's just like in those neorealistic movies!

RUSTY: It's not bad at the dump. You can take your pick— an old car seat or a baby carriage to sleep in. All you have to do is reach out your hand for a teapot, springs, tricycles. Little plants and lizards scramble among the chamber pots.

ANUNCIATTA: How sad!

RUSTY: On Sundays I look around for a tractor seat or a bidet and make myself comfortable. I smoke two or three cigar butts in the sun. I can see the rust slowly eating up each and every piece of iron. It's not bad. . . .

ANUNCIATTA: There are other ways of spending a Sunday.

RUSTY: That's Sunday for me. The smoke from the cigar butts, and Angel stretched out somewhere nearby. The little kids running around trying to find old bicycle wheels in the piles of junk. They always call out "Rusty!" and I tell them where they ought to look.

MONICA: It's too deadly! Alone in the middle of that scrap-iron cemetery. . . .

RUSTY: What a hope! Alone! In just one old locomotive boiler out there, three entire families are living and laughing and having more kids. And that's how it is in every ditch . . . and every milk pail practically!

MONICA: All that will change today. We'll make you over, Rusty. It'll be like those ads for developing the bust. Before and After.

JUSTIN: Rusty *before* the Ecumenical Institute, and *after* the Ecumenical Institute.

RUSTY: If it wouldn't be breaking any rules, do you suppose you could advance me—I mean like a retainer fee or something—a little piece of bread?

Voices are heard from offstage.

JUSTIN: It's not possible now. They're here. Rusty, get up on that pedestal. I'll cover you with this drape for the inauguration. (*He makes Rusty get up on the small pedestal and covers him with a drape such as is used for the unveiling of a monument or statue.*)

Enter Archimedes, followed by a Photographer and his equipment, and a Reporter carrying a tape recorder. Speaking to no one, the newsmen go directly to the canapés, sit down, and begin to eat.

ARCHIMEDES: Come in! Come right in, gentlemen! Please make yourselves comfortable.

JUSTIN: My very good friends, once more we have wished you to be the first to know of our anonymous labors, because we are, if you will permit me a metaphor . . .

REPORTER (*with his mouth full*): I will not permit it.

PHOTOGRAPHER: Where is the specimen?

MONICA (*singingly*): . . . that's for us to know, and you to find out!

The Photographer, upon noticing Monica, kisses her hand respectfully.

PHOTOGRAPHER: How are you, madam?

MONICA: Warm . . . warm . . . you're getting warmer . . .

REPORTER (*seeing the big gift boxes*): Is it somebody's birthday?

JUSTIN: My friend, this is only the first of a series of similar gatherings at which we shall make gifts and offer spiritual consolation to the forsaken.

REPORTER (*picking up a wine decanter*): White?

JUSTIN: *Without* prejudice, racial or political. (*Deeply serious.*) Thirty years ago the Ecumenical Institute was founded in the hope that it could offer a little . . .

REPORTER (*interrupting*): Mustard!

Anunciatta passes him the mustard.

JUSTIN (*immutable*): And so it was that fifteen years later a group of idealists motivated solely by their own restlessness and their sense of the . . .

PHOTOGRAPHER: Where's your toilet? I've got to . . . change my film.

ARCHIMEDES: This way. (*Exit Archimedes and the Photographer.*)

JUSTIN (*immutable*): . . . until this very day on which, thank God, we contemplate . . .

REPORTER (*looking at a canapé with a melancholy air*): If it weren't for my liver, I'd believe in God.

ANUNCIATTA (*annoyed*): Faith isn't a question of the bowels.

MONICA: Anunciatta, don't make rash statements! This is all coming out in the papers!

JUSTIN (*finishing up*): . . . with no other witnesses or judges than posterity. I have spoken. Now we shall proceed to the unveiling of this week's pauper! Even if I do say it, who shouldn't, very few institutions in our country have the privilege of reckoning with any such wretch as this one. Nevertheless, we must remember that somewhere inside those human dregs, there is a soul, a solitary soul that has found . . .

Enter Archimedes and the Photographer.

PHOTOGRAPHER (*angrily*): Cockroaches! Two in the lavatory and one in the toilet!

All applaud Justin.

I don't see that it's anything to celebrate.

JUSTIN: Anunciatta, the trumpets!

Anunciatta puts on a record of the incidental trumpet music. All except the newsmen wait, quite immobile.

Archimedes, uncover Rusty!

Archimedes uncovers him.

Ladies and gentlemen, you have before you an authentic pauper!

Rusty, with one trouser leg pulled up, is scratching his knee. He gets down from the pedestal and sits on it.

RUSTY: Five minutes more and I would have fallen headlong, curtain and all. My knees are giving out.

REPORTER: You want a cigarette, fella?

RUSTY: I want a leg of lamb.

REPORTER: Sorry. Only have Luckies.

JUSTIN: And now the drawing and the gifts! The modest contribution of the Ecumenical Institute. Anunciatta, Archimedes, if you please . . .

Archimedes gets Rusty to his feet. He removes Rusty's ancient army coat. Rusty stands there in absolutely nothing but his old trousers, which are constantly threatening to fall to the floor. He has to hold them up with both hands. He is a distressing sight. Archimedes prevails upon Rusty to draw a number from a metal box.

ARCHIMEDES: 25!

Anunciatta takes a fur coat out of one of the boxes.

ANUNCIATTA (*announcing*): Nutria!

JUSTIN: Liberalist animals of four continents send their small courtesies.

RUSTY: Thank you, sir. (*In spite of himself, Rusty draws out another number from the box.*)

ARCHIMEDES: 76!

Monica reaches into a box, brings out a riding boot.

MONICA (*announcing*): Plastic leather!

They put the boot on Rusty.

JUSTIN: The Ku Klux Klan's Department of Assistance to Inferior Races gives a boot!
RUSTY: Thank you, sir. (*Rusty selects another number.*)
ARCHIMEDES: 93!

Anunciatta takes a pith helmet from a box and puts it on Rusty.

ANUNCIATTA (*announcing*): Pith helmet!
JUSTIN: African missionaries of all creeds send commemorative stamps and pith helmets for our indigents.
RUSTY: Thank you, sir.
PHOTOGRAPHER: Don't move, please. (*Flash photo.*)
MONICA: Archimedes, the chicken!

Exit Archimedes. Anunciatta brings out an electric shaver from one of the boxes.

ANUNCIATTA (*announcing*): An electric shaver!
JUSTIN: An anonymous donation! . . . But remember friends, the *electromagnetic* shaver shaves *best*!
RUSTY: Thank you, miss, but . . . wouldn't you have even a *little* piece of bread? . . .
JUSTIN: Man does not live by bread alone.

Enter Archimedes carrying a tray on which is a whole broiled chicken, the rotisserie rod still through it. Rusty's eyes all but fall out.

ANUNCIATTA (*announcing*): Imported meat!
JUSTIN: From the aviaries of the Peloponnesian monks. Contribution of the Orthodox Church.
RUSTY: Thank you, sir. (*Rusty hungrily takes the chicken by one of its legs, and is just about to sink his teeth into it, when he is restrained by the Photographer.*)
PHOTOGRAPHER: Hold it! One moment! Let's have all the members of the Institute in this one, please.

The four Directors group themselves around Rusty.

That's it! Good! Now, let's see . . . (*Sights through camera.*)
MONICA: How do we look?
PHOTOGRAPHER: The chicken's not right. Lift it up a little.

Archimedes pushes Rusty's arm up.

Don't move! . . . Got it!

Anunciatta and Archimedes return to the boxes. Monica flirts with the Photographer. Rusty returns his full attention to the chicken, and is just about to bite in when he is interrupted again by the Reporter.

REPORTER (*turning on the tape recorder*): Rusty, would you be so kind as to give us an informal interview for network broadcast? (*Without waiting for an answer.*) Thank you. Most kind. What is your real name?
RUSTY: I don't know what you mean. All names are real names. My father was called "The Scab," and my grandfather was called "Wino." Those were their real names.
REPORTER: How did you have the good fortune to be found?
RUSTY (*pointing out Archimedes*): That nice gentleman there vomited on me.
REPORTER: How were you able to live alone for so long?
RUSTY: Alone? . . . I wasn't alone. A lot of people live with me . . . people like myself.
REPORTER: But in this day and time one can't find poor people even in the Museum of Natural History!
RUSTY: I don't know what you're trying to say, but I see them everyday.
REPORTER: It's one of your little jokes, of course. (*Addressing the listeners.*) As you can see, ladies and gentlemen, poverty does not destroy the sense of humor. Hungry people always make the best humorists. (*Addressing Rusty.*) Is there any special statement you'd like to make?
RUSTY: Would Ophelia be listening in?
REPORTER: We're the only ones listening at the moment, but perhaps she will hear the network broadcast later. What would you like to say to her?
RUSTY (*taking the microphone in both his hands, and speaking very rapidly*): Ophelia . . . I don't know where I am! . . . Some very attentive and educated gentlemen, and some goodhearted and sweet ladies . . . are killing me! . . . You have to *do* something! . . . Anyone who hears my voice . . . Anyone . . .

Justin grabs the microphone and tries to cover up.

JUSTIN: Enough, Rusty! . . . Modesty forbids that we go on listening.

The Photographer has come over to them.

PHOTOGRAPHER: One last picture now, but without the chicken. It's a little trite.

To Rusty's consternation he snatches away the chicken.

That's it! That anguished face. Very good. Ready . . .

ANUNCIATTA: There are still lots of gifts left.

MONICA (*announcing, as she brings an umbrella out of a box*): Surprise! An umbrella! With an exquisite card that says: "Contribution of the Democratic Ladies of Mississippi: To keep the Puerto Ricans from getting too dark in the sun."

Anunciatta take out a lace mantilla. Archimedes puts it around Rusty's shoulders.

ANUNCIATTA (*announcing*): Lace mantilla!

JUSTIN: A beautiful lace mantilla made by the handicapped of the Pentagon working only with their toes. And destined to add beauty to Rusty's life.

The Reporter returns with the tape recorder.

REPORTER: One word, please . . . just a word for the International Radio and Television Company of Five Continents, affiliated with the Program for the Improvement of the Human Condition.

RUSTY: Sh . . . Shh . . . Shit! (*Loaded down with presents, Rusty sways unsteadily and then slowly falls to the floor. He has not made the slightest sound. He remains stretched out, unconscious.*)

REPORTER: Thank you. The traditional eloquence of this town has synthesized your clear view of the problem.

The newsmen prepare to leave.

JUSTIN (*attempting to conceal Rusty's indisposition*): Just a moment . . . I still have one further surprise. The Ecumenical Institute will take happiness and food to the exiled cadaver of General Godofredo Batista, tragically assassinated by the C.I.A. guerrillas.

REPORTER: Did I hear that wrong, or did you say something about a general?

PHOTOGRAPHER: They're always so photogenic, especially in times of a coup d'etat.

JUSTIN (*gravely*): We are speaking, gentlemen, of the body of Godofredo Batista, for which we have more than one surprise.

PHOTOGRAPHER (*looking at Rusty*): The corpse is well preserved.

MONICA: All the poor thing lacks is human warmth.

REPORTER: Can he make a statement?

ANUNCIATTA: He is very reserved.

PHOTOGRAPHER: That stuff on his coat, are those stains or decorations?

JUSTIN: Please! The presents for the general!

Archimedes serves drinks to everyone, Monica passes around items from a box.

MONICA (*announcing*): Deodorant!

JUSTIN: A donation from the State Department, from the expert on Latin-American Affairs.

Now they are simply throwing the gifts upon Rusty's lifeless body. Anunciatta brings out little booklets.

ANUNCIATTA (*announcing*): Hymnbooks!

JUSTIN: Spiritual songs for morning gargling. UNESCO's offering to the Latin communities in the United States . . . Very touching. . . .

They throw them on the body. Archimedes brings out a plastic bag of white powder.

ARCHIMEDES (*announcing*): Bicarbonate!

JUSTIN: Personal contribution of our own secretary, Archimedes, for the gastric well-being of the needy.

Archimedes liberally sprinkles the white powder on the body. The Reporter, carrying the tape recorder, approaches the body and begins his interview.

REPORTER: . . . introducing Godofredo Batista. Would you give us your unbiased comment . . . just a word for the aficionados of these indigent celebrations?

A silence.

Thank you. Brief but to the point. Now the Radio and Press Association are pleased to present to the Institute, the saviors of our hero, this scroll with the simple and moving legend: "The Military Is Not Contagious." (*He exhibits the scroll and then presents it to Justin.*)

All applaud. The Reporter approaches the Photographer and interviews him as though he were Rusty.

Once again, our Poor Man of The Week! My good man, is there anything more you would care to add?

PHOTOGRAPHER (*imitating Rusty's voice and gestures*): Only that this is the happiest moment of my whole life. I can only compare it to my First Communion. (*The Photographer takes the microphone and interviews the Reporter.*) And what of your future life? Have you any plans?

REPORTER: I will educate my children in the faith of my elders, and become a Mason. High Mogul, Builder of the Great Triangle, Manes Tessel Phares.

PHOTOGRAPHER: Would you care to say a word of appreciation as you take your leave of the listening audience?

REPORTER (*speaking in the manner of a rude and ignorant person*): I wanta thank the Government and the authorities of the Ecumenical Institute. My situation has been changed like magic. Only yesterday I was an illiterate victim of German measles, syphilis, and scurvy. But today, culture, laxatives, and the Sunday Supplement have given dignity to my life and the life of my mate, unfortunately dead now in the fullness of her illness. Thank you again. Thank you. (*The Reporter weeps openly.*)

PHOTOGRAPHER (*in a low, respectful voice*): His emotions are stronger than his words. (*Changing tone and giving the Reporter a poke with his elbow.*) Wipe off that slobber and let's get out of here.

REPORTER: Yeah. Let's go. Next Saturday we'll crank out another Radio Feature on this social ulcer. We can do it sitting around after dinner.

JUSTIN (*snatching the microphone from the Reporter*): Until next Saturday then! Charity without the press is like love without antibiotics.

MONICA (*snatching the microphone from Justin*): And remember, a new pauper each and every week! And there will be prizes!

JUSTIN (*getting the microphone again*): Because only man can give dignity to man.

ANUNCIATTA (*snatching the microphone from Justin*): *Et retributionem peccatorum videbis. Fiat luce.*

*The newsmen have stuffed the remaining sandwiches into
their pockets and coats, and have taken a few bottles as well.
With the bottles in their hands, they speak directly to the
audience. One stands on the pedestal, the other just below.*

REPORTER: Until next week . . . and remember! to put pizzazz
  in your smile use Glimmer!
BOTH: Glimmer and grin!

*As a tape-recorded jingle is heard, the newsmen depart.
As all the others are occupied in saying their good-byes to
the newsmen, Archimedes takes advantage of the moment,
stealthily takes a piece of bread from an inside coat pocket
and gives it to Rusty. Rusty seizes it hungrily and takes an
enormous bite. In that moment the others turn around and
surprise Rusty and Archimedes.*

JUSTIN: Well, this is the limit, Archimedes! Doesn't it occur to
  you that you are killing the goose that lays the golden eggs?
ARCHIMEDES: You're the ones who are killing him . . . he's
  starving.
JUSTIN: If we allow Rusty to turn into a satisfied bourgeois
  he will automatically stop being the poor starved devil he is.
ARCHIMEDES: Well, but that's inevitable, isn't it?
JUSTIN: You insensitive! . . . Would you like to tell me what
  we're going to do then each week?
MONICA: It's very dangerous, Archimedes. With every donation, with every broiled chicken, we are killing in Rusty
  the very best thing he has—his poverty.
ANUNCIATTA: Archie, where would we get a new pauper?
ARCHIMEDES: Pardon me, but I think we should also give
  some thought to him.
JUSTIN: We are thinking of him! That's all we do! Rusty's
  poverty makes him depend on charity. At the same time,
  the survival of this institute of charity depends upon Rusty's
  poverty. In view of the alternatives only a nit as irresponsible as you could have any doubts. The works of welfare
  must be placed above any other consideration. Monica,
  Anunciatta, let us save the Institute! . . .

*The three throw themselves upon Rusty and strip him of
his fur coat, the pith helmet, the boot, the electric shaver.
They take all the gifts and drop them back into the boxes.
They back away with shame, and leave the stage.*

Rusty has offered no resistance whatever. Once again he is half nude, his trousers still threaten to fall off. Rusty's theme music is heard. The light fades on the stage, and a cold light illuminates the forsaken Rusty. He seems remote. Then silence.

RUSTY: I don't know if I was in a jail or a brothel. Now I know. I know what it is. Sometime, somewhere, one remembers and *knows*. I dreamed one time that they were tearing my clothes off, like now, and they were nailing me onto this old rusty gate or something. A locked gate. I had escaped through all this scrap iron, but they managed to smash me onto this gate, with my arms spread wide. I woke up screaming. I can still hear the hammer. Angel howled all that night long. (*Rusty looks at his hands and speaks to the dog lying at his feet.*) It's not blood, Angel. It's not blood. (*Shows his hands.*) It's only rust, see? (*To the audience.*) Anyone got a smoke?

A silence.

I have looked for rest, Angel. Someplace shady to wait, the way you do, wait for a blow, or a morsel. One makes mistakes, Angel. I thought we were living in a school for the retarded, but no. Now I know what it is. (*To the audience.*) No one got a smoke?

A silence.

(*He searches like a blind man for the dog at his feet.*) You there, Angel? . . . Someday I'm going to tell you about some holiday afternoons, sitting on the curbs. I had four grandparents with big feet, and they all spat and shouted. Now it's something else. Newly constructed ruins, laughter and shame. . . .
Yesterday I got lost among the junked bicycles, and down in a hole I found a man without a face and a woman whose breasts were rusted away. . . . You know, Angel, it was Ophelia. (*To the audience.*) Nobody got a smoke? . . .

A silence.

The light bothers you, Angel. I know. There's no shade here. If it isn't a school it must be a theatre. A theatre where they hand out prizes and punishments: empty jars, diplomas, and grimaces. No one . . .? No one's got a smoke?

A silence.

The only thing I'd really like to have is a safety pin. A simple and sure pin. I need it, Angel, I need it. You can find everything in a garbage can, but I've never found a pin.
Anyone here know . . . has anyone ever seen flesh, human flesh? Forget it, Rusty. Forget it all. (*To the audience.*) I don't want to bother you . . . but hasn't anybody . . . anybody at all . . . got a smoke?

A silence.

Angel! Angel! . . . Where are you? . . . Where? . . .

The lights go out softly. Rusty's theme music fades away. A great silence. Total darkness. Then voices are heard.

ANUNCIATTA'S VOICE: Where do you turn on the light, Justin?
JUSTIN'S VOICE: Behind those boxes, on the left.

Noise of falling boxes.

ANUNCIATTA'S VOICE: Oh! . . . . I can't find it.
JUSTIN'S VOICE: Here, let me. . . .

The light comes on. Rusty lies in a heap at the foot of the pedestal, covered by the canvas. Enter Justin, Anunciatta, and Monica. They have come in from the street. They wear coats. They remove them. Justin serves himself a drink. Enter Archimedes.

ARCHIMEDES (*flustered, removing his scarf*): It got late on me. I had to press my pants.
MONICA: I am worn out. I'm falling to pieces. Do we really have to go through it all again?
JUSTIN: Like every Saturday.
ANUNCIATTA: Where there is necessity, there are no clocks, no calendars, Monica.
MONICA: If we are going to keep our beneficence going at this pace, I'm going to have to have a vacation.
JUSTIN: There are always special study courses for intellectuals and sociologists at some European spa. They're fantastic for putting on weight.
MONICA (*raising the window shade ever so slightly*): Have you all noticed how much quieter Rusty seems each week? You'd almost think he wasn't happy.

JUSTIN: One needn't expect gratitude. It's a known fact that they repay a smile with a kick in the shins.

ANUNCIATTA: When I passed by with the sandwiches for the newspapermen, he scared me. He looked at me with resentment.

ARCHIMEDES: Maybe he's feeling sick to his stomach. Why not offer him some milk of magnesia?

MONICA: Not a bad idea.

ANUNCIATTA: Archie, how understanding!

ARCHIMEDES: Rusty's fainted! (*Archimedes lifts him up with difficulty.*)

JUSTIN: He seems to do that. Take him to the storeroom!

Archimedes takes him by the arms and drags him toward the door.

ARCHIMEDES: He doesn't weigh a thing.

Rusty finally manages with extreme difficulty to go out on his own two feet. Justin follows behind.

MONICA: I don't understand these faints of Rusty's.

ANUNCIATTA: Well, strong emotions and rats do the same thing to me.

MONICA: We've all but covered him up with presents for six months now. He's swimming in gifts.

ANUNCIATTA: Could he be an ascetic, or a yogi in disguise?

MONICA: Even our luck couldn't be that bad, sweetie!

Enter Justin.

JUSTIN: All right, we've completed one stage just as planned.

MONICA: Yes, but at what a cost in sacrifice! Even though I shouldn't be the one to say it.

ANUNCIATTA: Justin, I need to have a serious talk with you.

JUSTIN: I'm listening, my good friend.

ANUNCIATTA: Archie and I have been thinking something.

MONICA: Something indecent, no doubt.

ANUNCIATTA: We've made up our minds.

JUSTIN: Speak, I'm keeping a moment of silence.

ANUNCIATTA: Archie and I want to adopt Rusty.

MONICA: You want to WH-A-A-T???

ANUNCIATTA: Adopt Rusty. We've come to the conclusion that what he needs is a mother, a father, and a barking dog.

JUSTIN: Fantastic! Absolutely sensational!

MONICA: What's so sensational about it?

JUSTIN: At the closing meeting of the Poverty Congress, before seventy-thousand emotion-choked persons, we shall process the legal adoption.

ANUNCIATTA: We wanted it to be rather private.

JUSTIN: Of course, completely private. May I be the godfather?

ANUNCIATTA: It would be an honor for our little Rusty.

JUSTIN: It's a stroke that will impress every sociologist and pediatrician working in the Congress.

MONICA: Are you sure that bleary-eyed old thing needs adopting?

Enter Archimedes.

Congratulations, Archimedes! You know, you've got a marvelous face for a father. . . .

ANUNCIATTA: They know, Archie.

ARCHIMEDES: Everything?

ANUNCIATTA: Almost.

MONICA: So sweet . . .

ARCHIMEDES: Who?

MONICA: That mangy orphan of yours. And while we're on the subject, what time is it?

JUSTIN: If I may be permitted a metaphor: a quarter past eight.

MONICA: Then it's time I asked you for something I've been putting off.

JUSTIN: Anything you like, Monica, anything you like.

MONICA: A week ago Jeronimo was poisoned.

JUSTIN (*hopefully*): Your husband? . . .

MONICA: No, unfortunately. My watchdog. He guarded the estate. I was thinking you could lend me Rusty. It's a simple job. He will be given affection, food, and a roof over his head. All he'll have to do is bark every half hour. And naturally, he will be free to go out every fifteen days or so to mount a bitch.

ARCHIMEDES: Ta, if we are going to adopt him, I don't think we can allow . . .

JUSTIN: It's a very convenient offer, Monica. And yours is very generous as well, Anunciatta, but the truth is I need Rusty myself.

MONICA: You need him?

ANUNCIATTA: May one know what for?

ARCHIMEDES: He never said anything . . .

JUSTIN: Yes. I need Rusty. The best of a man is in his work. A trade gives a man dignity. And Rusty has one. I'm going to set up an artificial eye factory. I'll flood the market in no time. Rusty will work without pay, of course.

MONICA: The redemption of the proletariat, by means of work. . . .

ANUNCIATTA: A notable idea, Justin! A pity it's so devious and filthy.

MONICA: Oh, Justin! your idealist's dream come true at last— getting rich at someone else's expense!

ARCHIMEDES: Typical of you, Justin. You're all heart and scrotum.

MONICA: Naturally, Justin darling, I shall oppose you.

ANUNCIATTA: And so will I!

ARCHIMEDES: And I!

JUSTIN: I am not frightened by the rumblings of domestic animals. I shall have the ten tons of eyes that I need.

MONICA: A dog is a dog and I will not let him be poisoned again!

ANUNCIATTA: Baby! . . . Our little boy!

ARCHIMEDES: I won't surrender even one of his little feet!

JUSTIN (*raising his voice*): Stupid chickens!

MONICA: Stupid chicken corrupter!

ANUNCIATTA: Gutless apostle!

ARCHIMEDES: Denationalized!

JUSTIN *and* ARCHIMEDES: Women!

MONICA *and* ANUNCIATTA (*together*): Men!

JUSTIN: This is senseless! Rusty prefers me.

MONICA: I promised him an old-age policy!

ANUNCIATTA: He only has to see me to start making little faces. . . .

ARCHIMEDES: He's already signed the papers for me.

JUSTIN: Impossible. We have a contract.

MONICA: I've already put a collar on him.

ANUNCIATTA: I put a tattoo on his chest.

JUSTIN (*yelling*): He's mine!

ANUNCIATTA: Mine!

MONICA: Mine!

ARCHIMEDES: Mine!

All are talking and shouting at once. Suddenly they stop. There is a brief silence.

(*In a normal voice.*) Why don't you ask him?

ANUNCIATTA: Who?

ARCHIMEDES: Rusty.

JUSTIN: What?

ARCHIMEDES: What he wants to do.

JUSTIN: It's not a matter of what *he* wants to do.

MONICA: We could ask him who he promised first—even though it was me.

ANUNCIATTA: Me.

ARCHIMEDES: Me.

JUSTIN: Me.

MONICA: All right. Let him just signal with one finger, and we'll know what to abide by.

JUSTIN: Go and get him if you want to. But I'll brook no interference.

MONICA: I'm going. (*Exit Monica.*)

JUSTIN: As for you, you turtledoves, what you're trying to hatch is an ostrich egg, and it's hollow.

ANUNCIATTA: Your crude and indelicate insinuations are making me . . .

A scream of horror is heard. They stand up expectantly. Enter Monica, very pale and unsteady.

What is it?

JUSTIN: Did he attack you?

MONICA: No.

ARCHIMEDES: Has he escaped?

MONICA: He's right where you left him. . . . Hanged.

JUSTIN: What did you say?

MONICA: Hanging from a rafter. He still has a big tear on his cheek, and a green bubble in his mouth.

A silence.

JUSTIN (*in a hushed voice*): A tear?

ARCHIMEDES (*in a hushed voice*): Then, he wasn't happy?

JUSTIN: A bubble?

ANUNCIATTA: Was he trying to tell us something?

A long silence.

ARCHIMEDES: We know what we can abide by now. He's showing us with one finger, just as we wished.

JUSTIN: An accident. It's imprudent to raise oneself up to the rafters.

MONICA: He was imprudent.

JUSTIN: How is it he didn't think of the Institute, when he owed it so much?

ANUNCIATTA: He was selfish.

JUSTIN: We all have our problems, but we cope. We eat. We sweat.

ARCHIMEDES: He was weak.

JUSTIN: The interviews the last few weeks went to his head. Fame can be dangerous.

ANUNCIATTA: He was an exhibitionist.

JUSTIN: And above all, how is it he didn't think about me? . . .

MONICA: And me.

ANUNCIATTA: And me.

JUSTIN: And the factory.

MONICA: And the estate.

ANUNCIATTA: And the cradle.

ARCHIMEDES: Maybe he did think about all that, up until the last moment.

MONICA: We never meant a thing to him.

JUSTIN: Raise crows and they'll pick out your glass eyes.

ANUNCIATTA: Now what are we going to do?

ARCHIMEDES: I'm going to go and take him down. (*Exit Archimedes.*)

ANUNCIATTA: I meant what are we going to do about the Congress of Poverty? The principal actor is missing.

MONICA: The foreign delegates are arriving tomorrow.

JUSTIN: It's grotesque! Three Doctors of Philology are being sent from Louvain to write up the new Allied Declaration of Human Rights . . . and what does Rusty think up to do? He winds up a childish tantrum hanging from a rafter!

ANUNCIATTA: You and your putting on airs! You got half the world involved in this gathering, and all based on the premise that we had the "last pauper," the last person in the world for whom we could do our acts of charity. Well, now, that last pauper has hanged himself. Instead of decorating you, they're going to prosecute you for embezzlement of funds.

JUSTIN (*frightened*): Really?

ANUNCIATTA: It's perfectly clear. Furthermore, they'll dissolve this Institute for lack of reason for being.

JUSTIN (*collapsing*): My God, this is terrible. I'm liquidated!

MONICA: I've never seen such a jellyfish!

JUSTIN: You despise me too, Monica? Just the same, we'll all be falling into the same grave.

MONICA: As a Director of twelve institutions besides this one, I know very well how to get out of the grave. Where is the Declaration of Principles of the Ecumenical Institute? I want to check something.

Justin, still quite crestfallen, takes a folder out of the desk and hands it to Monica.

JUSTIN: That was drawn up by our founder, but he couldn't have imagined that the last poor man would be so completely irresponsible.

MONICA (*finishing reading the Declaration*): Just as I thought! Listen to this: "A secondary samaritan activity of the Institute, but no less important, shall be the merciful burial of persons without resources who demonstrate a clear condition of rigor mortis" . . . Isn't this fantastic?!!!

ANUNCIATTA: Sinister, is more like it.

JUSTIN: Exactly what are you trying to say?

MONICA: It's very simple. Rusty is dead. But we haven't really lost him yet. We have his body. The body of a pauper, needing prompt, simple, and economical burial. We shall keep to the highest purposes of the Institute . . . and save our charitable Saturday afternoons.

JUSTIN: Do you mean to say bury and . . . unbury Rusty . . .?

MONICA: That is a question of procedure.

JUSTIN: It is convenient. Imagine it. The interment of a pauper, each week, and everything done with a classic dignity. . . .

ANUNCIATTA: It's not bad. Weekly prayers for the dead in the solemn atmosphere of the catacombs. But . . . will he really lend himself to all that?

MONICA: Who?

ANUNCIATTA: Rusty.

JUSTIN: Now that he's dead, I'm of the opinion that we needn't ask him. Setting to one side the bothersome ethical implications of the situation, we must recognize that what Monica proposes is exceedingly practical. To have the body of an authentic pauper in the warehouse, ready at all times to be the beneficiary of an economical and dignified burial, is a true luxury for such an institute as ours.

ANUNCIATTA: I can see that it's possible, but how long can a rotating charity like that go on?

MONICA: What do you mean?

ANUNCIATTA: Monica, even our most beloved debtors, like Rusty, after a time suffer . . . transformations.

MONICA: Oh, that! Well, I don't think he'll smell any worse than he did when he was alive. He did give off a strong zoological emanation.

JUSTIN: I don't know if it's carrying our zeal too far, but obviously if we stuffed Rusty, we'd have "Indigence" preserved and stored away, beyond danger of spoiling.

ANUNCIATTA: Have him *stuffed*?

MONICA: That hadn't occurred to me. Like Rameses II in his golden cage.

JUSTIN: They stuffed Rameses?

MONICA: Rameses II, a canary I had once. It's expensive, but it's worth it. They put in little glass eyes.

ANUNCIATTA: Who would have thought that that sweet Rusty would end up with glass eyes?

MONICA: That's morbid thinking, sweetie.

JUSTIN: And it's not getting us anywhere. The truth is that Monica has come up with a happy idea that no doubt will be imitated in the future by all institutions destined for the ultimate in social work.

Well, let's be getting on to the taxidermist's! . . . (*Justin goes to the door and calls out.*) Archimedes!

Archimedes comes forth very slowly. He stands motionless in the doorway. He will remain there. He has a rope in his hands.

Archimedes! Bring one of those coffins the U.N. sent us on the Better Latin America Program. The Ecumenical Institute bids Rusty farewell . . . for the first time! Oh, and remember, from now on, on Saturdays—interment!

Blackout.

A discordant funeral march is heard. Nothing on stage undergoes any change, except that now there is a coffin made of the boards of an old packing crate right in the middle of the stage.

The Reporter and the Photographer are standing together on one side of the stage. Standing before the coffin are the two women. They are wearing long black veils over the same dresses they wore in the previous scene. Justin is ending an unintelligible funeral speech. The funereal music accompanies the address.

. . . grandiose spectacle . . . natural selection . . . survival of the species . . . some of them are burned . . . tumulus . . . or simply on the bare ground . . . Out of order . . . spent resources . . . believe in his immortality . . . serve two masters . . . gigantic institution . . . magnitude of his success . . . in the same verse . . . farming almanac . . . unrecognizable hat . . . Martha, rambling rose of the wildwood . . . In need of the needy . . . a minimum . . . or a nest of eggs . . . it happened suddenly . . . more difficult for a rich man . . . in addition . . . attributing to them a soul . . . but zeal, excessive or indiscreet . . . because of this latest example, I mean this, our brother, was the *jewel* of a blind civilization. I shall not tire of repeating it: he was the jewel, he was the jewel, he was the jewel. Yes, . . . he was the jewel . . . Because I still haven't tired of repeating it: he was . . . (*He is interrupted by Monica.*)

The actors speak all the following dialogue in hushed and low voices. Still, they are perfectly audible. They parody the false pretense of respect so often shown in the presence of the dead.

MONICA (*interrupting*): Justin, please! All this is very painful!
REPORTER: It's life, Ma'am. A paradox. In China old ladies have twins every five minutes, and they die the first leap year. On the other hand, here a pauper dies every week. It's incredible. We can't even see his face. (*He approaches the coffin.*)
ANUNCIATTA (*startled*): No! Please. This is very difficult for me! And besides, he looks a lot like that man last week.
JUSTIN: I shall not tire of repeating it: he was the jewel, he . . .
MONICA (*interrupting, and directing herself to the newsmen*): Would you care for a whiskey and Bitter Lemon?
REPORTER: Don't go to any trouble. Just any little imported thing you happen to have.

Anunciatta moves to get the drinks.

PHOTOGRAPHER (*to Monica*): One picture, please. Next to the coffin.

MONICA: With what expression?

PHOTOGRAPHER: Controlled grief.

Monica fixes an adequate expression. The Photographer takes the picture.

That's it. Goes very well with the clear sense of the horizontal the poor man gives.

MONICA: The last time you photographed me all you could see was my shoes.

PHOTOGRAPHER: At the Inaugural Session of the Poverty Congress tomorrow, I'll get you with a telephoto lens.

Anunciatta serves drinks to the Photographer and the Reporter.

ANUNCIATTA (*to the Photographer*): I always sit at the very end of the table at conventions. For modesty's sake. Don't forget where I am.

REPORTER (*to Justin*): What was that you were saying about a jewel??? I didn't quite understand that . . .

JUSTIN: I got tired of repeating it.

REPORTER: That happens a lot. Happened with an uncle of mine. Strong as a bull. He absolutely squandered his good health. What happened was simply that one morning—poof!—without so much as a murmur, we found him in bed. . . . more alive than ever, reading the paper.

JUSTIN: It's terrible when a thing like that happens. Particularly for the mother.

MONICA (*gesturing toward the coffin*): At three o'clock he asked for some comic books. At three thirty he whispered "Call Amanda." At four o'clock Amanda arrived. At four thirty, in a dying state, he left all he had to Amanda. And at five o'clock . . . it was all over.

REPORTER: He died?

MONICA: No. Amanda had a heart attack and died in his arms . . . right there in the midst of all those comic books. . . .

ANUNCIATTA: Only four days ago we ran into each other at the hairdressers. He said, "I've come to get my hair cut for Saturday . . ." and who would have thought it would be for his own funeral.

JUSTIN: That's how he was. (*Takes out a photograph.*) His aunt took this bare-tail picture of him when he was little. He hasn't changed a bit, has he?

REPORTER: Nobody can be sure about his life. You can go to bed singing one day, and the next day, you've got a note due at the bank.

PHOTOGRAPHER: We have to be going.

REPORTER: Now please, if there's anything at all you need, don't hesitate to 'phone me. I won't be in anyway.

JUSTIN: Thank you. Thank you, my good and faithful friends.

The newsmen leave. Justin takes off his jacket, makes himself comfortable on the sofa. Anunciatta and Monica remove their veils. Now they speak in their normal voices.

MONICA (*sipping her drink*): I've still got three inaugurations today, and a meeting with a depressed young intellectual. I have to inspire him every fifteen days.

ANUNCIATTA: Aren't you a little frivolous, Monica? You ought to read more.

MONICA: I know I should, but I've discovered it affects me the way fish does . . . gives me blackheads. Doesn't it you?

ANUNCIATTA: Certainly not.

MONICA: Maybe it's those cheap paperbacks that do it. They say Bible paper is marvelous for the skin.

ANUNCIATTA: Underneath that skin you've got an illiterate, Monica.

MONICA: Don't be so waspish, for goodness sake! Why don't you read some newspaper ads, and buy yourself a dress— not quite so ordinary.

JUSTIN (*who has been looking over some notes and sketches*): What do you think of this as a theme for the first meeting of the Poverty Congress: "On Interior Generosity," or, "How To Avoid Contamination by the Poor"?

Hurried footsteps are heard, and the voice of Archimedes. Enter Archimedes.

ARCHIMEDES (*excited*): Justin! Justin! There are more of them!

MONICA: Archimedes again, tearing the doors down to get in! It's practically a complex he's got!

JUSTIN (*to Archimedes*): Don't shout! Show a little respect. There are ladies here . . . and the deceased.

ARCHIMEDES (*lowering his voice*): Quite a lot of them, Justin.

ANUNCIATTA: A lot of what?

ARCHIMEDES: Paupers.

ANUNCIATTA: Paupers? . . . Are you sure, Archie?

ARCHIMEDES: I found them in the street. They need help. They asked me for food and clothing.

JUSTIN: Delirium tremens.

ARCHIMEDES: They're not visions. They pulled at my sleeve.

ANUNCIATTA: I don't think he's inventing this.

ARCHIMEDES: Come out to the street, Justin. They're milling around out there. A lot of them. They're as poor as Rusty.

MONICA (*touching up her makeup in her tiny mirror*): Can you tell me, Archimedes, what we need with them?

ARCHIMEDES: Well, . . . I don't know . . . The Congress . . . charity, and things like that.

MONICA: You have no feelings, Archimedes. It's really sadistic collecting hungry people the way you do.

JUSTIN: Let them go away, and not bother us!

ARCHIMEDES: But . . . what about the Institute? And our subsidy?

JUSTIN: Don't worry about it! We've got Rusty embalmed! An incorruptible pauper, always at our service! . . . Charity is henceforth assured!

The newsmen burst in from the orchestra, applauding. The actors take bows. The Photographer carries a bouquet of flowers that he gives to Monica. The Reporter pins a medal on Justin. Archimedes has left the stage. He returns with a banner reading: "World Congress of Poverty." Monica takes one end of it, Anunciatta the other. Justin steps forward, addresses the audience.

With this small representation, Sociological Assemblies have their beginnings; and we have given it the name, The First Congress of Poverty. You have witnessed a little allegory of the activities of the Ecumenical Institute and the fervent spirit that animates it. Now, as spokesman of the forum that will be held later on, I shall briefly review the theme for today: "On Interior Generosity," or, "How To Avoid Contamination by the Poor." (*Calls out toward the semi-darkness.*) Archimedes! The chart, please!

Exit Archimedes.

Permit me, here at the beginning, a digression. Only a moment ago a colleague, a foreign delegate, whom I see seated out there with you, this colleague and I were discussing my theme for today, and he said to me: *"Mevianizco orto proni, on boria eli sigma sarratua tauro or tapisco ilia. . . ."*

I suggested that that might be a snap judgment, but he added: *"Nisim, nisim, ta siloi enema barium onta servilin cresta. . . ."*

I couldn't believe it, but he went on to repeat his lapidary statement. There, in a word, you have Europe's opinion of us. *Servilen cresta!* . . . And they are quite right! There is one thing we should learn once and for all regarding international solidarity, and that is: to safeguard human dignity from all contamination. And the poor in their period of incubation and proliferation are particularly dangerous.

Enter Archimedes wearing his sandwich board.

We see an explanatory drawing, similar to the one of the cow seen in Act One. This chart however shows Rusty in anatomical sectional view. It is of oblong shape, as Rusty is shown on all fours. On the exterior he is shown in rags. The visceral parts all have their anatomical names, etc. Some words in Latin, various scientific legends. Again Justin uses the pointer as he explains the chart.

In this viscera the highly contagious bacilli are incubated. I have no wish to be an alarmist. I simply wish to point out Poverty and its bubonic carrier: *"el indigentis homunculo,"* an all but extinct mammal, which has found in our country an ideal climate for its breeding ground. The Institute over which I preside, and which has organized this meeting of sociologists, has demonstrated the vertiginous ovulation and gestation of this biped before the highest authorities of the land. We have received these consoling and clairvoyant declarations from His Excellency, the President of the Republic:

> "It is a corollary to the shift of the world economic frontiers as the whole epicenter of world affairs rotates toward the area whence it started."

These words give an incentive and a hope for us all. I move on now to the Forum for tonight. We have the following agenda:

1. New Concept of man-cipher-ovum-excremento.
2. Interior Generosity, or social expectoration.
3. Charity, as therapy for guilt complexes.

Ladies and gentlemen, there you have it. . . . I urge you to reflect deeply, but not to despair, because today there are vaccines for everything, and dehydrated solidarity works miracles.

Now you have the word. Insult. Blaspheme. Smile.
You are within your rights.
This is a public forum.

Goodnight!

Justin begins to close the curtains.

THE END

THE CRIMINALS

JOSÉ TRIANA

Translated by Pablo Armando Fernandez
and Michael Kustow
Adapted by Adrian Mitchell

José Triana was born in Bayamo, Cuba, in 1931; after his studies in Santiago de Cuba he spent several years in Spain where he published a book of poetry, *De la madera del sueño* (1957), and wrote his first play, *El general mayor hablará de teogonía* (1957). Triana's dramatic output is still quite limited and his early works show a disparity and confusion in handling certain elements of structure, as when he attempts to imitate the style of the European absurdists in dealing with the themes of noncommunication or the ineffectiveness of orthodox religion. He is sensitive, however, not only to the specifics of the Cuban environment and value systems, but also to the broader implications of morality and metaphysics. His current success lies precisely in his ability to combine these elements into dramatic statements about the violence and cruelty of the world. Using undignified characters from the lower social strata of contemporary Cuba, he surpasses the conventional style of direct social criticism to express indirectly his concerns with archetypal patterns of irrationality and moral decay. Some critics were superficially reminded of *Electra Garrigó* (1948) by Virgilio Piñera when he premiered *Medea en el espejo* in 1960, in that he adapted the passion and tragedy of a classical Greek figure to a lower-class Cuban environment. *La muerte del Ñeque* (1963) also contains overtones of Greek tragedy and the violence and criminality of the Cuban underworld, while prefiguring the importance of game symbolism in his theatre.

Triana's most mature play to date is *The Criminals* (*La noche de los asesinos*), written in 1964 and produced in the Latin American Theatre Festival in 1966 after it won the Casa de las Américas annual theatre contest the previous year. This is a brutal play involving three "adolescent adults"—two sisters and their brother. In their restrictive basement room, they perform a ritualistic act in preparation for their crime—the murder of their parents. The myth of conflict develops in an impassioned way as they exorcise their conscience before the grisly act. Disgusted and disillusioned by the established order represented by the parents, they repeatedly enact this ceremony in search of independence or self-identification. Triana does not attempt to establish blame, however;

the squalid, petty lives of the parents are equally as disgusting as the spoiled, mocking attitudes of the children. The character doubling and constantly changing roles give emphasis to the shifting dimensions of reality within the multiple levels of this very complex and very violent "game."

Triana, in daring to expand the conventional limits of theatrical violence, has made an unmistakable contribution to contemporary Cuban dramaturgy.

Characters

LALO
CUCA
BEBA

Time

Around the 1950s.

Set

A room. A table, three chairs, rolled-up carpets, dirty curtains with large floral patterns, flower vases, a small bell, a knife, and other objects that are not used.

ACT I

LALO: Shut the door. (*Beats his chest. Exalted, eyes wide open.*) A murderer. A murderer. (*He falls to his knees.*)

CUCA (*to Beba*): What's all this?

BEBA (*indifferently, watching Lalo*): The performance has begun.

CUCA: Again?

BEBA (*annoyed*): Of course. It's not the first time.

CUCA (*pleading*): No.

BEBA: Don't be childish.

CUCA: Father and mother haven't gone out yet.

BEBA: So?

LALO: I killed him. (*He laughs. Stretching his arms solemnly toward the audience.*) Can't you see them? Two coffins. Look: candles, flowers. We filled the room with gladioli—mother's favorite flowers. (*Pause.*) They can't complain. We've finally made them happy. I've just been pulling the clothes on their bodies, they were all stiff and sticky . . . and I dug a deep, deep hole. Earth, more earth. (*He gets up.*) Nobody knows yet. (*He smiles. To Cuca.*) What's on your mind? (*Caressing her chin as if she were a child.*) I know: you're scared. (*He moves aside.*) Oh, you're hopeless.

CUCA (*dusting the furniture*): Don't like all this nonsense.

LALO: Nonsense? You call a crime nonsense? You're cold, very cold. Nonsense? You really think so?

CUCA (*firmly*): Yes.

LALO: Then what *is* important?

CUCA: You've got to help me. We must put this house straight. This room's a pigsty. Mice, cockroaches, moths, and caterpillars—the whole bloody lot. (*She moves an ashtray from the chair and puts it on the table.*)

LALO: How far can you get with a feather duster?

CUCA: Better than nothing.

LALO (*authoritatively*): Put the ashtray back where it belongs.

CUCA: The ashtray should be on the table, not the chair.

LALO: Do what I tell you.

CUCA: Don't start again, Lalo.

LALO (*takes the ashtray and puts it back on the chair*): I know what I'm doing. (*Takes the vase and puts it on the floor.*) In this house the ashtray goes on the chair, the vase goes on the floor.

241

CUCA: And the chairs?

LALO: On the tables.

CUCA: And what about us?

LALO: We float. We float with our feet in mid-air and our heads hanging downward.

CUCA (*annoyed*): Marvelous—why don't we try it? What would people think if they could hear you now? (*In another tone of voice. Harder.*) If you keep pushing me there's going to be trouble. Leave me alone, Lalo, I'll do what I can.

LALO (*deliberately*): Don't you want me to help you?

CUCA: I said leave me alone.

LALO: Don't spoil things. I want the ashtray there. Vase there. Leave them where they are. Stop giving orders.

CUCA: Me? We must put this house straight.

LALO: You're not listening.

CUCA: What do you mean?

LALO: You heard.

CUCA: I don't understand. Don't know what you want. It all sounds mad. Confused. Can't say anything. Can't do anything. And if it's what I think it is, well, it's horrible.

LALO: You're scared. Do you want to live? Then you have to forget that you're scared.

CUCA: It sounds easy.

LALO: Do it then.

CUCA: Leave me alone. Don't preach, it doesn't suit you. (*Dusting a chair.*) Look at this chair, Lalo. Hasn't been cleaned for ages. Cobwebs. Ugh.

LALO: What a bloody mess. (*Going carefully nearer. Deliberately.*) The other day I said to myself: "We ought to clean up," but then we got sidetracked into some nonsense or other and . . . look, look at that . . . (*Pause. Deliberately.*) Come on, why don't you join in?

CUCA (*almost on her knees, cleaning the chair*): Leave me out.

LALO: Try.

CUCA: Don't force me.

LALO: Just a little—

CUCA: I'm not strong enough.

Beba, who has been upstage cleaning some old furniture and pots and pans with an old rag, comes forward; her movements, for a moment, remind us of Lalo.

BEBA: Those corpses are fantastic! Really spectacular. They give me a feeling . . . I don't want to think anymore. I've never been so happy. Look at them, they're disintegrating.

LALO (*grandly*): Have our visitors arrived?

BEBA: I heard them on the stairs.

LALO: Who?

BEBA: Margarita and old Pantaleon.

Cuca doesn't stop work, although she pauses once in a while to look at them.

LALO: I hate those two. (*In another tone of voice. Violently.*) Who told them?

BEBA: How should I know? . . . Don't look at me like that. It wasn't me.

LALO: Then it must have been her. (*Points to Cuca.*) Her.

CUCA (*still cleaning the furniture*): Me?

LALO: You. Yes, you.

BEBA: Perhaps they weren't told at all. Perhaps they're just dropping in.

LALO (*to Beba*): Don't protect her. (*To Cuca, who gets up and dries the sweat on her forehead with her right arm.*) You're always spying on us. (*Starts walking around Cuca.*) You watch every step we take, everything we do, everything we say, everything we think. You hide behind the curtains, the doors, the windows . . . (*With a sly smile.*) Look at you, a spoiled, coddled little girl playing detective. (*Laughing violently.*) Two and two make four. Sherlock Holmes thoughtfully tunes his Stradivarius. (*Abruptly.*) It's very nasty. (*In another tone of voice, softly, like a stalking cat.*) You're never satisfied are you? What are you trying to find out?

CUCA (*frightened, not knowing what to do*): Nothing, Lalo, nothing . . . I promise. (*Brusquely.*) I said, leave me alone.

LALO: If you're staying out of it, why do you watch us? And why do you make up to such grotesque people?

CUCA (*about to cry*): I didn't mean any harm—

LALO: Then you should have thought about it.

CUCA (*trying to stay on the right side. Insolently*): They're my friends.

LALO (*angrily, contemptuously*): Your friends. I'm sorry for you. (*With a triumphant smile.*) Don't try to fool me. You're absurd. Hit and run. You're not even brave enough

to call things by their right names. (*Pause.*) If you're
against us, show us your teeth. Bite. Rebel.

CUCA (*losing control*): Stop it!

LALO: Come on, come on.

CUCA: You're trying to drive me mad.

LALO: Come on, you're not scared, come on.

CUCA (*stifled*): Forgive me.

LALO (*imperatively*): Come on, up you get.

BEBA (*to Lalo*): Don't hurt her.

LALO (*to Cuca*): Look at me.

CUCA: My head's hurting me.

LALO: Look at me.

CUCA: Can't.

BEBA (*to Lalo*): Give her a few moments.

CUCA (*sobbing*): It's not my fault. That's how I am. Can't
change. Wish I could.

LALO (*annoyed*): You're just a fool. (*He moves away.*)

BEBA (*to Cuca*): Come on then. (*Takes her aside and walks
her over to a chair.*) Let's dry those tears. Aren't you
ashamed? He's right, you know. You're being difficult.
(*Pause. She smoothes her hair with her hands.*) Come on,
then, come on. (*In a friendly voice.*) Don't look at me like
that. Come on, give us a smile. (*In a motherly voice.*) You
shouldn't do it, but now you've started, you've got to finish
it. (*Joking.*) Your nose is all red, just like a little tomato.
(*Stroking her nose with her index finger.*) Oh, you're being
so silly.

CUCA (*staying close to Beba*): Don't want to look at him.

BEBA: Try to relax.

CUCA: Don't want to listen to him.

BEBA: He won't eat you.

CUCA: My heart . . . listen to it, listen, it's going to blow up.

BEBA: Don't be such a baby.

CUCA: It is, it is.

BEBA: You should be used to it by now.

CUCA: I want to run away.

BEBA: It's always like this at first.

CUCA: I can't stand it.

BEBA: It gets easier as it goes along.

CUCA: I feel sick.

LALO (*holding a vase in his hands, making an invocation*):
O Aphrodite, inspire our curses tonight!

CUCA (*to Beba, upset*): He's starting.

BEBA (*to Cuca, in a conciliatory way*): Sh. Don't listen.

CUCA: I want to spit at him.

BEBA: Don't attack him, or he'll—

LALO (*like a Roman emperor*): Come to my assistance: I'm dying of boredom.

Cuca, unable to share this attitude, mocks him.

CUCA: What a performance! Just like your Uncle Chico. (*To Beba.*) Isn't he? (*Disgustedly.*) You monster.

LALO (*self-importantly*): When the gods are silent, the people shout. (*He throws the vase toward the back.*)

CUCA (*imitating her mother. Sarcastically*): That's right, throw things about, break up the happy home, you won't have to pay for a new one.

LALO (*smiling, facing the door*): What a delightful surprise.

BEBA (*to Cuca*): Feeling better?

Cuca nods.

LALO (*as if greeting imaginary people*): Do come in, come in . . . (*Shaking hands with imaginary people.*) How are you? . . . How are you?

BEBA (*to Cuca*): Sure?

Cuca nods.

LALO (*to Beba*): They've arrived.

BEBA (*to Lalo*): Don't talk to them, they'll go away.

CUCA (*to imaginary people*): Good evening, Margarita.

LALO (*to Cuca*): They've come to sniff out the blood.

BEBA (*to the imaginary people*): How are you?

CUCA (*to Lalo*): You always think the worst of people.

BEBA (*to Cuca, imitating her mother*): That's enough. (*To the imaginary people.*) Asthma is such a spectacular disease. No wonder it appeals to so many people.

LALO (*to Cuca*): I won't forgive you for bringing them in.

CUCA (*as if paying attention to the imaginary people, with an insolent smile at Lalo. Between her teeth*): Pretend you didn't hear.

LALO (*to Beba*): It's awful. (*In another tone of voice, with a hypocritical smile to the imaginary people.*) And how *are* you, Pantaleon? It's been such a long time. Where have you been hiding?

BEBA (*pursuing the imaginary people*): How's your urine? They told me the other day . . .

CUCA (*pursuing the imaginary people*): How's your bladder doing?

BEBA (*amazed*): What? They still haven't operated on your sphincter?

CUCA: And how's the old hernia?

LALO (*with a hypocritical smile*): Margarita, you're looking better than ever. Is that growth of yours still growing? (*To Beba.*) You look after them.

BEBA (*to Lalo*): I've run out of things to say.

LALO (*whispering, pushing her*): Say anything. Whatever you do, it'll be wrong.

BEBA (*looks at Lalo, upset. Pause. Immediately afterward she throws herself into a make-believe comedy*): You look superb. I suppose it's the spring. I don't know . . . There's a special look about you . . . Oh, it's so hot. I'm absolutely drenched in perspiration. (*She laughs.*) Ooh, Pantaleon, what are you up to? You're such a sensual . . . Yes, you are . . . You . . . Don't look so surprised. Oh, what a pretty little wart.

LALO (*imitating Pantaleon*): No, no, I don't believe a word of it. The years, my dear child, the passing years corrode a man and he ends up like a limp old dish rag. (*He laughs maliciously.*) But if you'd seen me in my prime, the good old days, the Roaring Twenties . . . Ah, if only they'd come roaring back again. But I'm crying for the moon, as they say. (*In a special tone of voice.*) Today I have a little pain, just here . . . (*Pointing to his stomach. He sighs.*) I'm an old man now, nothing but a dried-out bag of bones. (*In another tone of voice.*) And every day it gets worse. Our children—they're so disrespectful, so unmerciful.

BEBA (*imitating Margarita, annoyed*): No, don't say that; it's not fair. (*Whispering.*) People visiting glass houses shouldn't throw—(*With a smile.*) What will these pretty children think? (*To Cuca.*) Come here, darling, why are you hiding from Auntie Margarita?

Cuca doesn't move.

Come on, what's the matter, am I an ugly old lady? Come on, don't be naughty, my pretty little baby. Tell me, how are mommy and daddy? Where's your mommy?

LALO (*jumping from the chair. Violently to the audience*): You see? What did I tell you? That's why they came, I know them. I was right. (*To Cuca.*) They're *your* friends.

Get them out. They want to shove their noses into everything. (*Screaming.*) Tell them to go to hell. You hear me? It's all over.

Cuca doesn't know what to do. She moves about, gesticulates, she wants to say something but either can't or doesn't dare.

BEBA (*imitating Margarita. To Cuca*): I don't want to leave just yet. We just dropped in as usual. We've been promising to come for weeks. And anyway, I feel a little sick. Some rosemary leaves and mint would make me feel better, perhaps your mother . . .

LALO (*desperately*): Cuca, make them get out. Tell them to go to hell. (*As if he had a whip in his hand and threatened them.*) Out! Out of here. Into the street.

CUCA: (*to Lalo*): Don't be so rude.

BEBA (*imitating Margarita, with suffocated screams of outrage*): They're insulting us. It's outrageous. What horrible children!

CUCA (*to Lalo. In control of the situation*): You've got a terrible temper.

BEBA (*to the imaginary visitors*): Please forgive him.

CUCA (*to Lalo*): What have they done to you?

BEBA (*to the imaginary visitors*): He's so high-strung.

CUCA (*to Lalo*): You're so inconsiderate.

BEBA (*to the imaginary people*): Doctor Mendieta said he must take a good rest.

CUCA (*to Lalo*): So tactless, so bad-mannered, so . . .

BEBA (*to the imaginary people*): Such an unexpected attack . . .

CUCA (*to Lalo, with a reserved smile*): God will never forgive you for this.

BEBA (*to the imaginary people*): Bye, Margarita. Good night, Pantaleon. Don't forget, mother and father went away to the country and we're not sure when . . . Oh, they'll be back soon, I expect. Bye-bye. (*She blows a kiss with false emotion. Pause. To Lalo.*) Why do you make things so difficult for me? (*She sits at the back and starts to polish some shoes.*)

CUCA (*threatening subtly*): When mother finds out . . .

LALO (*angrily*): Go on, then, tell her. (*Calling.*) Mother, father. (*Laughs.*) Mommy, daddy. (*Defiantly.*) Don't wait. Go on. Run and tell them. I'm sure they'll be grateful. Go on, run along. (*He takes Cuca by the arm and leads her to the door and then returns to the center.*) You're no use. You never really commit yourself. You want to, you don't want to. You are and you aren't. Do you think that's living? If you want to come to life, you have to take risks. All the time. Doesn't matter if you win or lose. (*Sarcastically.*) But you want to be safe. You want the easy way. (*Pause.*) You dither and dither and suddenly find you're hovering helplessly in mid-air. You don't know what to do, don't know what you are, and, worst of all, you don't know what you want.

CUCA (*sure of herself*): And what about you?

LALO: Whatever you do, you'll never save yourself.

CUCA: And what about you?

LALO: Maybe not, but you won't stop me.

CUCA: Every day you'll grow older . . . Here, always here, locked up with the dust and the cobwebs. I know it, I see it, I sense it. (*She smiles wickedly.*)

LALO: And so?

CUCA: You're sinking, sinking . . .

LALO: That's what you'd like to see—

CUCA: Sinking, sinking . . .

Lalo laughs.

Sinking, sinking . . .

LALO: You don't—

CUCA: Sinking, sinking . . .

LALO: —know anything . . .

CUCA: Sinking . . . sinking . . . Now I'm doing what I want to do.

LALO: You're beginning to bite.

CUCA: I'm saying what I think.

LALO: You don't, you don't understand. Look this is the only possible way. (*He takes the chair and moves it about in the air.*) I want this chair to be here. (*Suddenly placing the chair in a different place.*) And not over here, because here (*Quickly returning it to the first place.*) it's more useful to me. I can sit down more easily and quickly (*Putting the chair in the second spot.*) while over here it's useless, there's no point to it . . . (*Putting the chair back in the first place.*) Our parents don't, they don't allow it. They think I'm totally illogical. Everything has to stay where it is, nothing must move from its place . . . And that's impossible: because you and I and Beba . . . (*With a scream.*) It's intolerable. (*In another tone of voice.*) They think I'm trying to contradict them, fight them, humiliate them . . .

CUCA: In a house, the furniture . . .

LALO (*to Cuca*): Are you a vase? Would you like to discover that's all you are? And for most of your life you've been treated like a vase? Do you think I'm a knife? And you, Beba, are you a happy little ashtray? No, no. That's stupid. (*In a mechanical rhythm.*) Come over here. Get over there. Do this. Do that. Do the other. (*In another tone of voice.*) I want my life. Every day of it, every hour, every minute. I want to do what I want to do. But my hands are chained up. My feet are chained up. There's a blindfold around my eyes. This house is my world. And this house is getting old, it's rotting away. Because of them. Them. They never ask themselves what's wrong. And neither do you. And Beba's even worse . . . If Beba plays our game it's only because there's nothing else she can do.

CUCA: But why blame them for everything?

LALO: Because they made me into a useless thing.

CUCA: Liar.

LALO: Why should I tell lies?

CUCA: Self-defense.

LALO: I'm trying to be honest.

CUCA: You're as demanding as they are. Remember the games you invented? You took our dolls and smashed in their faces, you forced us to go through rituals as complicated as nightmares. You wanted to make us exactly like you.

LALO: I was starving for freedom.

CUCA: They've always looked after you, they've always loved you.

LALO: I never wanted that kind of love. They've seen me as everything except a human being.

Beba, at the back, cleaning the shoes, imitates her father.

BEBA: Lalo. Starting today you're responsible for scrubbing the floors. You'll mend my clothes and you'll mend them properly. Your mother's not well and it's the least you can do. (*Beba goes to the back and continues shining the shoes.*)

CUCA: They gave you everything . . .

LALO (*to Cuca*): How much did it cost them?

CUCA: Lalo, remember what father earned? When he was young—a junior clerk. As he approached senility—a junior clerk. What more could he have given you?

LALO: They always told me: "Don't walk home from school with whatshisname." "Don't play with so and so." "Thingemmybob is a bad influence." I wasn't better than anyone else. Why should I say: thanks for my room, thanks for my bed, thanks for my food?

CUCA: Try to understand them . . . That's the way they're made. And since they're like that, you were bound to rebel.

LALO (*shakes head*): I believed in them too much. (*Pause.*) But what happened to the things I wanted?

CUCA: You just wanted your own way.

LALO: "You've got to do this." And, if I got it wrong: "I might have known." And then I was beaten.

CUCA: That's what parents do. But you don't have to turn the whole house upside down.

LALO: Cuca, I want things to make sense. So we can say: "We'll do this" and we do it. And if it doesn't work, we say: "Too bad. Better luck next time." And if it comes out right: "Fine! Let's get on to the next thing." Just to be able to do something and alter it as you go along. Not having to think: "I've got no right to my life. It's just lent to me." Don't you ever want to grab your independence?

CUCA: You know we can't . . .

LALO (*violently*): Can't, can't, can't . . .

CUCA: They're right.

LALO: I'm right too.

CUCA: You're fighting them?

LALO: Yes.

CUCA: You're fighting everything?

LALO: Yes.

At this moment Beba repeats the imitation of her father.

BEBA: Lalo. Wash the clothes. Then you can iron them. Mother and I decided. Here, take them, sheets, curtains, tablecloths, and my trousers for the office . . . Clean out the toilets. Eat in the corner of the kitchen. Learn, damn it, learn. Do you hear me? (*She goes upstage.*)

CUCA: Why not leave home?

LALO: Where the hell can I go?

CUCA: You could try.

LALO: I've tried. Don't you remember? I always come back.

CUCA: Try again.

LALO: No . . . Look, I get . . . confused. Lost. When I walk out of here, I seem to fade away. They never taught me anything. I don't even know how to walk down a street.

CUCA: Then how can you make decisions and give orders.

LALO: I've decided for myself.

CUCA: Ready to start again?

LALO: As often as I have to.

CUCA: You'll carry right through to the end?

LALO: It's the only way out.

CUCA: And what about the police?

LALO: I don't know. Maybe . . .

CUCA: How can you beat them?

LALO: Wait and see.

CUCA: I'm not helping. Understand? I'll defend them as hard as I can. I believe in them. They don't interfere with me. They give me what I want. So leave me out, I'm not obstinate. Cats close their eyes when you give them food. You're about as grateful as a cat. (*He takes a few steps.*) Go away. I won't play your game. (*To Beba.*) Don't you rely on me either. (*In another tone of voice.*) Oh, dear God, get me out of this. (*Pause.*) They're older than we are, they know more about life than we do. They struggled. They made sacrifices. At least they deserve our respect. If things go wrong in this house, it's because something was bound to go wrong . . . No, no, I can't fight them.

LALO (*happily. Applauding*): Encore. A fine performance.

BEBA (*happily. Applauding*): You deserve an award.

LALO: We'll have to invent one.

BEBA: She's promising.

LALO: But she's a fool.

BEBA: She's sensational.

LALO: She's an idiot.

BEBA: She's a saint.

They applaud furiously and mockingly.

CUCA: Go on, laugh. When my turn comes I won't have any pity.

LALO: What do you mean?

CUCA: I'll do what I like.

LALO: Try it.

CUCA: You can't push me around. (*She walks back*).

LALO (*sarcastically*): You're getting scared. (*Laughs.*)

CUCA (*furiously*): I've got hands. Nails. Teeth.

LALO (*challenging aggressively*): I give the orders.

CUCA: Don't come near me.

LALO: Do what I tell you. (*He takes her by the arm and they begin to struggle.*)

CUCA (*angrily*): Let go.

LALO: Do what I tell you.

CUCA: Bully.

LALO: Do what I tell you.

CUCA: You're hurting.

LALO: Yes or no?

CUCA: It's not fair . . . (*Totally defeated.*) All right.

LALO: Quick. Get up.

CUCA (*to Beba*): Help me.

Beba walks to Cuca. Lalo stops her with one movement. Cuca pretends that she can't get up.

LALO: She can get up.

BEBA (*to Lalo*): Forgive her.

LALO (*with a scream*): Keep out of this.

BEBA: You're always shouting. I can't take any more. I wanted to help you. I wanted to enjoy it. I don't know what else to do . . . And round and round we go. If we don't obey, we get screamed at for nothing—a glass of water, a bar of soap on the floor, a grubby towel, a broken ashtray. Surely there are more important things in the world? I sit and I ask myself: what's the use of clouds and trees and rain? What are the animals for? Shouldn't we stop just long enough to think about them? So I look out of the window and I begin to think—but then they start yelling: "Dust! Soot! The girl's dreaming! Pull your head in, shut the window or you'll catch your death." So I wander into the living room and switch on the radio. "You're using electricity and last month and the month before that we used so much and we can't go on like this and switch it off the noise is driving me mad." Sometimes I start singing that little song you made up for us: "The living room is not the living room." And then the whole house shakes like a capsized ants' nest, and they shout, mommy and daddy shout at Lalo, Lalo shouts at mommy, mommy shouts at Lalo, Lalo at daddy, daddy at Lalo, and

I'm right in the middle. And in the end I come and hide here . . . but you don't even notice that, you just go on arguing, as if this house could be put right with words. You end up fighting just like they do. I can't stand any more. (*Decisively.*) I'm getting out.

Lalo takes her by the arm.

Let me go. I don't want to listen to you. Deaf, blind. Dead. Dead.

LALO (*affectionately, but firmly*): Don't say that.

BEBA: That's what I want.

LALO: If you helped me, perhaps we could save ourselves.

BEBA (*looking at him, amazed*): What do you mean? (*She holds onto his arms.*) All right. We can do it, Today.

Lalo quickly takes two knives. He looks at their edges and then rubs them against each other.

(*To Lalo.*) You're going to do it again?

CUCA (*to Beba*): Quiet.

Beba moves about the stage. Each character takes up a definite position.

BEBA (*imitating a gossiping neighbor*): Shall I tell you something, Cacha? It was in all the papers. Yes, my dear, yes. But you know old Margarita who lives on the corner, and Pantaleon, who's only got one eye, well, they saw everything, right down to the last drop of blood. And they told me all about it.

LALO (*rubbing the knives together*): Ric-rac, ric-rac, ric-rac, ric-rac, ric-rac, ric-rac.

BEBA (*imitating a drunken shopkeeper*): Old Pantaleon and Margarita, they know everything. That's the kind of kids there are in the world nowadays. Try to tame wild animals, they'll turn on you everytime. (*She laughs mockingly.*) Have you seen the pictures on the front page?

LALO (*rubbing the knives together*): Ric-rac, ric-rac, ric-rac, ric-rac, ric-rac, ric-rac, ric-rac.

BEBA (*imitating Margarita talking to her friends*): We dropped over there around nine thirty . . . usual time . . . Soon as I set foot in the house I said to myself: "Well, well, well. There's something funny going on here." You know me. I'm sensitive to these things . . . and sure enough. Oh, what a sight! Blood everywhere. Look at my hair.

Still standing on end. Count my goose pimples . . . Well I
don't know how to describe it, dear, you should have
seen . . . try to imagine it . . . Just impossible to . . .
Horrible. Quite horrible, my dear . . . and such a mess,
you wouldn't believe it . . . I think there were some
syringes, and those things you fill them with, ampoules,
yes . . . Those children are wicked, wicked. Ask Consola-
cion, ask Angelita what she saw the other day . . . disgusting! And such good dedicated parents. But that Lalo,
he's the ringleader. No doubt about it. It was him, him
and nobody else . . . phew you should have seen that knife
. . . What a knife! Dear God, a butcher knife.

LALO (*in his own world*): Ric-rac, ric-rac, ric-rac, ric-rac,
ric-rac, ric-rac, ric-rac, ric-rac, ric-rac.

BEBA (*imitating Pantaleon*): I said to Margarita: "Hold your
horses, woman." But she burbled on about the younger
generation, how awful they are nowadays . . . You know
Margarita. Talk the hind leg off a . . . They . . . no, not
they . . . that's a lie, him, that Lalo . . . well sometimes I'm
inclined to believe that, well God alone knows who did it
. . . but I . . . my boy, I'd swear to it . . . because the
girls . . . how could they have done it? but if you'd seen
Lalo's face. It was incredible. Such fury. Yes, yes, the
devil himself. Almost assaulted us . . . And me with my
arthritis . . . But I don't stand for that sort of nonsense . . .
I don't care what else he does, that's his funeral. But
bossing us around, God forbid, the degenerate son of a
bitch. If you'd seen that room swamped in blood, if you'd
smelled that stench . . . All seems very strange, doesn't it?
(*With a hysterical laugh.*) Be grateful you missed it, it was
gruesome, yes, gruesome, that's the word . . . We should
do something. (*Pompously.*) Should we lodge a protest
against him? (*In another tone of voice.*) What do you
think?

LALO (*continuing his game*): Ric-rac, ric-rac, ric-rac, ric-rac,
ric-rac, ric-rac, ric-rac, ric-rac, ric-rac, ric-rac, ric-rac, ric-
rac, ric-rac.

*Lalo hasn't stopped rubbing the knives together. This act
begins to create, along with the sounds that Lalo makes,
a delirious climax. Cuca becomes a newspaper boy. Beba
goes to the back.*

CUCA (*shouting*): Read all about it! Murder on Apodaca Street! Read all about it! Here you are, ma'am. Thank you, miss, don't miss any of the details. Son butchers both his parents . . . Here take a look . . . see all the blood? Plenty of pictures in the supplement. (*In singsong.*) Stabbed them forty times. Read all about it. EXTRA, EXTRA. Pictures of the innocent parents. Don't miss it, lady. It's terrible, mister. *Chronicle.* (*She goes toward the back.*) EXTRA! (*Her voice drifts off.*) Father murder! Mother murder! Awful butchery. Mother father murder . . .

Pause. Beba walks from the back to center downstage.

BEBA (*imitating her father*): Lalo, what've you been up to? Take that look off your face. What are you staring at? Who've you been with? Knives? What do you think you're doing? I want an answer. Don't just stand there. Why are you home so late?

LALO (*like a teen-ager*): I bumped into some friends, father, and . . .

BEBA (*imitating her father*): Give those to me. (*Takes the knives violently.*) Fidget, fidget, fidget! (*Checking the sharpness of the knives.*) Sharp, that's sharp. Planning to kill somebody? Come on, don't just stand there like a bit of furniture. Who do you think you are? Permission, why don't you ask my permission? If I've told you once, I've told you a hundred times—this is no time to come home. (*She slaps him about.*) When are you going to learn obedience? How many more times have I got to tell you? I warned you, didn't I warn you? Are you going to learn sense? Yes? No! What do you think your mother feels? You're breaking her heart. Do you want us both to die of broken hearts? What are you trying to do to us? You've got no consideration . . . Take that look off your face. (*She pushes him toward the chair.*) Sit down. Do you want to be locked up in the dark again?

Lalo makes a gesture.

Don't answer back. Dumb insolence. I gave you everything. There's something wrong with you. Yes, there's something funny about you. All those sacrifices . . . Yes and your mother attacks me for staying late at the office. Talks about other women. Other women—huh, more than one

business deal has gone kaput because of you and the rest
of my family. Can't you see the sacrifices I'm still making
for you? Forty years . . . forty years behind a desk developing my ulcers, pushed around, doing without . . . I
haven't even got a suit, haven't even got a decent pair of
shoes . . . And this is all the gratitude I get. Forty years
is no joke. Forty years, all for you. And my son turns out
to be an irresponsible layabout. Doesn't feel like working,
doesn't fancy studying . . . Well what do you want? And
what have you been up to?

LALO: We were reading . . .

BEBA (*imitating her father*): Reading? I'll give you reading.
What do you mean, reading?

LALO (*thoughtfully*): A magazine.

Cuca comes from the back. Beba retires to the back.

CUCA (*imitating her mother*): Magazines. Magazines. Magazines. That's a lie. Tell us another. Tell us the truth.

Beba, imitating her father, approaches Lalo aggressively.

No, Alberto, don't hit him. (*To Lalo in another tone of
voice.*) I'm glad that happened to you. I'm very glad indeed. (*In another tone of voice.*) Where's the money I
hid in the dresser?

Lalo makes a gesture.

Did you take it? Did you spend it? Did you lose it? (*With
hatred.*) Thief. You shameless little bastard. (*Tearfully.*)
I'll tell your father. No, don't make things worse.

Lalo makes more silent gestures.

It's shocking. (*In another tone of voice.*) If he finds out,
he'll kill you. (*In another tone of voice.*) O Mary Mother
of God, what have I done to be punished like this? (*Furiously to Lalo.*) Give it back or I'll send for the police. (*She
searches Lalo's pockets, while he submits humbly. She yells.*)
Thief. Dirty stinking thief. I'll tell your father. I ought to
beat you. I'll have you put in a home.

Lalo has his back to the audience.

BEBA (*from the back like a child*): Mommy, mommy, is this
an elephant?

LALO (*imitating his father*): Beba, come here, show me those hands.

Beba comes forward and shows him her hands.

Those nails are too long . . . They make you look like a . . . (*To Cuca.*) Pass the scissors, woman.

Cuca approaches Lalo and whispers in his ear.

What? What's that? . . . Is that true? And Lalo? Where's he gone.

Cuca and Lalo look at Beba wickedly.

Is it true what your mother says? Come on, own up. Own up or . . . So, you lifted your skirt and showed your knickers to a bunch of filthy louts, did you?

Silence, gestures by Beba.

You dirty little animal.

Cuca imitates her mother laughing.

You want to grow up to be a slut? Over my dead body. (*Shaking her by the shoulders.*) Listen you little whore, I'm going to kill you. (*Pause.*) Where's your brother? (*Calling him.*) Lalo, Lalo! (*To Cuca.*) You say he went through your purse?
BEBA (*as herself*): It's no good. My head's exploding.
LALO (*ordering*): Go on, it mustn't stop.
CUCA (*sarcastically*): Do what he says.
BEBA (*in agony*): Air, I want some air.
LALO (*to Beba*): Doorbell's ringing.

Beba collapses on the chair.

CUCA (*imitating her mother*): Have you heard, Alberto?
BEBA (*desperately*): Honestly, I think I'm going to be sick.
LALO (*annoyed*): She spoils everything.
CUCA (*imitating her mother*): Sh. There goes the doorbell again.
LALO (*imitating his father, greeting an imaginary person who enters through the door*): Come in Angelita, nice to see you . . .
CUCA (*imitating her mother. To Beba*): Do tell me, you can

tell me, dear. Are you really feeling all right? (*Mimicking saintliness and care.*)

LALO (*imitating his father, to imaginary people*): Don't stand on ceremony, Angelita. (*He seems cordial and spontaneous.*) Make yourself at home, take a pew.

CUCA (*imitating her mother*): Make yourself comfortable. Would you like a cushion? (*Sincerely.*) Are you sure you're comfy? Why don't you lean back and relax?

LALO (*imitating his father*): And Lalo . . . Where's he hiding? (*To the imaginary person.*) You know what children are, Angelita. Only three of them but they're more trouble than an army.

CUCA (*imitating her mother. To Lalo*): Alberto, I think I'd better . . . (*To the imaginary person.*) I'm sorry, Angelita, I'm not looking after you very well, but I think the child is sick; something wrong with her tummy . . .

LALO (*imitating his father*): Have you taken her temperature?

Cuca nods.

CUCA (*imitating her mother*): Oh, how embarrassing.

LALO (*to the imaginary people*): You see what I mean? They're little devils. But luckily I'm bigger than they are. You have to rule with a rod of iron, as they say.

CUCA (*imitating her mother*): She won't eat anything.

LALO (*imitating her father*): Force her.

CUCA (*imitating her mother*): She throws it all up.

LALO (*imitating her father*): Give her some broth.

CUCA (*imitating her mother*): Oh Angelita, you don't know how I suffer. Why does anyone have children?

LALO (*imitating his father. Grasping a cup and forcing her*): Drink it all up.

Beba rejects the cup.

You'll get it down and keep it down.

BEBA (*with a yell. As herself*): Leave me alone. (*She gets up angrily. Center stage.*) Monster. You're both the same. (*Screaming, toward the back.*) I want to go. Let me go.

Lalo and Cuca try to stop her, but she gets to the door, screaming.

Mommy and daddy, get me out of here.

LALO (*imitating his father*): What's all this then?

CUCA: Quite a performance. (*Approaching Beba.*) You, it would be you . . . You always push me into it: "Come on, don't be silly. You know you'll enjoy it." And now look at you. Come on, up you get. (*She helps Beba up. Imitating her mother.*) Don't forget we've got visitors. (*To the imaginary visitors.*) Such spoiled children, so tiresome . . . (*To Beba, returning her to the chair where she was sitting.*) There's a nice little girl, there's a good girl, what a well-behaved little girl . . .

BEBA (*imitating a child*): I want to go.

CUCA (*imitating her mother*): Where do you want to go, my pet?

LALO (*as himself, violently*): It's all going wrong. It's no use.

CUCA (*imitating her mother*): Don't get excited, Alberto.

LALO (*as himself*): I could kill her.

CUCA (*imitating her mother*): We must be patient.

BEBA (*crying*): I'm scared.

LALO (*as himself*): What of? Why's she crying?

CUCA (*imitating her mother*): Take no notice. That's the best thing, Alberto.

LALO (*imitating his father, with clumsy gestures*): It's just that sometimes . . . (*Smacking his right knee.*) You don't understand me, woman.

CUCA (*imitating her mother*): How can I help understanding you? (*Sighs.*) Alberto, you're such a child. Isn't he, Angelita?

BEBA (*angrily, getting up*): I must do something. I'm going to burst. I want to go. I can't stand being caged up. Suffocation. I'm going to die and I don't want to be trapped and crushed in this room. Anything else, but no more of this. I don't want it. Please, please leave me alone, just let me go, let me go.

Cuca approaches Beba and puts her arms around her. She fakes tenderness.

CUCA (*imitating her mother*): You must go if you have to, darling. You're just a little upset.

Beba stays upstage in the dark. Cuca comes back with a smile that turns to laughter.

Have you ever seen anything like it. It's almost as if she expects to be hit. Children, they're so overimaginative . . .

(*She sits down and fixes her hair.*) Look at me. I must look like an unmade bed. I've hardly had time to turn around today. Such a struggle, Angelita, such a struggle! I'm sorry I've been looking after you so badly, but you're just like one of the family. (*She smiles hypocritically.*) All the same, I do like to be polite . . . Don't I, Alberto? Please, dear. We must all keep perfectly calm.

Lalo gets up.

Where are you going? Be careful.

Lalo looks at her very deliberately.

Oh yes, I understand.

Lalo walks to the dark part of the stage.

He's gone to keep an eye on those little imps. They're such a strain. You need four eyes, what am I saying, four, five, eight, *ten* . . . You have to watch them, watch them all the time. They can be very very naughty.

Lalo enters wearing an old and worn-out bridal veil. Lalo imitates his mother in her youth, on her wedding day in church. At the back Beba sings the wedding march. Lalo's movements should not be exaggerated. On this occasion a certain ambiguity is preferred.

LALO (*imitating his mother*): Alberto, I'm so nervous. The smell of the flowers, the music . . . So many people, aren't there? Your sister Rosa didn't come, I see. Nor did your cousin Lola . . . They don't love me! I know, Alberto, I know! They've been gossiping about me. They say I, they say my mother's no better than she should be . . . Do you really love me, Alberto? Do you really think I'm pretty? . . . Oh, my tummy hurts. Smile. There's that monster Dr. Nuñez and his wife . . . Do you think people are counting the months? If they find out, I'll die of shame. Look, Espinosa's daughters are grinning their heads off . . . little whores . . . Oh, Alberto, I'm dizzy, my stomach hurts, hold on to me, don't tread on my train or I'll fall over . . . Oh, darling I want to get rid of this baby . . . I know you've made up your mind to have it, but I don't want it. Oh, I'm going to faint . . . Alberto, Alberto, I'm so stupid. We

shouldn't have got married today, another day would have
been better . . . Oh, that music, the smell of those flowers
. . . Here comes your mother, that vicious old . . . Oh,
Alberto, I need air . . . My damned belly! I'd like to tear
it open!

CUCA (*imitating her mother. With hatred, chewing her words*):
You make me sick. (*She rips the veil off violently.*) I
don't know how I gave birth to such a monster. I'm ashamed
of you, ashamed of your whole life. You want to save
yourself? Forget about being saved. Why don't you drown
yourself? Die. How dare you criticize me, tear me to
pieces in front of visitors? Don't you know what you are?
You don't know your ass from your elbow. (*To an imaginary person. In another tone of voice.*) Please excuse us,
Angelita. Please don't go. (*Harshly, firmly.*) I kept asking
you to help me. There's so much to clean in this house,
the dishes, the cupboards, the dust, and those marks on
the mirrors. So much to be done: mending, sewing, em-
broidery . . .

Lalo approaches Cuca.

Get out. You want to turn this house upside down, but I
won't allow it. Not even after I'm dead. The ashtray goes
on the table. The vase goes on the table. (*She puts the
vase on the table.*) Who do you think you are? I'll tell your
father. (*Rancorously.*) You fool, what would you be without us? What are you moaning about? Do you think we're
stupid? Yes? Well we're no better or worse than anyone
else. But if you think we'll let you order us around, you're
very much mistaken. So you know what I've sacrificed to
keep this house going? You want to go? Let me pack your
trunk. There's the door.

*Cuca has her back to the audience. Lalo approaches the
table and looks at the knife indifferently. He takes it and
caresses it. He stabs it into the center of the table.*

LALO: How much longer? How much longer?
BEBA: Don't rush.
LALO: If we could only do it today.
BEBA: Give it time.
LALO: Now. (*Lalo gets up quickly. He grabs the knife from
the table. He looks at his sisters and runs upstage.*)

BEBA: Don't do it.

CUCA: You'll be sorry.

BEBA: Careful.

CUCA (*sings weakly*):
>The living room is not the living room,
>The living room is the kitchen.

The two sisters are in position, Beba on stage right, Cuca on stage left. They have their backs to the audience. Simultaneously they give a shattering scream. Lalo enters. The two sisters fall to their knees.

LALO (*knife in his hands*): Quiet.

CUCA *and* BEBA (*beginning to sing quietly*):
>The living room is not the living room,
>The living room is the kitchen.
>The bedroom is not the bedroom,
>The bedroom is the lavatory.

LALO: Now I feel calm. I'd like to sleep, sleep; sleep forever . . . Tomorrow, I shall sleep tomorrow. Today there's too much to be done. (*The knife slips from his hands and falls to the floor.*) How easy it is . . . You simply walk into the room. Slowly; tiptoe. The slightest noise would be disastrous. So you move quietly, suspended in midair. The knife doesn't tremble, your hand doesn't tremble. You are sure. Wardrobe, bed, curtains, vases, carpets, ashtrays, chairs. They all push you toward the naked bodies, as they sweat so nastily in the darkness. (*Pause. Decisively.*) And now we must clean up the blood. Wash them . . . dress them up. Fill the house with flowers. Later on, we will dig a deep deep hole and wait until the morning. (*Thoughtfully.*) Simple . . . terrible.

The sisters have finished singing. Cuca picks up the knife and begins cleaning it on her apron. A long pause.

CUCA (*to Beba*): How do you feel?

BEBA (*to Cuca*): Normal.

CUCA (*to Beba*): It's hard work. It's tiring.

BEBA (*to Cuca*): The worst thing is, you get used to it.

CUCA (*to Beba*): But some day . . .

BEBA (*to Cuca*): It's like everything else.

LALO: Open the door. (*He beats his chest. Exalted. With his eyes wide open.*) A murderer. A murderer. (*He falls on his knees.*)

CUCA (*to Beba*): What happens now?

BEBA: The first part has ended.

CURTAIN

ACT II

When the curtain rises, Lalo is on his knees, back to the audience, head bent low. Cuca is standing, looking at him and laughing. Beba takes the knife impassively from the table.

CUCA (*to Beba*): Look at him. (*To Lalo.*) That's how I like to see you. (*Laughing.*) Now it's my turn. (*Long outburst of laughter.*)

LALO (*imperiously*): Shut that door.

CUCA (*to Lalo, closing the door*): I can't stand you.

BEBA (*to Cuca, looking contemptuously at Lalo*): It's all so pathetic.

CUCA (*to Lalo*): What's the matter now? Listen to this: We've got to go on. We've always stopped halfway but not this time. I'm tired of leaving everything in midair.

LALO (*thoughtfully*): We always have to begin again.

CUCA: Right. I agree; but this time . . .

LALO (*annoyed*): Yes, yes . . . whatever you want.

CUCA: No, not what I want—just, what has to be done. Or are you putting me in charge? That's funny.

BEBA (*annoyed, to Cuca*): But you love it . . .

CUCA (*offended*): What do you want, little girl?

BEBA: I'm not going to do it.

CUCA: But we're already doing it, and this time we have to take it right through to the end.

BEBA: You know I'm right.

CUCA: It doesn't matter.

BEBA: Then I'll be off.

CUCA: You stay here.

BEBA: Don't make me angry.

CUCA: Don't threaten me.

BEBA: I can scratch and kick.

LALO: That's enough.

CUCA (*to Beba*): You're going to be very quiet.

BEBA: You think so? Look, can't you understand that I can't do it? I'm not staying in this room till I rot. I hate these walls. If you want to stir up trouble, you deal with it. I'm young. One day I'll walk out and never come back and then I'll be able to do what I like. All right? (*Pause.*) You didn't want to do it at first, did you? But now you're ready to kill. As if you were gambling for your soul. All right, go on, save yourself. Don't look at me like that. Save yourself, but from what? Maybe you just want to save your own skin? (*Deliberately.*) That's why you're calling the police. That's why, in a few minutes, we'll have the investigation and the interrogation. Did you do this? No, no. You didn't, eh? Hey, officer . . . It's impossible. Ah, look, we've found a clue. Fingerprints. One of the people in this room must be the criminal. Do you think we're cretins? Do you think you can fool us? (*Changing her tone.*) I don't want to be mixed up in all that.

CUCA: We've got to go through to the end.

BEBA: It doesn't end.

CUCA: Don't give up.

BEBA: I'm tired. It's always the same. Do this! Do that! Why do we go on like this? (*Changing her tone, more intimate.*) I don't want to be involved . . . (*In a different tone.*) I'm not enjoying it.

CUCA: Nonsense. I know you better than that. (*Imitating her mother.*) What a precious little jewel you've turned out to be! (*In another tone of voice.*) Do you think I sit back and twiddle my thumbs after what this boy's done? I will defend the memory of my mother and father. I will defend them at any price.

BEBA: Don't touch me.

CUCA (*imitating her mother, authoritatively*): Put the knife back.

Beba obeys. She drops the knife on the floor.

Not like that.

BEBA (*furiously*): Then do it yourself.

CUCA (*with a malignant smile*): Control yourself. (*In another tone of voice.*) Please, let's have everything where it belongs. (*Changing tone.*) We haven't reached the best part yet.

Beba replaces the knife on the table.

We must take every precaution.

BEBA (*furiously*): Count me out.

CUCA (*mentally assessing the room*): The lamps, the curtains . . . It's simply a mathematical problem.

BEBA (*furiously*): Find someone else, or do it yourself.

CUCA: You've been with us from the start. Too late to pull out now.

BEBA: We'll see.

CUCA (*imitating her mother*): Everything's going to be all right.

BEBA: Well I hope you get a surprise.

CUCA: But I can use surprises as well. (*To Lalo.*) Up you get.

Lalo doesn't answer.

BEBA (*furiously*): Let him be. Can't you see he's suffering.

Lalo sighs or groans.

CUCA: Keep out of this.

BEBA: Better wait. Maybe . . . in a moment.

CUCA: I know what I'm doing.

BEBA (*sarcastically*): All right, but remember I'm on my guard, I'm ready any time . . .

CUCA (*quickly, angrily*): To do what?

BEBA: To break out.

CUCA: So you're really against it? Listen, listen very carefully: I'm not going to let you interfere. You're just a cogwheel, a spoke, a spring, a piston, a valve . . . (*In a different tone of voice.*) You should be happy about the way it's going. (*Pause, in another tone of voice.*) Don't make that face. (*In a threatening tone.*) All right, but you'll have to take the consequences. Everything in this house is part of it. (*She moves about the room, straightening the vase and other objects and listing them.*) Vase. Knife. Curtains. Glasses. . . . The water. The pills. Soon the police will be here. . . . The hypodermic. The ampoules. And all we have to do is vanish, become invisible, evaporate if necessary.

Beba moves toward the door. Cuca stops her.

No darling. None of that. You understand? (*Cuca's sarcastic tone makes Beba flinch.*) What's this? You don't like what we're doing? You want to play at sabotage? But we'll disappear. Have you anything to add? Are you trying to change sides. (*To Lalo.*) Get up. It's late. (*To Beba.*) Are you going to defend the indefensible? He's a murderer, isn't he? (*To Lalo.*) Smarten yourself up. You look like a corpse.

Lalo gets up awkwardly, to Beba.

I never thought it would be so difficult.

LALO (*still with his back to the audience*): Bring me water.

CUCA (*imperiously*): No, that's not allowed. (*Gets close to Lalo and straightens out his clothes. Tenderly.*) You've got to wait. (*Imitating her mother.*) That collar's a national scandal. You look like a tramp.

LALO: My mouth's dry.

BEBA (*imitating her mother, tenderly*): You slept badly, didn't you?

LALO: I've got to go out for a bit.

CUCA (*violently*): You won't get out of here.

LALO: Just for a minute . . .

CUCA: Just for nothing! Everything's ready. What's wrong with you? Are you trying to spoil it for me? I'm not going to let you.

Cuca tries to stop Lalo, who tries to escape. She grabs the collar of his shirt. They both struggle violently. Beba is confused for a second. Then she becomes interested in the fight and starts to walk around Cuca and Lalo.

LALO: Let go.

CUCA: Make me.

LALO: Don't be too sure of yourself.

CUCA: You're afraid to risk your neck.

LALO: You're scratching me.

CUCA: That's nothing. This is life or death. You can't escape. I'll do anything to see you punished.

Beba runs back toward the door.

BEBA (*screaming*): The police! The police!

The two stop fighting. Lalo falls into a chair, beaten. Beba is beside the closed door. On the other side, upstage, is Cuca.

CUCA (*angrily*): I'll never forgive you. It's your fault, your fault. If you want to die, all right, go ahead and die.
BEBA: Shut up. Quiet. (*Long pause.*)

Beba and Cuca move about in slow motion. They are now the two policemen who discover the crime.

CUCA: Dark in here.
BEBA: Smells bad.
CUCA: Bloodstains everywhere.
BEBA: Looks as if they slaughtered a couple of pigs.
CUCA: Piggish people?
BEBA: Heartless people.

The two walk on as if in a darkened gallery. Lalo doesn't move from his chair. The sisters stop in front of him and pretend to shine a torch at him.

(*Triumphantly.*) Got him.
CUCA: Gave us a bit of trouble, didn't he. (*Violently, to Lalo.*) Get up, come on, move.

Lalo, annoyed by the light, tries to cover his face with his hands.

BEBA (*roughly*): Listen to this . . . One move and I'll shoot.
CUCA (*rudely*): Come on, get up.
BEBA (*rudely*): It's all over.

Lalo stands and puts up his hands.

We'd better be quick.
CUCA: Search him.
BEBA: Looks dangerous. (*Searches him.*) Your papers? (*Takes out an imaginary piece of paper.*) What's your name?

Lalo doesn't answer.

Don't you understand—you're under arrest? When an officer asks you a question, you answer and you answer fast. Who screamed?

CUCA: Who did you kill?

BEBA: Where's the blood from?

CUCA: You live with your parents?

BEBA: Brothers and sisters?

CUCA: You killed them, didn't you?

BEBA: Better confess now.

CUCA: We'll make things easier for you.

LALO (*vaguely*): I don't know.

BEBA: What do you mean, you don't know? Do you live alone?

CUCA: What are all these clothes for? . . . (*In another tone of voice.*) Leave him alone. (*She smiles.*) He'll have plenty of time to talk.

BEBA: Nobody can save him now. (*She laughs, rudely.*) A hardened criminal. Probably started by robbing them—that wasn't enough so he decided to kill them. (*To Lalo.*) Your own parents? . . . I can imagine. Poison? (*Takes the pill box from his hand and returns it to the table.*) How many pills?

Lalo doesn't answer. He smiles occasionally.

CUCA: A thoroughly vicious crime. (*To Lalo.*) Where are the bodies? (*To Beba.*) Not a sign of them.

BEBA: Where did you hide them? Did you bury them?

CUCA: We'll search the whole house. Every corner . . .

BEBA: Why did you kill them? Come on: were they bad to you?

LALO (*dryly*): No.

CUCA: It's time to talk. Why did you kill them?

LALO (*self-assured*): I didn't do it.

CUCA: Don't waste our time.

BEBA: Were they asleep?

CUCA: Don't try to look tough. So you haven't killed anyone? What about your parents? Your brothers or sisters? Some other relation?

Lalo shrugs his shoulders.

Then what did you do?

BEBA: Suffocated them with a pillow?

CUCA: How many times did you stab them?

BEBA: Five? Ten? Fifteen?

CUCA: Don't tell me that it was a game. There's blood all over the house. And you're covered with blood. Are you denying it? Aren't you going to answer any questions? (*In another tone of voice.*) I've never seen such a crime . . . (*Suddenly.*) Where are your parents? Stuffed in a trunk? (*Pause, reconstructing the scene.*) You walked slowly, tiptoe, trying to make no noise in the dark . . . your parents were snoring and you held your breath and the knife in your hand didn't even tremble.

LALO (*proudly*): That's not true. . . . You're a liar.

CUCA: Then . . . what did happen? (*Exhausted.*) This house is like a maze.

BEBA (*who has been studying the room carefully*): Evidence. (*Pointing to the knife.*) We're on our way . . . (*Bends to pick it up.*)

CUCA: Don't touch it.

BEBA: Better check it for fingerprints. (*Takes the knife in a handkerchief and places it on the table.*)

CUCA: If he insists on pleading "Not Guilty" . . .

BEBA (*angrily*): Don't bother. I'll look after him. (*To Lalo.*) Come here. Have you decided to talk . . . or . . .? Do you think we're just here for decoration? (*Menacingly and persuasively.*) You may as well talk, we'll make it worth your while. You've had plenty of time to think. (*In a friendlier voice.*) Better tell us, it's for your own good. (*Looking at Cuca.*) It'll be taken into consideration. Don't worry.

Cuca goes to the side of the stage as if looking for something.

You'll feel much better when you've told us all about it. It's so easy. (*Almost familiarly.*) How did you do it? Why did you do it? Did they swear at you or . . .? Did somebody steal something? What really happened? You haven't forgotten have you? Try to remember . . . take your time.

LALO (*arrogantly*): You wouldn't understand.

BEBA (*persuasively, smiling*): What makes you think that? . . . (*More intimately.*) Come on, own up.

CUCA (*offstage, shouting*): Don't worry, Beba, I've found the mess. (*Comes onstage, rubbing her hands together.*) You ought to see it! Disgusting, horrible! Anyone'd be shaken. (*Reconstructing the scene.*) There's a shovel and pick. . . .

He dug a deep grave. Don't know how he managed by himself. . . . And there, down at the bottom, are the two bodies with a little earth sprinkled on top. (*Approaches Lalo and slaps him on the back.*) So the poor little boy didn't do anything at all?

Beba looks in the direction of Cuca. She is excited.

Of course, I understand. (*With a satisfied smile.*) The boy's innocent. (*In another tone of voice.*) All right . . . (*She looks at him with contempt.*) Time's running out. (*Rudely.*) You've just signed your own death warrant.

BEBA (*entering. Not acting as a policeman*): This is awful.

CUCA (*as a policeman, rudely*): Stop acting.

BEBA: It made me shudder.

CUCA (*as a policeman*): There's something strange about this boy.

BEBA: It really shook me.

CUCA (*as a policeman, to Beba*): Come on, wake up. Pull yourself together . . . (*To Lalo, contemptuously.*) You're a . . . I'd like to . . . (*To Beba.*) Let's draw up the charge.

BEBA: What? . . . But he hasn't confessed yet.

CUCA (*as a policeman*): That won't be necessary.

BEBA: I think it will be.

CUCA (*as a policeman*): We've got all the evidence we need.

BEBA: We ought to try . . . (*Approaching Lalo.*) Lalo, you've got to talk, you've got to confess. Why? Lalo. Why?

CUCA (*as a policeman*): Don't let up now.

BEBA (*to Lalo, almost begging*): Don't you understand it's just a formality? A confession's important. Say what you like, whatever comes into your head, logical or not. But please say something.

Lalo doesn't move.

CUCA (*as a policeman*): Down to the station. The charge. The report . . .

Beba seriously walks to the table and sits down. The scene should now acquire a new dimension, an eerie strangeness. The elements used are: vocal sounds, taps on the table, and rhythmic footsteps, first Beba's and then Beba's and Cuca's. These should be used to the greatest possible extent.

(*Dictating automatically.*) On the third day of April at six in the evening at the city police headquarters . . .

BEBA (*moving her hands automatically over the table*): Tac-tac-tac-tac. Tac-tac-tac-tac. Tac-tac-tac-tac.

CUCA: In the presence of the duty officer, we, the signatories, Officer 4216 Cuco and Officer 5390 Bebo brought in a citizen alleging that his name was . . .

BEBA (*as before*): Tac-tac-tac. Tac-tac-tac-tac. Tac-tac-tac.

Cuca keeps moving her lips as if continuing with the dictation.

Tac-tac-tac.

CUCA (*as before*): The officers affirm that as they were patrolling in the neighborhood of city police headquarters . . .

BEBA (*very rhythmically*): Tac-tac-tac-tac. Tac-tac-tac-tac. Tac-tac-tac-tac. Tac-tac-tac-tac. Tac-tac-tac-tac.

Cuca moves her lips as if still dictating.

CUCA (*as before*): Hearing raised voices, considerable disturbance . . .

BEBA (*as before*): Tac-tac-tac-tac. Tac-tac-tac-tac.

CUCA (*as before*): Fighting and screaming . . .

BEBA (*as before*): Tac-tac-tac-tac. Tac-tac-tac-tac.

CUCA (*as before*): And a cry for help . . .

BEBA (*beating the table and tapping her feet very rhythmically and automatically*): Tac-tac-tac-tac. Tac-tac-tac-tac.

Cuca moving her lips as if still dictating.

Tac-tac-tac-tac.

CUCA (*as before*): Entering the house . . .

BEBA (*as before*): Tac-tac-tac-tac. Tac-tac-tac-tac.

CUCA (*as before*): They found two corpses . . .

BEBA (*as before*): Tac-tac-tac-tac.

CUCA (*as before*): Contusions and first-degree wounds . . .

BEBA (*as before*): Tac-tac-tac-tac. Tac-tac-tac-tac.

Cuca begins tapping and beating the table like Beba until the scene reaches a delirious frenzy that lasts a moment. Pause. Beba and Cuca return to their usual positions. Cuca shows a piece of paper to Lalo.

CUCA (*authoritatively*): Sign here.

Pause. Lalo looks at the paper. He looks at Cuca. Takes the paper with contempt and studies it closely.

LALO (*angrily, firmly, defiantly*): I don't accept it. Understand? It's trash, nothing but garbage. (*Pause, mockingly.*) You're wonderful, really wonderful, trying to catch me in your nasty little man-traps. I suppose it's all you can expect. Almost . . . natural. But what do you want? You think I'm going to sign that shitty piece of paper? You call that law? You call that justice? (*Screams, ripping the paper.*) Crap, crap, crap. This is the only dignified thing to do. As a good example. The only thing people will respect. (*Stamps angrily on the ripped-up paper. Pause. In another tone of voice, with a bitter smile, almost crying.*) Now wouldn't it be nice and dignified and a good example to everyone if you simply said: "Guilty." That's that: next case, please. But what you're doing now . . . (*To Cuca.*) Aren't the facts enough for you? Why try to make me fit into your thickheaded fantasies? Do you think I'm a lunatic? . . . What do you want? (*Mockingly.*) You think I'm dying of fright yet? Listen: No. I'm not scared.

Beba hits the table with the gavel.

I'm guilty. I'm guilty. So judge me. Do what you like. I'm entirely in your hands.

Beba bangs the gavel, imitating a judge. Lalo in another tone of voice, less violently, but always arrogantly.

If Your Honor will permit me . . .

BEBA (*imitating a judge*): The public will maintain silence or the Court will be cleared and the session will be held behind closed doors. (*To Cuca.*) You may proceed.

CUCA (*to Beba*): Thank you, Your Honor. (*To Lalo.*) The accused may be aware of the difficulties that we have encountered in our attempts to clarify the incidents that occurred in the ominous dawn . . . of . . .

Beba bangs her gavel.

BEBA (*as judge*): I must ask the prosecution to be more specific and clear in the formulation of questions.

CUCA (*as prosecutor*): Excuse me, Your Honor, but . . .

BEBA (*as judge, to Cuca. Banging on the table*): Keep to the point.

CUCA (*as prosecutor. Solemnly*): Your Honor, I repeat that the accused has systematically obstructed all attempts to reach the truth. For this reason I submit for the consideration of the Court, the following questions: Can he and should he be permitted to mock the law? Is not the Law the Law? If we mock the Law, does the Law stop being the Law? If we can mock the Law, does the Law become something else, which is not the Law? . . . In short, members of the jury, must we all become clairvoyant?

BEBA (*as judge. Implacable, banging on the table*): I must ask the prosecution to stop changing the subject.

CUCA (*as prosecutor, showing off her theatrical courtroom manners*): Ladies and gentlemen of the jury, the accused, in common with all guilty men, fears the great weight of Justice . . .

LALO (*furious, but keeping control*): You're cheating. I know what you're trying to do. You're trying to swamp me, but I won't let you.

CUCA (*as prosecutor, angrily, with great solemnity. To Beba*): Your Honor, the accused is behaving irreverently. In the name of the Law, I demand decency and respect. Why is the accused trying to disrupt this Court? If that is what he wants, we publicly condemn such an intolerable attitude. The processes of Law and Justice are logical. No one can complain about their methods. They were made to suit man. But the accused apparently doesn't understand, or perhaps he doesn't want to understand, or perhaps he is temperamentally inclined to violent outbursts . . . or it may be that he wants to hide something from us, befog us with a smokescreen of nonsense and abuse. I must ask the members of the jury to examine these attitudes carefully and, when the time comes to pronounce a verdict, to remain calm and implacable. Ladies and gentlemen of the jury, on the one hand the accused openly declares his guilt; that is to say, he confesses that he has killed. This monstrous act exceeds the natural limits of humanity and cannot be tolerated by the man in the street. On the other hand, the accused denies everything, indirectly of course, changing the order of events, using false arguments, contradictions, banalities, and ridiculous expressions. Phrases like: I don't know; maybe; could be; yes and no. Are these answers? Note also the familiar use of: I don't really remember. Gentlemen of the jury, this is inadmissible. (*Ad-*

*vancing to the center of the stage with great theatrical
effect.*) The Law cannot stand by passively, faced with a
case so pregnant with degradation, malice, and cruelty.
Standing before you, ladies and gentlemen, you see the
most repulsive murderer in history. Look at him. Could
anyone help feeling disgusted, confronted by this wretch,
this sickening little rat, this slippery gob of spittle? Shouldn't
we want to vomit and curse him? Can Justice stand back
with folded arms? Ladies and gentlemen of the jury, can
we allow such a person to share our hopes and ideals at
a time when humanity, that is to say, our society, should
be marching toward a shining future, toward a golden
dawn?

*Lalo tries to say something, but Cuca's torrential speech
prevents any act, gesture, or word.*

Look at him. Indifferent, imperturbable, alien to any feeling
of tenderness, understanding, or compassion. Look at that
face. (*Yelling.*) The stony face of a murderer. The accused
denies that he committed the murder for money, that is
to say, for gain, in order to steal, or so that he would
inherit his parents' pathetic little pension. And so we must
ask ourselves, why did he kill? We cannot be absolutely
sure about a single one of his motives. Must we agree that
he did it out of hatred? Revenge? Or out of pure sadism?

*Pause. Lalo moves impatiently in his chair. Cuca, in a
circumspect tone of voice.*

Can Justice permit a son to kill his parents.
LALO (*to Beba*): Your Honor . . . I would like, I want . . .
CUCA (*as prosecutor*): No, ladies and gentlemen. No, members of the jury. One thousand times no. Justice cannot
accept such an obscenity. Justice sustains the family. Justice has created order. Justice is eternally vigilant. Justice demands good manners. Justice guards man from his
own corrupt and primitive instincts. Can we show pity for
a creature who violates the natural principles of Justice?
I ask you, ladies and gentlemen, members of the jury, can
we allow ourselves the luxury of compassion? (*Pause.*) Our
entire city rises in indignation, a city of proud and silent
men advances, determined to claim for Justice the body

of this monster . . . demanding that his body should be exposed to the righteous fury of real human beings whose only desires are for peace and tranquillity. (*In a grandiose tone of voice.*) And so, and so I demand from the accused that he help us to discover the truth. (*To Lalo.*) Why did you kill your parents?

LALO: There was some reason or other . . .

CUCA (*violently*): That's not an answer. (*Quickly.*) How did you do it then? Did you give them something to drink first, some poison? Or did you stifle them with pillows as they lay there so defenselessly and then finish them off afterward? What did you do with the pillows? What was the point of these syringes and pills? Are they simply red herrings? Explain yourself, prisoner at the bar. (*Pause.*) Did you kill them in cold blood, planning the details of the crime step by grisly step, or was it done in some ecstasy of violence? Tell us, did you do all that damage with this knife? (*Exhausted.*) And finally, prisoner at the bar, why did you kill them?

LALO: I felt that I was being persecuted and harassed.

CUCA (*as prosecutor*): Persecuted? Why? Harassed? Why?

LALO: They wouldn't leave me alone.

CUCA (*as prosecutor*): Nevertheless, the witnesses testify . . .

LALO (*interrupting*): The witnesses are lying.

CUCA (*as prosecutor. Interrupting*): Are you denying the statements of the witnesses?

LALO (*firmly*): Nobody was there that night.

BEBA (*as the judge. To Lalo*): The accused must be more accurate in his replies. That is absolutely essential. Is what you have just said entirely true? . . . The jury demands both truth and precision. The jury hopes that the accused will accept, willingly, these requirements of order. . . . The prosecution may continue.

CUCA (*as prosecutor*): Now, let us turn to your close relatives. . . . Your grandmother, for example, your aunts . . . your nearest and dearest. Did you see them often? What sort of relationship did you have with them?

LALO: None.

CUCA (*as prosecutor*): Why?

LALO: My mother hated my father's family and my father didn't get along with my mother's family.

CUCA (*as prosecutor*): I have been led to understand that your parents complained about you . . .

LALO: All my life, as long as I can remember, I've been hearing the same complaints, the same sermons, the same litany.

CUCA (*as prosecutor*): They must have had some reason for these complaints.

LALO: Sometimes yes, sometimes no. . . . But when reasons are hammered home endlessly, they become unreasonable.

CUCA (*as prosecutor*): Were your parents so demanding?

LALO: I don't understand.

CUCA (*as prosecutor*): This is the question: what kind of relationship did you have with your parents?

LALO: I thought I'd explained: they questioned me, they made demands on me, they spied on me.

CUCA (*as prosecutor*): What did they ask you? What demands did they make? Why were they spying?

LALO (*desperately*): I don't know. Don't know. (*Repeating in an automatic voice.*) Wash the dishes, wash the tablecloths, wash the shirts. Polish the cutlery, clean the toilet, polish the floors. Don't sleep, don't dream, don't read. You're no damn good.

CUCA (*as prosecutor*): Ladies and gentlemen, members of the jury, do you believe that these are motives capable of provoking an individual to such a degree of alienation that he feels driven to commit a murder?

LALO (*stammering*): I wanted . . .

CUCA (*as prosecutor*): What did you want? (*Pause.*) Answer me.

LALO (*sincerely*): Life.

CUCA (*as prosecutor, sarcastically*): And did your parents stop you living? (*To the audience.*) Isn't the prisoner at the bar evading the issue?

LALO (*intensely*): I wanted, I wanted, I longed desperately to do things for myself.

CUCA (*as prosecutor*): And your parents prevented you?

LALO (*convinced*): Yes.

CUCA (*as prosecutor*): Why?

LALO: They said I was stupid, said I was lazy, said that I'd never amount to anything.

CUCA (*as prosecutor. With much restraint*): Well, and what did you want to do? Would the accused like to explain himself?

LALO (*tormented. With great effort and a little confused*): It's very hard . . . I don't know. There was something. You know? Something. How can I express it? I *know* it exists, it's there; but I can't, not now.

Cuca smiles maliciously.

Look . . . I know this isn't it, but it's just . . . (*Assured.*) I tried, every way I could think of, tried to please them. . . . Once I caught pneumonia. . . . No. I shouldn't be saying this . . . it's just that . . . Everything always went wrong. I didn't want it to be like that; but I couldn't do anything else; and then . . .

CUCA (*as prosecutor*): And then? Are you sure about what you're saying?

LALO: I'm sure now.

CUCA (*as prosecutor*): Go on, go on.

LALO: I felt that everything was collapsing.

CUCA (*as prosecutor*): I don't understand. What exactly are you trying to say?

LALO: Those walls, those carpets, those curtains and lamps, the armchair where my father used to take his nap, the bed and the wardrobe and the sheets.

CUCA (*as prosecutor*): You hated them? And of course, you hated your parents, too, isn't that right?

LALO (*his attention wandering*): Maybe I should have just left. Gone anywhere, to hell or Timbuktu.

CUCA (*as prosecutor, with a declamatory air*): Ladies and gentlemen, members of the jury . . .

LALO (*continuing as if hypnotized*): One day, when I was playing with my sisters, I suddenly found out . . . (*Pause.*)

CUCA (*as prosecutor, taking a sudden interest in Lalo's digression*): What did you find out?

LALO (*same tone as before*): We were in the living room; no, I'm wrong . . . We were in the back room. We were playing . . . I mean, we were acting . . . (*Smiles idiotically.*) It might seem silly to you, but . . . I was being father; no, I'm wrong. I think at the time I was being mother. It was just a game. (*Different tone.*) But there, just at that moment, I got this idea . . . (*Again smiles idiotically.*)

CUCA (*as prosecutor, with growing interest*): What idea?

LALO (*with the same smile*): It's very simple, but it keeps getting complicated. You're never sure of saying what you feel. I . . . (*Moving his hands as if trying to explain things with this movement*.) I knew that whatever my parents were giving me wasn't life, and couldn't ever be life. Then I said to myself, "If you want to live, you have to . . ." (*He stops and makes a stabbing gesture, or clenches his fists as if tearing something apart.*)

CUCA (*as prosecutor*): And what did you feel at that moment?

LALO (*like a fool*): I don't know. You guess.

CUCA (*as prosecutor*): Weren't you frightened?

LALO: I think so, for a moment.

CUCA (*as prosecutor*): And then?

LALO: After that I wasn't frightened at all.

CUCA (*as prosecutor, ironically*): You got used to the idea?

LALO: I got used to it.

CUCA (*as prosecutor. She reacts violently*): What? (*Banging the table.*) Members of the jury, this is unheard-of.

LALO: It's true. I got used to it. It seems terrible, I mean I didn't want it to be like that; but the idea buzzed around and around in my head, coming and going and coming back again. At first I wanted to get rid of it . . . you understand? But it kept insisting: "Kill your parents. Kill your parents." I thought I'd go mad. I threw myself into bed. I started running a temperature . . . suddenly I was full of fever. I thought I'd pop like a balloon, thought I'd explode, thought the devil was signaling to me; I shivered as I lay between the sheets. . . . You should have seen me . . . couldn't sleep; night after night lying awake. My whole body was shaking. It was terrifying. I saw death crawling toward me, inch by inch, from behind the bed, in between the curtains, among the clothes that were hanging in the wardrobe; death became my shadow and whispered to me from inside the pillows: "Murderer!" and then suddenly disappeared; and I sat in front of the mirror and I saw my mother dead in her coffin and I saw my father hanging by his neck, and they were laughing and shouting at me; and every night I felt my mother's hands rise out of the pillows to claw my face.

(*Pause.*)

Every morning I woke up in agony; it was like rising out of a grave, my ankles gripped by the two corpses who always chased me through my nightmares. Sometimes I was tempted. . . . But no . . . no . . . Leave the house? . . . How could I? I knew what happened when I tried. I always had to come back, always had to promise: never again. I wasn't going to try that. Anything else, not that. Then the idea drifted into my head that I should rearrange the house to suit me, take control of things. . . . The living room is not the living room, I said. The living room is the kitchen. The bedroom is not the bedroom. The bedroom is the lavatory.

(*Short pause.*)

What else could I do? If I didn't do that, I'd have to destroy everything, everything; because every object in the house was involved and they all conspired against me and understood my thoughts. If I sat in a chair, the chair wasn't the chair, but my father's corpse. If I took a glass of water, what I held in my hands was my mother's damp neck. If I played with a vase, an enormous knife would suddenly fall out of it on the floor. If I cleaned a carpet, the job could never be finished because the carpet was one huge woven clot of blood.

(*Pause.*)

Haven't you ever felt like that? I was suffocating, suffocating. I didn't know where I was or what was happening. And whom could I tell? Was there anyone I could trust? I was stuck in a pit and I couldn't get out.

(*Pause.*)

But I had this crazy idea that I could save myself. . . . From what? I don't know . . . well, maybe, in a way. . . . You start to explain it all, and somehow, right from the beginning, you get it wrong. Maybe I wanted to save myself from that suffocating, from that pit. . . . Soon after, without knowing why, I began to change. One day I heard a voice and I didn't know where it was coming from. And then I heard my sisters' laughter all around the house. And mixed in with their laughter, I heard thousands of voices repeating in unison: "Kill them. Kill them." No, I'm not inventing this. It's the truth. Yes, the truth. (*As if inspired.*) From that moment I knew what I had to do. Gradually I discovered that everything, the carpets, bed, wardrobes, mirror, vases, glasses, spoons, and my shadow—they were all whispering, all demanding: "Kill your parents." (*Almost musical ecstasy.*) "Kill your parents." The whole house, everything, everything, was crying out to me for this heroic act.

(*Pause.*)

CUCA (*violently*): I'm off. You're cheating.

LALO: We've got to go through to the end.

CUCA: I can't let you take over . . .

LALO: You've often tried to make it go your way—

CUCA: What you've done is unforgivable. We each had a part; we agreed.

LALO: Did we? All right, then . . .

BEBA (*like a judge, banging her gavel*): Silence in Court! I must ask the Court to comport itself with dignity . . .

CUCA (*as her mother, to Beba*): Your Honor, forgive my interruption. But I must ask for a thorough investigation of the whole affair, right from the beginning. I demand a retrial. That's why I'm here. My son is posing as a victim, but that's the exact opposite of the truth. I demand that justice should be done.

Beba starts to imitate the sound of a typewriter. Exaggerated.

You ought to hear what this creature did to us. It was terrible, so . . .

BEBA (*as the judge*): Go on . . .

LALO (*almost out of the game*): But mother, I . . . (*Feels that he's cornered.*) I . . . I promise . . .

CUCA (*as the mother*): Don't give me your promises. You'd like to fool us. I know all your tricks, all your games, all your dirty little swindles. I know them all—because I had to give birth to you. Nine months of dizziness, vomiting, pains. Those were the warnings that you were on the way. Are you trying to confuse me? All these promises to tell the truth, what do they add up to? Do you think you've won over the audience and saved yourself? Tell me, saved yourself from what? (*She laughs uproariously.*) What sort of world are you living in, little boy? (*Mocking.*) O my little angel, I'm so sorry for you. You really are—well, I won't say what you are. (*To Beba.*) Your Honor, can I tell you something? One day he decided that we should rearrange the whole house to suit him . . . Soon as I heard of this mad idea, I put my foot down, hard. His father shouted fit to raise the roof. But what did it look like? You can't imagine. . . . The ashtray on the armchair. The flower vase down on the floor. What a mess! And then he started singing at the top of his voice, running all over the house. "The living room is not the living room. The living room is the kitchen." When that happened I pretended not to hear, pretended I was listening to the rain. (*Hard, dry.*) You only told your side. . . . Why didn't you tell the rest? (*Mocking.*) You've talked about your martyrdom, now talk about ours, your father's and mine. I'd like to refresh your memory. (*Transformed.*) You Honor, if you knew the tears I've wept, the humiliation, the hours of agony, the sacrifices . . . Look at my hands . . . it breaks your heart to look at them. (*Almost with tears in her eyes.*) My hands . . . if only you'd seen them before I got married . . . I've lost everything: all my youth, all my happiness, all my little pleasures. I've sacrificed them all for this animal. (*To Lalo.*) Aren't you ashamed? You still think you've done something heroic? (*Disgustedly.*) I don't know how I carried you in my belly all those months. I'll never know why I didn't strangle you at birth.

Beba bangs the gavel.

LALO: Mother, I . . .

CUCA (*as mother*): Shut up, shut up, you're not worth your weight in dirt. You're not even worth one of the contractions I had when I gave birth to you. . . . Because you, you, you're the guilty one. The only one who is guilty.

LALO (*violently*): Leave me alone.

CUCA (*as mother, violently*): I'm getting old. You want to think about that and make some sacrifices. You think I've got no right to live? You think I'm going to spend my life in nonstop agony? Your father doesn't look after me and neither do you. Where will I end up? Yes. I know you're all waiting for me to pass away, but I won't give you that satisfaction. I'll shout to the neighbors, to all the passersby. You'll see. That'll be my revenge. (*Shouting.*) Help! Help me! They're murdering me! (*Bursts into tears.*) I'm a poor old woman dying of loneliness.

Beba bangs the gavel.

Yes, Your Honor, I'm caged up by four dirty walls. I never see the sunlight. My children have no consideration. I'm getting wrinkled, I'm drying up . . . (*As if before a mirror, she starts stroking her face, ending by slapping it.*) Look at those lines! (*Pointing out her wrinkles with rancor and disgust.*) Look at that flab. Your skin will be like that one day. All I want from the world is that everything that ever happened to me should happen to you. (*Arrogant.*) I've always been a woman who respects Justice, Your Honor.

LALO (*mockingly*): Are you sure? Think carefully, mother.

CUCA (*as mother*): What's that? What are you talking about?

LALO (*sarcastically*): I mean I know you're lying. Once you accused me . . .

CUCA (*as mother; interrupting him with a cry*): Lalo! (*Pause, smoothly.*) Lalo, can you really say that? (*Pause; she walks a few steps; once again she seems agitated.*) Oh, Lalo . . . (*Wiping her tears away.*) You mean that I, Lalo . . . (*With obvious doubt.*) You think that I . . . could I have done that? Probably I did . . . but, look, it wasn't serious . . . (*She laughs vulgarly.*) You see, I fell in love with this beautiful red taffeta dress, a dress in the window of the New Bazaar. My husband earned next to nothing. I had to work miracles every week to make ends meet. I'd made my bed, and I had to lie in it. A junior clerk at the Ministry, Your Honor, that's all he was. So, as I was saying . . . I was desperate, crazy for that dress. I dreamed about it . . . I even saw it reflected in the soup. And at last, one day, I decided, just like that, to buy the dress out of the housekeeping. So I invented a story.

BEBA (*as judge*): What story?

CUCA (*as mother, very freely*): When Alberto came home . . . Blind drunk as usual . . . I said to him: Listen dear, talk to your son . . . (*She approaches Beba to whisper in her ear.*) . . . because I think that he's been stealing from us.

BEBA (*as judge*): Why did you do it?

CUCA (*as mother, vulgarly*): I don't know. . . . It was easier that way . . . (*She ends the story with great exaggeration.*) So Alberto took a piece of rope, and I'd hate to tell you how many times he hit poor little Lalo . . . The truth was, he was innocent, but . . . I wanted that red dress so badly. (*Approaching Lalo.*) Do you forgive me, my son?

LALO (*hard*): I don't have to forgive you.

CUCA (*as mother, hysterical*): Have some respect, Lalo. (*Dramatically.*) I'm not what I used to be. I'm fat and ugly . . . ugh, this body!

LALO: Forget it.

CUCA (*as mother, firmly*): Show some respect.

LALO: I was only playing.

CUCA (*as mother, hard, imperative*): Don't start your acting again. Your father spends his life chasing daydreams, the old lunatic. Just like you. Let him be a lesson to you. He's playing the part of "the man who can do everything" and really he's worth nothing. A piece of shit. Absolutely useless. He's always been *nobody*. His whole life has been talk, and he thinks he can go on like that. Sometimes I wanted him to die. Why did I have to marry a man who couldn't give me a better life than this? (*Pause*). Come on. (*Pause*.) If it wasn't for me, Your Honor, this house would have tumbled down, Your Honor . . . Yes, me, me . . .

LALO (*as father, with a firm, almost terrifying voice*): She's lying, Your Honor.

CUCA (*as mother, to Lalo*): How dare you?

LALO (*as father, to Beba*): It's true. She's trying to paint everything black. She only sees the mote in someone else's eye. As a father, I was sometimes guilty. But so was she. (*His voice grows more assured.*) Like all parents, we've sometimes been unjust and sometimes we've done unforgivable things.

CUCA (*as mother, with hatred*): You came home with makeup all over your shirt and handkerchief.

LALO (*as father, violently*): Shut your mouth. You don't want me to tell the truth.

CUCA (*as mother, violently*): Your Honor, his drinking, his friends, his guests at all hours of the night.

LALO (*as father, violently*): Who wears the pants?

CUCA (*as mother, violently*): I'm in charge.

LALO (*as father, violently*): That's it. "I'm in charge." Yes, you, you're in charge all right. That's all your life amounts to. You made fun of me. You humiliated me. That's the truth. Domination. (*Brief pause.*) I've been a real idiot, I've eaten all that shit. If you'll excuse the word, members of the jury.

CUCA (*as mother, sarcastically*): Well, well. So at least you accept it.

LALO (*as father, violently*): Yes. Why deny it? (*Pause, organizing his thoughts.*) I went into marriage with some illusions. If I said I went into it with my eyes closed, I'd be exaggerating, and lying as well. I went into it like most people, thinking it would solve a few problems for me:

clothes, food, stability . . . a little company . . . and at last
. . . a few little liberties. (*As if hitting himself internally.*)
Idiot! You idiot! (*Pause.*) I never imagined what it would
be like.

CUCA (*as mother, violently*): You never imagined anything.
"You have your fun, I'll have mine," a lot of people think
like that. But I wasn't going to allow that.

LALO (*as father, bitter*): You're right there. It certainly wasn't
like that. Days before our wedding the rows began: the
church was too suburban, it wasn't fashionable enough,
the wedding dress didn't have a long train, your sister
said this, your mother said that, your cousin, your aunt,
your friends were thinking something else, your grandmother said that we ought to have invited Mr. and Mrs.
whatstheirname, the cake was only nine tiers high, your
friends ought to dress more formally . . .

CUCA (*as mother, provocatively*): Go on, go on . . . say it all.
Throw it all up, don't keep anything down. At last I can
see that you hate me.

LALO (*as father, firm, decisive*): Yes, that's true. And I don't
know why. But that's how it is. When we were engaged you
jumped into bed with me because you knew that was the
only way to catch me. That's the truth.

CUCA (*as mother*): Go on, go on, don't stop.

LALO (*as father*): You didn't want to be an old maid. You
hated children. But stay single? No, no. You had to have
a husband. Didn't matter who. Having one was all that
mattered.

CUCA (*as mother*): I hate you, I hate you, I hate you.

LALO (*as father*): A husband would give you security. A
husband would make you respectable. Respectable . . .
(*Pause.*) I can't explain . . . Anyway, this is what life's
about, so you'd better put up with it . . .

CUCA (*as mother, desperately*): Lies, lies, lies.

LALO (*as father*): Are you going to let me finish?

CUCA (*breaks situation*): You're cheating again.

LALO (*as father*): You don't want people to know the truth.

CUCA (*out of situation*): We were discussing something else.

LALO (*as father*): You're afraid to see it through to the end.

CUCA (*out of situation*): You just want to squash me.

LALO (*as father, violently*): And you, what have you been
doing? Tell me, what have you done to me? And to them?

(*Laughing.*) "I'm getting ugly, Alberto. I'm swelling up. We can't keep going on your wages." (*Pause.*) And I never knew your motives, your real reason. But today, I'm telling you. "Place your hand on your heart and answer me DID YOU EVER LOVE ME?" (*Pause.*) Doesn't matter. Don't say anything. I can see it all clearly. It's taken a long, long time for me to wake up.

CUCA (*as mother*): Oh, Alberto, these children . . . I feel terrible. I can't stand them. You look after them. I'm all alone and I can't cope. You understand? I can't. Bring an ashtray. Bring a towel, bring my slippers. I spend the whole day rushing about. Your sister rang today, the cunning bitch . . . I'm desperate, Alberto. I wish I was dead . . . And there you are, happily sitting at the Ministry, all calm and cozy, while I'm being eaten alive. . . . Here I am stuck inside a house that I loathe, this prison, this hell . . . with no visits to the movies, no parties, nothing. . . . Go on then, tell me I'm selfish, tell me I expect too much. But what are you doing to help us? Go on, tell me when you've ever lifted a finger to help us.

LALO (*as father*): That's enough. I'll go mad.

CUCA (*as mother*): That's it, go on, go on! Why don't you get out of this house for good?

LALO (*as father*): That's what you'd like, isn't it? But I'm going to stay here till I drop. If you only knew . . . there are other women . . . you're not the only one. (*To the audience.*) I can't stand it, I want to get away, fly away, and all this . . . But I'm afraid, and that fear paralyzes me. I can't make up my mind, I stop halfway; think one thing and do another. It's terrible to have to admit it. But I can't do it. (*Shouting.*) Lalo, you can if you want to. The question is: why didn't I take up every one of my thoughts, every one of my desires, and live them out? And the answer is: I was afraid, afraid, afraid.

CUCA (*as mother, sarcastically*): Can't blame me for that, little boy. (*Pause, challenging.*) What did you want me to do? Those children are devils. They turned my house into a pigsty. Lalo tore the curtains and broke the cups; Beba wasn't satisfied with ripping up the pillows . . . and you expect to come home and find everything where you want it. You remember when Beba peed in the living room?

LALO (*as father*): And what did you do about it?

CUCA (*as mother*): Me?

LALO (*as father*): Are you a vase? Are you a picture on the wall? Nothing like that ever happened in my house.

CUCA (*as mother*): What did you expect me to do? Do you think it's my fault? If I put a chair over here, I find it over there. . . . Tell me, what do you want me to do?

LALO (*defeated*): The house had to be cleaned. Yes . . . the furniture had to be changed, sure . . . (*Pause, with great sadness.*) But what we really needed was to build a new house. (*Pause, slowly.*) But we're old already and we can't do it. We're dead. (*Pause, violently.*) You always thought you were better than me.

CUCA (*as mother*): I've wasted my life on you.

LALO (*as father, vengefully*): You can't escape. Go on. Go on. Go on.

CUCA (*as mother, between sobs*): You ink-blooded little pen-pusher. I wish all of you were dead.

BEBA (*imitates Lalo, shouting and moving in circles around the stage*): We've got to roll up the carpets, pull down the curtains. The living room is not the living room. The living room is the kitchen. The bedroom is not the bedroom. The bedroom is the lavatory.

Beba is at the opposite end of the stage from Lalo with her back to the audience. Lalo, also with his back to the audience, doubles up slowly. Beba gives a terrible cry.

Ayyyyyyyyyyyyy! (*Sobbing.*) I see my mother dead. I see my father beheaded. We've got to pull this house down.

LALO: Open that door. (*He falls to his knees.*)

Cuca gets up slowly, goes to the upstage door, opens it. Pause. She comes to the table and takes the knife.

BEBA (*normal voice*): How do you feel?

CUCA (*normal voice*): Stronger.

BEBA: Satisfied?

CUCA: Yes.

BEBA: Truly?

CUCA: Truly.

BEBA: Ready to do it again?

CUCA: You don't have to ask.

BEBA: One day we'll do it properly . . .

CUCA (*interrupting*): Without anything going wrong.

BEBA: Weren't you surprised you could manage it?

CUCA: I'm always surprised.

LALO (*sobbing*): Oh, if only love could do it . . . If only love . . . Because, in spite of everything I love them.

CUCA (*playing with the knife*): I think that's silly.

BEBA (*to Cuca*): Leave him alone, poor fool.

CUCA (*to Beba, laughing mockingly*): Look at him. (*To Lalo.*) That's how I like to see you.

BEBA (*serious again*): All right. Now it's my turn.

CURTAIN

I TOO SPEAK OF THE ROSE

EMILIO CARBALLIDO

Translated by William I. Oliver

Pero mi rosa no es la rosa fría . . .
Xavier Villaurrutia
But mine is not the frigid rose . . .

Amago de la humana arquitectura . . .
Sor Juana Inés de la Cruz
Portent of our human architecture . . .

The vitality and inventiveness of Emilio Carballido, born in Córdoba, Veracruz, Mexico, in 1925, have placed him in the first rank of the contemporary Mexican theatre movement. The most frequent critical observation regarding his dramatic production has been the simultaneous dual track that he has followed: from the time of his earliest plays he has developed a realistic style while at the same time venturing into fantastic realms characterized by abstract and imaginative beings and situations. These two veins, originally dichotomized, were joined for the first time in *The Golden Thread* (1956); since that time Carballido has mixed forms, experimenting with various possible combinations. He runs the gamut from serious drama through adaptations of the classical Spanish allegorical-religious plays to slapstick farce, and from full-length plays to brief one-acters. His sources of inspiration are equally varied: from Greek myths through the Mexican colonial past to present-day provincial or urban problems. In all, he shows himself to be a master technician. Although especially facile with female characterization involving sexual or marital frustrations, he creates equally authentic characters from various social levels whose problems are typically but not uniquely Mexican: family or individual situations involving guilt, greed, lust, or simply the eternal pursuit of happiness against immeasurable odds. Without being didactic, Carballido employs different degrees of social satire in order to present a contemporary Mexican consciousness, whether realistically or through surrealistic flights of fancy.

I Too Speak of the Rose (*Yo también hablo de la rosa*, 1966) is a felicitous and mature combination of his two tendencies: a basically realistic incident is contained within a highly imaginative structure. The central issue, frivolously conceived but with grave consequences, concerns two mischievous youngsters who are jailed for accidentally derailing a train. An elaborate probing of the complexities of human motivations ensues. The Freudian psychiatrist and the Marxian economist offer theories that produce not valid explanations, but parodied versions of the human condition. Reality clashes contrapuntally with the mythical visions of the mysterious

Medium who speaks metaphorically of the categorization of human behavior, and its instinctive character, which defies logical interpretation. The language is rich, expressive, and appropriate to the social milieu of the participants. Through the hypothesis of the symbolic rose, the play speaks eloquently about Carballido's talents as an interpreter of the human condition, and is a compelling answer to the modern-day technocrats whose expertise would neatly resolve all problems through systematic computerization of human behavioral patterns.

Characters

THE MEDIUM
TOÑA
POLO
MAXIMINO GONZÁLEZ
FIRST PROFESSOR
SECOND PROFESSOR
ANNOUNCER
MALE PEDDLER*
WOMAN PEDDLER
NEWSBOY
FIRST MALE SCAVENGER
SECOND MALE SCAVENGER
FIRST FEMALE SCAVENGER
SECOND FEMALE SCAVENGER
MALE STUDENT
FEMALE STUDENT
OWNER OF THE GARAGE (Spaniard)
GENTLEMAN
LADY
A POOR BOY
A POOR GIRL
A POOR MAN
A POOR WOMAN
TEACHER
TOÑA'S MOTHER
POLO'S MOTHER
TOÑA'S SISTER
THE TWO WHO DREAMED

* A boy, a girl, two men, and two women will suffice for the bracketed roles.

Harpsichord music. Silence. Darkness. A spotlight comes up on the Medium. She is seated in a wicker chair and is dressed in peasant costume. She wears a white blouse and a skirt as dark as the rebozo that covers her head.

THE MEDIUM: I heard my heart beat all afternoon. After my chores I sat here, like this, quietly, looking with bleary eyes, listening to my heart beating gently against my breasts, like a timid lover knocking at my door or a chick pecking the walls of its egg, trying to burst into the light. I conjured up an image of my heart . . . (*She brings her hand to her breast.*) a sea anemone . . . complicated, delicate colors, hidden in its cave, an efficient and methodical thing, devoted to the task of regulating endless and crepuscular canals, some wide enough for royal barges, others only wide enough for rowing vegetables and food to market by the slowest stroke of oars . . . all pulsing evenly, in time. Locks that open and then close in rhythm, all to the powerful flowering of my heart. But then I thought . . . What if all the hearts of the world were to cry out at once? . . . But more of that later. I thought then too of the air . . . it smelled of smoke and stale food . . . but I was like a fish, sitting in my chair submerged . . . in the air. I could feel it on my skin. I could feel it brush against me and snarl the petals of my heart. Air that swirls and pounds. And then I began to recall all that I know . . . and I know many things. I know about herbs; some that cure, others that taste or smell sweet, some whose effect is miraculous for they reconcile . . . some cause death or madness, and others simply grow heavy with tiny flowers. And I know more. I store within me part of all I've seen: faces, crowds, views, the feel of rocks, corners . . . many corners . . . and gestures, contacts! I also store memories, my grandmother's memories, my mother's, my friends' . . . many memories which they, in turn, had stored from friends and old, old folk of long ago. I know books, writing, and illusions! . . . I know how to go places, I know roads! But knowledge, like the heart, is hidden and beating, glowing imperceptibly, regulating canals that travel back and forth and flow into one another in sudden floods and currents. All manner of news daily comes to me . . . events . . . they take all shapes, they sound and flash and make themselves explicit . . .

293

oracular. They intertwine and they germinate. Things happen . . . I hear them . . . I receive them! I assimilate them! I pass them on! I behold them! (*She gets up.*) News!

Darkness.

We hear the racket and screech of a train derailment, whistles, shouts, iron scraping upon iron, crashes, silence. Lightning flashes.

Darkness.

The Newsboy enters, running.

NEWSBOY: The *Daily Press*, sir! Get your paper now! Delinquents derail a train! Read all about the terrible disaster! It was only a freight train! only a freight train! but what if it had been a pullman?! Buy your copy of the *Daily Press*! Today's *Daily Press* . . .

He goes off. Darkness once again. The stage lights come up. A street. We see a telephone booth. Polo, standing on a box, is trying to extract the coins from the telephone with a wire. Toña stands guard.

TOÑA (*speaking rapidly*): Hurry! Hurry up! Someone's coming! . . . Hold it! Hold it! There's an old man! He's going to use the phone! I can tell. He's looking at a little notebook.

Polo comes out of the booth and stands next to the girl. A Man enters and heads for the telephone. He steps inside the booth and the children look at him.

TOÑA: The telephone doesn't work. It's out of order.

The Man was about to drop a coin in the slot. He stops and looks at the children.

MAN: Out of order?

POLO and TOÑA: Umhum.

He hangs up and goes off. Polo returns to his task. Toña keeps watch as before. Finally he manages to extract a coin from the telephone. They examine the coin and are pleased.

TOÑA: What'll we buy?

POLO: Bananas?

TOÑA: Candy! Candy's better.
POLO: All right.
TOÑA: There's another telephone on the avenue.
POLO: There're too many people there. They'd see me.
TOÑA: Not at night.
POLO: Come on, let's spend it.

They walk toward a Candy Vendor who approaches them with his tray of sweets.

POLO: How much is the sesame candy?
VENDOR: Five, ten, and twenty.
POLO: Two fives.
TOÑA: Why don't you flip him for them.
POLO: You wanna flip.
VENDOR: For what?
TOÑA: Twenty!
POLO (*doubtful*): I better flip for ten, uh?
VENDOR: Don't back out! Twenty! Here goes.
POLO: Heads!
VENDOR: Tails!

They examine the coin. The Vendor picks it up and walks off. Silence. Toña and Polo walk on.

TOÑA: I just thought that . . . Well, you *could* have won. You would have too if *you'd* flipped.

Silence. They walk on, scuffling and kicking things.

TOÑA: Well? . . . You should have told him to let you flip! . . . And why did you play for twenty? . . . All I did was mention it, that's all!
POLO: Shut up!

Silence.

TOÑA: Flip him again.
POLO: With what?
TOÑA: I've got my bus fare.
POLO: And how will you pay for the bus?
TOÑA: Well . . . you'll win, won't you?
POLO: Sure. Easy.
TOÑA: But *you* flip this time. Here.
POLO: Hey! Hey! You! I'll flip you again.

The Vendor comes back.

VENDOR: You want to try again?

POLO: But *I* flip this time.

VENDOR: For what?

TOÑA: Twenty!

POLO: Twenty. Here goes.

VENDOR: Tails!

They look at the coin. Tails! The Vendor picks up the coin.

TOÑA: Here, let me. There, see. Flip! Heads.

They look.

I won.

VENDOR: But if you flip you can't call. Flip again.

TOÑA: Oh, yeah! Just because *I* won it's not worth anything,
is it?

POLO: She's just a girl, she doesn't know.

TOÑA: So? I won, didn't I?!

VENDOR: Oh, get out of here! What do you want?

TOÑA: Two ten-centers. (*She takes the candies.*)

VENDOR: Want to flip again?

They look at each other.

POLO: OK. For twenty-centers. Here goes. (*He flips.*)

VENDOR: Tails.

They look at the coin. Tails!

Once more?

They say no; he picks up the coin and moves off.

TOÑA: Why did you flip again? We'd already won! So there
you are, you're broke! I don't have enough to pay the bus
fare, and it's late! How do I get to school now?

They eat their candies.

Anyway, I didn't do my homework. (*She wipes her hands
on her dress.*) Aren't you going to school?

POLO: Haven't got any shoes. Can't buy any until next week.

TOÑA: Go barefoot . . . the way you are.

POLO: The teacher stands at the door to check to see if
we've polished our shoes. . . . I'll be damned if I'm going
to polish my feet.

TOÑA: I still got twenty cents. Let's buy some *jicama*.[1]
POLO: All right.

A little Woman comes on. She's selling jicama.

POLO: Two, five-centers.
OLD WOMAN: They cost ten.
TOÑA: Gee, they're expensive! What about two for fifteen, hum?
OLD WOMAN: All right.
TOÑA: With chile?

The Old Woman prepares them and hands them to the children. They pay and eat.

POLO: We got five left.
TOÑA: Save it for later.

They come to the telephone booth.

POLO (*gets an idea*): Maybe somebody's used it since we got the coin? (*He goes inside the booth, lifts the phone, and puts it back on its hook. He gets twenty cents change. He takes it out, astonished.*) Hey! It came out all by itself! Twenty cents, all by itself. Look, twenty cents. I lifted it up and it came out all by itself.

Toña comes running. She jiggles the hook up and down, up and down. She bangs the phone, shakes it. She dials, pushes the return button, she jiggles the hook once more very quickly and with great violence. She hangs up.

TOÑA: No more.
POLO: Hey, here comes Maximino. Hi!

They greet him as Maximino comes on. He is about twenty-three years old. He wears a somewhat dirty white sweat-shirt, old denim pants, and tennis shoes.

MAXIMINO: Hi!
TOÑA: We got twenty cents out of the telephone! He just picked up the phone and out it came.
POLO: And I got twenty more out of it with a wire!

---

[1] A starchy potato-like root, often sold by street vendors, and eaten raw with salt, lemon, and chili powder.

MAXIMINO: Good for you! Keep it up . . . 'til they catch you.
TOÑA: What would they do?
MAXIMINO: They'd lock you up for five years . . . more!
TOÑA: For twenty cents?
MAXIMINO: Sure!
TOÑA: All I did was to stand guard.
MAXIMINO. Accomplice . . . four years.

There is an awkward silence.

POLO: And your motorcycle?
MAXIMINO: Ran it too long without oil. It threw a rod and the kick pedal stuck.

Toña laughs.

Get her. What's so funny?
TOÑA: Kick pedal! You make it sound like a scooter.
POLO: What a stupid broad! Kick pedal is a starter!
TOÑA: A lot you know about it.
POLO: You going to fix it at home?
MAXIMINO: No, in the shop. The whole thing has to be overhauled.
TOÑA: The trouble's that motorcycle's no damn good!
POLO: You just can't keep your big fat mouth shut, can you? You don't know a damn thing about it!
TOÑA: But you know it all, don't you? Next thing you're going to say it's a great motorcycle! . . . It's just an old beat-up rattletrap!
MAXIMINO (*proudly*): Two hundred and fifty cubic centimeters per cylinder and sixteen horsepower, that's all!
TOÑA: What does that mean?
MAXIMINO: That means it's very good!
TOÑA (*convinced*): Oh? It looked kind of old to me.
MAXIMINO: What are you kids doing here anyway? Didn't you go to school?
POLO: I haven't got any shoes and she spent her bus fare.
TOÑA: He spent it! He gambled it away, flipping coins.
POLO: What a goddamn liar. *She's* the one who wanted to flip.
MAXIMINO: I'll give you your bus fare.
TOÑA: I haven't done my homework. Why don't you write me an excuse instead? . . . Please . . . huh?
MAXIMINO: All right, what'll I say?
TOÑA: I'll dictate it later.

MAXIMINO: Where do you plan to hang out all morning?

POLO: I don't know. Down by the railroad tracks.

TOÑA: That's the garbage dump!

POLO: We might find something. You can see the train go by.

TOÑA: Whatcha got here? Let me see! (*She pulls Maximino's wallet out of his back pocket.*)

POLO: I bet you he's broke.

TOÑA: Let's see.

She opens the wallet and examines its contents. Maximino and Polo watch her with masculine patience.

TOÑA: Hey! You turned out real handsome in this picture. Let me have it.

MAXIMINO: Yeah! The camera broke. Why do you want it?

TOÑA: Because I do. Give it to me.

MAXIMINO: I'll need it later on . . . and if I do then I won't have it.

TOÑA: Oh, come on, give it to me. I'll stick it on the mirror in my room.

POLO: She'll show it to her friends and tell 'em you're her sweetheart.

TOÑA: That's a lie. It's none of your business anyway. Oh, come on, give it to me.

MAXIMINO: All right, take it.

TOÑA: But you've got to write something on it. Please.

Maximino finds this very difficult. He takes his pencil and starts to write something.

MAXIMINO: Oh, what the hell, take it the way it is.

TOÑA: Go on, write something. Write something!

Maximino thinks. He sits down and writes with great effort. Then he stops, thinks again, and writes some more. Then he signs it with a great flourish that barely fits on the little piece of cardboard. He hands it to the girl somewhat shamefacedly.

(*Reading.*) "To my little friend Toña with sincere appreciation. Your friend Maximino González." Oh! I'm going to stick it on the mirror in my room, you'll see.

POLO: Friend isn't spelled with a "ph."

TOÑA: Aren't you the smart one! I suppose that's why you're still in the fifth grade. Let's see what else you've got. These your folks?

MAXIMINO: Yes.

TOÑA: Look, if these are your parents, who's this?

MAXIMINO: My girl friend.

TOÑA: That little skinny thing? Oh, she's ugly! . . . She's cross-eyed too!

MAXIMINO: You're the one who's cross-eyed. (*He takes the wallet away from her and puts it back in his pocket.*)

TOÑA: She *is* cross-eyed! One eye points to the north and the other one to the south.

Maximino takes his wallet out and examines the photograph. Then he holds it out.

MAXIMINO: Come on, where is she cross-eyed. Show me! Like hell she is! (*And he puts the wallet away.*)

TOÑA: She's cross-eyed.

MAXIMINO: I'll be seeing you.

TOÑA: Oh, I'm just kidding. She's not cross-eyed. Don't go!

MAXIMINO: I have to go change. It's late.

POLO: Go on.

MAXIMINO: I'll be seeing you. (*He starts out.*) Don't you need bus fare?

TOÑA: Yeah . . . but I didn't do my homework.

Maximino starts out.

Hey, when I have *my* picture taken I'll give you one. But you've got to carry it in your wallet, huh?

MAXIMINO: OK. (*He goes off.*)

TOÑA (*calling after him*): Be sure to say hello to little Miss Cockeyes for me. (*She laughs.*)

POLO: She really cross-eyed?

TOÑA: Sure! . . . Nah. (*She looks at the photograph.*) I'm going to stick it on my mirror.

POLO: Maximino's a great guy. He's all right.

They go off. The lights go off on them and come up on the dump. It is a great carpet of garbage surrounded by a few plants and branches. In the background we see the railroad tracks. It is bright daylight. The Scavengers walk about examining the garbage, picking up papers and stray bottles. They save some and discard others. One of the Scavengers steps on a piece of glass and hurts her foot. She exclaims softly, and goes off limping and grumbling. The man looks at the woman but goes on scavenging. He kneels down

*amid the garbage and discovers a shoe. He examines it
but leaves it behind. Polo and Toña enter upstage balancing
on the railroad track. The Scavenger was about to leave.
He has been gathering the things he wanted to save when he
sees the kids. He speaks to them.*

SCAVENGER (*in need of a drink*): Say, uh . . . you wouldn't
have five cents, would you?

POLO: No.

SCAVENGER: I need it . . . you know for a cure. I'm in a bad
way, sonny.

Polo shakes his head. The Scavenger starts off.

TOÑA: Oh, mister . . . Go on, Polo, give it to him! Mister,
come here!

Polo makes a face but gives him the money.

SCAVENGER (*mumbling so that he is scarcely understood*):
God bless you. Bless you. (*And he goes off.*) Yeah.

TOÑA: Did you give him everything?

POLO: Sure.

TOÑA: He only asked for five cents! Oh, you're so stupid!

POLO: You told me to give it to him!

TOÑA: But not everything . . . he only asked you for five
cents!!

POLO: You're crazy . . . and what's worse, you're dumb!

TOÑA: That's what you say . . . God, what a stink.

POLO: Garbage.

TOÑA: Smells of weeds, too. Real . . . real stinky weeds . . .
see them over there!? And it smells of . . . oh, look at the
flies! There's a dead animal somewhere, for sure! (*She
breaks into song, imitating some orchestral arrangement of
a dance tune.*)

POLO: You crazy?

TOÑA: You know how to dance? My sister taught me this one.
Look. (*She executes a step while she sings.*) You know
how?

POLO: Yes. (*He dances with her for a while and then he
backs away letting her dance by herself.*) Here's part of
an engine. (*He reaches into the garbage and pulls out an
unrecognizable piece of steel. He turns it about in his hands
examining it.*)

TOÑA: What's it for?

POLO: An engine. I'll take it to Maximino. (*He puts it down to one side.*)

TOÑA: I'm going to pick some flowers. (*She begins to pick the tiny, little flowers. All of a sudden she screams.*)

POLO: What's wrong.

TOÑA: I got pricked. It's got thorns. OOoogh, my, my, my! (*She sucks her finger then, truculently.*) Look . . . it drew blood. (*She sings and dances a new step, and picks more flowers.*)

POLO: I went to see the *Masked Avenger Against the Monsters* yesterday.

TOÑA: On Sunday I went to see the *Black Shadow of the Mansion* . . . Frightened me so much I screamed that night because I was having dreams.

POLO: What did you dream of?

TOÑA: I don't know. It was ugly . . . Those are wasps. Oh, look! There's lots of them. They sting!

POLO: Only if you're afraid of them. (*He balances on the railroad track.*) I hear there are guys that walk on a wire way up high and they carry a stick so's to hold their balance. They walk across the wire. You think it's true?

TOÑA: Sure. I've seen them in the movies.

POLO: Yeah, but in the movies that's all tricks.

TOÑA: I saw a woman who climbs up on a horse and stands up, you know. And then she stands on one foot like this and the horse runs around. I saw her . . . a circus.

POLO: When did you go to a circus?

TOÑA: Once . . . my father took me!

POLO: Your father's dead.

TOÑA: He took me before he died! He was pretty nice, my father. And there was a bear on a little bicycle . . .

POLO: What's so hard about riding a bicycle?

TOÑA: Well, it was damn hard for the bear. Look at the little flowers I got . . .

POLO: Not many.

TOÑA: I'll pick more later on. I don't want to be stung by a wasp. Hey . . . see that tub over there? That would be great for planting flowers! Gee, you could put a big plant inside of that one. (*It's a round zinc washtub. She goes to pick it up but she cannot lift it.*) It's heavy!

POLO: I'll bet! (*He gives her a Bronx cheer.*) What's the matter, can't you pick it up? (*He goes to her. He tries but cannot lift it. He tries again. It won't budge. He straddles it. He can't move it.)*

She laughs so hard she drops her flowers. She continues laughing as she picks them up.

What the hell! What's the matter with this thing, huh? (*He is actually scared of it.*)

Toña suddenly stops laughing. She too senses something unreal about the weight of the object.

TOÑA: Can't *you* move it?
POLO (*worried*): No.

Toña exclaims and moves away from it holding the flowers to her breast.

TOÑA: Gee, it's funny it should weigh so much!
POLO: Chicken! (*But he, too, moves away from the tub. There is a pause.*) Let's find out what the hell's the matter with it.
TOÑA: You'd better leave it alone.
POLO (*walking beside the tub cautiously*): I wonder why it's so heavy? (*Then, understanding.*) It's full of cement.
TOÑA: Yeah? I wonder why.
POLO: Must be one of those things bricklayers use or masons for . . . well I don't know . . . something. Look, it's full of cement!
TOÑA: So that's it. (*She examines it.*) Yeah, it *is* full of cement. You couldn't plant any plants in that. (*She starts singing and dancing again and puts some of the flowers in her hair.*) What do you think?
POLO (*pushing the tub with his foot*): Hey, you can roll it! Want to help me? Come on!
TOÑA: Wait a minute. (*She puts some more flowers in her hair.*) All right.

She helps him and the two of them push the tub.

TOÑA: Where will we take it?
POLO: To the other side of the tracks.

They roll the tub upstage.

It's harder if we go that way.

They push the tub in the most difficult direction, upstage and to the left. We hear a train whistle.

TOÑA: The train's coming! Hurry up!

They hurry. They are now at the very highest point. We hear the train whistle again. They look at each other.

THE TWO OF THEM: Let's put it on the tracks!

The idea makes them giggle nervously and happily as they push the tub. It is heavy and there are obstacles in the way. It starts to roll back but they push. The train whistles once more, closer. They push the tub, then run off. Whistles. The train approaches, the lights dim, and we hear the racket of a derailment. Darkness.

Flashes of lightning reveal the young pair as they stare with fascination. Darkness.

NEWSBOY (*we hear him in the dark*): Read all about the derailment! Great losses! Great losses! Disaster caused by delinquent children! The *Daily Press!* Get your *Daily Press!*

A spotlight comes up. The Medium now stands before an enormous book, which rests on a stand. She points out the enormous, yet meticulous engravings that are to be found on each page. They are perhaps old engravings in the style of Dürer, or of certain botanical and zoological illustrations of the German school of the nineteenth century, or of any old Mexican codices—perhaps all three. They are delicately tinted. She now wears somewhat lighter clothing.

THE MEDIUM: This book is full of animals. (*She opens it.*) I'll tell you about them. It's written here that a dog guards the physical integrity of his master. Alone among the beasts it is he who has a sense of property. He seems to intone, "My house, my patio, my tree, my money, my master, my love." He guards these things and defends them like a mad miser; *he* is the *first* to discover thieves, beggars, and creditors. He barks at them! attacks them! "I protect my love and I protect the world." His house is the hub of the world, he thinks. (*Another page.*) The cat, however, watches over the spiritual integrity of those to whom it has been assigned. He gathers up shadows and purges evil wills by making small, bloody sacrifices for the good of the home. He kills scurrying rat and shrill bird and startled chick and then, his prize between his teeth, he performs his ritual. When night falls, he climbs to the rooftops and there he analyzes the halos of the moon and waves of light . . . radio waves . . . vapors. He consults with the air and is given secret assignments. Then he runs off howling hair-raising cries and perpetuates himself . . . or he might succumb to the corrupt seduction of some secret ray destined for a person that is dear to him. That's why certain cats appear enigmatic. (*Another page.*) The hen is a storehouse of nourishment. Daily and with sweet efforts it gives us eggs that satisfy a rigorous aesthetic and encase within their shells an enormous explosion of chicken coops and such eternal questions as "Who was first, the chicken or . . ." But beware in cracking an egg, if the whites are cloudy or if the yolk is murky, some old crone may have used that egg to draw away a bodyful of passions and diseases! You may have broken the small box of a local Pandora! And while she enjoys her new-found health, we may be just a spoon away from swallowing her old evils. (*Another page.*) Beware of goldfish. They swim in little circles—weaving and unweaving! The twists and turns of oceanic writing! They see beyond the crystal with little dead eyes and wave their fins invitingly summoning scaly maladies. They turn, go, and come making signs that one should best ignore, signs we understand when it is too late. Beware of aquariums, their best sentinels are cats. (*Another page.*) Butterflies are most profound, saying such things as "fleetingness" . . . and "mystery." They say, "We love surprises!" They say, "Everything is possible!" They say, "All things matter!" (*Another page.*) And there are snakes, with a dark and burning secret on the tips of their tongues. (*Another page.*) The bees . . . know *all* about solar energy and light. Things we don't suspect! Oh, there are many, many books and many, many warnings. (*She nods her head and brings her finger to her lips as the lights dim out.*)

A vertical light falls upon the forestage. We see a newsstand. The boy who sells the papers stands to one side. A Gentleman and a Lady stand examining the display of newspapers.

LADY (*eating something*): There's not a word about the trunk murder . . . the body was cut into bits!

GENTLEMAN: Seems that a pair of delinquents derailed a train. Barbaric! Absolutely barbaric! Seems that they rolled a tub full of cement onto the tracks.

LADY (*her mind on something else*): Little savages, that's what they are. All of them. They're all a bunch of savages. (*Then suddenly interested.*) Any casualties?

GENTLEMAN: No, it was a freight train. The cars were overturned. . . . Look at their faces, will you! Says here that they were twelve and fourteen years old . . . They look forty.

Projected on the background we see two blowups of Toña and Polo, as sinister as all police mug shots. They look frightened and much older. Photographs taken at the moment of some nervous twitch.

LADY (*absentmindedly*): It's just vice and crime . . . vice and crime! Those people are criminal from the day they are born.

GENTLEMAN (*looking to see if the bus is coming*): It's poverty that does it.

LADY: Oh, yes, their poverty's something awful. But they didn't say anything about the trunk murder, huh?

GENTLEMAN: Here comes a bus. (*They move off to get on the bus.*)

THE NEWSPAPER PEDDLER: *Daily Press*! Get your *Daily Press*! Latest news!

Blackout.

The lights come up on the Teacher who walks downstage. She is densely powdered, tightly permanented, with a small red mouth, about sixty years old.

TEACHER: Before we start class, I must inform you of some very sad and shameful news for this school. One of your companions, Leopoldo Bravo, has committed a criminal act and now finds himself in prison. As the newspapers put it, it was all due to idleness and . . . (*She reads.*) and "loose living!" That boy was repeating fifth grade and I haven't the faintest idea why he was readmitted! Next year and in the future we are not going to readmit students that have been flunked out! Is that clear! Idleness and stupidity

and well, lack of civic spirit! (*She reads.*) "The juvenile
delinquents stayed by the side of the railroad tracks to
witness their ghastly deed. They were easily captured."
(*She grunts and looks for another passage.*) "One must also
blame the lack of parental supervision." (*She grunts her
approval again.*) "One must attack those parents who allow
their children to drift into idleness as well as the irrespon-
sibility of the schools and the teach . . ." (*She stops speaking suddenly and folds the paper.*) Well, now you know all
about it. I brought it to your attention because it contains
a lesson for all of us. The dangers of idleness. You,
Martínez Pedro, who never do your homework, take it to
heart! Your chum, your "buddy," is in jail! And you,
Antúnez, take care. If you fail you will not be readmitted
to this school and be sure to remember that you must all
of you have your white uniforms by Monday. No later!
If you don't have them you will not be admitted! There are
no excuses and don't tell me that you don't have enough
money to buy them! You certainly have enough money for
other things. And now let us examine fractions. Let me
see . . . you, Antúnez! Tell us, what is a common denominator? . . .

Blackout.

*The lights come up on university students reading a news-
paper.*

GIRL STUDENT: Did you see this? A couple of little squirts de-
railed a train. Look at 'em. See?
STUDENT: Hey, wild! Anyone killed? (*He reads.*)
GIRL STUDENT: No. Fortunately. It was a freight train.
STUDENT: God. What knuckleheads. They really did it up
good. (*He laughs.*)
GIRL STUDENT: Two cars overturned . . . the engine smashed
through a tree. It's a mess! (*She laughs.*) Anyway, it would
be fun to do a thing like that, wouldn't it?
STUDENT: Wild, man, wild!
GIRL STUDENT: What kids! That's what I call inspired!

They laugh. Dim out.

*The lights come up in the shop. Maximino is working on
a motor. The telephone rings.*

MAXIMINO: Hello? Larranaga's Garage. Speaking. Yes, I'm

Maximino. Oh, hi! Friends of mine? Which ones? In jail!
That can't be! You mean the kids? Oh, I bet they caught
them in the telephone booth. They did . . . what? A train?
You mean to say that they derailed a train! You sure?
Well, where did they take them? Ooooh sssh . . . (*Then he
whistles.*) That's rough! Oh, how can that be? Oh, well,
I'll have to see what I can do. Yeah, they're friends of mine.
Thanks for calling. Yeah, good-bye. (*He hangs up. He
stares for a moment, thinking.*)

*The owner of the garage enters. He is dressed in denim
trousers and shirt.*

MAXIMINO: Hey, Don Pepe, I've got to take off. They've
arrested a couple of friends of mine.

DON PEPE: What have you got to do with it?

MAXIMINO: They just called me up to let me know. They're
just kids . . . you know. I take care of them, like wards,
you know?

DON PEPE: What did they do? Why did they arrest them?

MAXIMINO: They derailed a train.

DON PEPE (*terrified*): Communists!

MAXIMINO: No, no! Two little squirts, that's all. You know,
kids. You know them, I bring them here sometimes on the
motorcycle. Polo and Toña.

DON PEPE (*moving his head*): You must be wrong. Just
something to a street car, hitching a ride . . . or something
like that.

MAXIMINO: No, a train. A railroad train. They say they derailed it . . . overturned it . . . I . . . I don't know.

DON PEPE: All right, take off. But be back in an hour . . .
and finish that job. It was a rush order.

MAXIMINO: Sure, sure.

DON PEPE: And if you're late, stay after hours.

MAXIMINO: Oh, sure, sure. (*He starts out.*) Don Pepe, if
they should need it, uh, well, could you . . . could you
lend me some money?

DON PEPE: I knew that was coming . . . I could feel it in
my bones! What's the matter, don't they have any family?

MAXIMINO: Well, I don't think they can afford it.

DON PEPE: We'll see. We'll talk about it later. We'll see.

MAXIMINO: Thanks. (*He goes out.*)

DON PEPE: But what the hell were they doing around a train?!

Dim out.

Lights up on the dump. A happy male Scavenger is coming from the train, carrying a large pack or sack.

SCAVENGER: Hurry up, woman! There are a whole bunch scattered over there in front of the car!

WOMAN SCAVENGER (*comes running over to the train*): I carried off a whole sack of beans.

SCAVENGER: And there's sugar too. This train was loaded with food! (*They run off opposite sides of the stage.*)

A poor Boy and a Girl enter.

GIRL: You're sure it's all right?

BOY: There's no one around. Go on, go on. Look, the car's open.

GIRL: It's overturned.

BOY: What did you expect. And there's no one to stop us! Hurry up! The police will be here any minute.

GIRL: Weren't there any people on the train?

BOY: They went off to testify. (*They run off.*)

The Woman Scavenger returns carrying two large sacks. She can barely carry them. She sees two other people coming and she says to them.

WOMAN SCAVENGER: Hurry up . . . there are all kinds of things!

A Woman enters covered with a shawl. She is very poor.

WOMAN: Holy Mother of God, isn't there anyone standing guard?

WOMAN SCAVENGER: They left a few guards but when they saw the food they picked up some sacks and ran off with them. Took them home. (*She has caught her breath and now runs off.*) There's no one here now.

WOMAN: Holy Virgin, Mother of God! But this is nothing less than stealing! (*She speaks to a Man who is approaching.*) Sir, sir . . . will it be all right to take something from the train? . . . What do you think?

MAN: What? . . . You mean you can?!

WOMAN: They say there's no one standing guard. I don't think it would be stealing, do you?

MAN (*thinks about it*): Well, as I see it . . . It's stealing. No two ways about it.
WOMAN: Oh, dear God. (*She crosses herself.*)
MAN (*trying to convince her*): Absolutely.
WOMAN: Those bags look so heavy!
MAN: . . . I'll help you. Where do you live?
WOMAN: Over there, by the outskirts.
MAN: I live there too. Come on, come on!
WOMAN: But my husband's so respectable, so jealous! What if someone told him that they saw me come in with you? Oh, that would be the end of me!

They go running off. The poor children come back carrying sacks.

GIRL: Hurry before they take it all away!
BOY: They can't . . . not in twenty trips!
GIRL: I'm going to fetch my sister. She's little but she can carry something.

They run off and the Man and Woman come back loaded down.

WOMAN: Oh, Virgin Mary, Mother of God, I really do think this is stealing!
MAN: Stealing . . . shmealing . . . what the hell! It's corn and beans!
WOMAN: Oh, I'm going to tell my brothers. They've got so many children! It's a pity mine are in school. They could help. Oh, but this is heavy!

They go off and meet the Scavengers on the way.

SCAVENGER: I'm going to put it all inside my pack.
WOMAN SCAVENGER: And we'd better cover it over with newspapers in case they catch us. I told my sister-in-law. I mean, she's got a right to her slice of the cake, huh? And the kids will be here in a minute.
SCAVENGER: We've got to tell all of them! There's enough for everyone!

They run off. Dim out.

The Medium enters. Her clothes are even lighter colored than before. Her story will be illustrated by two dancers.

THE MEDIUM: Now I'm going to tell you the story of the two who dreamed. They were good men . . . full of faith. One of them lived in the town of Chalma, famous for its sanctuary, and the other in the town of Chalco, also famous for its sanctuary. In one version of the story we are told that these men were brothers. Another version claims that they were twins and resembled each other amazingly. And yet another version says that they were just friends. It came to pass that these two men had a dream, during the same night, at the same hour, each in his own town . . . they dreamed. And this was the dream they dreamed: a wonderful figure, radiant and covered with miraculous signs, warned each of them. "Go at once to your brother's town. Before three days pass, you must be with him. The two of you together must dance and pray at the great sanctuary next to your brother's house." And then, in their dream, they knelt to the figure and agreed. Then the figure thundered, "Before three days have passed . . . no later! The two of you, together, not separately, but together . . . and at the great sanctuary next to your brother's house!" They awoke, amazed, and told their wives of their dream, and as they told it they still could hear the sound of many bells and the music of a flute. Each set out from his town, one from Chalma on the way to Chalco, the other from Chalco on the way to Chalma in order to tell the other the news and carry out the miraculous command. After a day's journey they met at the very midpoint of their route. In turn each told the other his dream and they were alike . . . like a mirror with two opposing images . . . for they could not then know to which town to go. Was it Chalma or Chalco? They tossed a coin in the air but it fell to the ground and was lost in a crevice of the earth. "It's a sign," they said, and so they made camp on that very spot to wait for yet another sign . . . another dream. They ate, they slept, and then woke up. Their time was running out. No sign came. Their fear . . . their terror of that perplexing vision grew in them, but the sign did not come. Soon it was time to go to the sanctuary but there was no time to reach either one. The sign never came and so they fulfilled their command where they were. It was a barren place covered with weeds and rocks. They cleared it with machetes and moved enough rocks aside to make a space the size of an atrium for a

small . . . a very small church. Night came upon them and
a gentle breeze dried the sweat of their bodies. They had
a few drinks of mescal and then danced and prayed. They
danced in that complicated rhythm inherited from their
ancestors. They prayed the prayers they had learned in
childhood. Two tired, dirty men adorned with feathers and
mirrors danced and prayed in nocturnal ambiguity, in that
wilderness . . . without answers. There under a shower of
pollen sprayed from the goldenrod they prayed. Their time
was up and they knew no better way of satisfying the
arbitrary being that had spoken in their dream. They said
farewell and took their leave, long before the sky was
shattered by the dawn. They left—both feeling the designs
of providence had been only half-fulfilled. (*She starts to
go off. When she is almost off, she stops and turns around.*)
And do you know what happened to that plot the two
men had cleared for their dance and prayers? (*She is
silent. She looks at everyone. A teasing smile creeps across
her mouth.*) But that's another story. Just another story.
(*She goes off hurriedly.*)

Dim out.

NEWSBOY (*holding out his newspapers*): Delinquent rascals!
Read all about the young rascals! Half a million dollars
damage! Half a million lost in prank by delinquent kids!
News! News! Get your *Daily Press*. (*He goes off.*)

*Lights come up on Toña's Mother. She is packing a small
bag of food and carries several packages. One of her
daughters (Paca) comes in. She is carrying a newspaper.*

PACA: Here's another picture of Toña.
MOTHER: Let's see. Oh, that's awful! She looks ugly!
PACA: She looked better in the other one. What are you
taking to her?
MOTHER: A wrap, some clothes, and candy . . . the kind she
liked. But it's so far away. I'll try to make it on time today.
If I'm late they won't let me in. You'll have to take my
place at the hospital tomorrow. That's the only way I'll
get there in time to see your sister. I've already told them
about it.
PACA: You mean I've got to empty those garbage pails?
MOTHER: If your mother can empty them you can too!

PACA: But I wanted to go with you to see Toña.

MOTHER: You're going to stay here and take care of your sisters. And make sure *they* don't go around derailing trains.

PACA: But what a crazy thing for Toña to do! (*She laughs.*)

MOTHER: Don't laugh. It's no joke.

PACA: But who'd ever think of a thing like that? Toña's crazy.

MOTHER (*almost laughing*): Oh, Toña. She was always one for getting into trouble. (*She thinks about it.*) But I don't think they'll let her out soon.

PACA: You mean they're going to keep her in prison?

MOTHER: It's not a prison! It's a . . . well . . . like a boarding school. (*She wipes her eyes.*) She needs her father, that's what. Oh, why did she have to go and do a thing like that?!

PACA: The paper says some awful things about her.

MOTHER: Give it here. (*She is about to tear it up in her anger.*)

PACA: Wait! Let me cut the picture! And look at how funny Polo looks! What a face!

MOTHER: Oh, the poor girl! The one who helped me most. Such a good girl. Poor thing.

PACA (*tearing out the picture*): Well, I think they're going to let her out. I mean, why would they keep her locked up? Fat chance she'll ever pay for the train!

MOTHER: They say it's to keep her from doing it again. (*She takes the newspaper and tears it up without conviction, sadly, slowly, into several pieces.*)

PACA: Oh, well, if she's going to go on derailing trains . . .

MOTHER: Oh, it's so late I don't think we can ever get there in time today. Yesterday a man at the gate told me to leave the things with him. Fat chance. They're a bunch of thieves! All those guards!

PACA (*taking off her pin*): Here, give her this pin. She always liked it and I used to get angry at her when she put it on. Tell her it's a gift.

MOTHER: All right. We've got to tell the school we don't know when she's going to come back. I think she's going to lose the year, that's what. (*They go out.*)

The lights change and come up on Polo who sits in one chair, his Mother is in another under the shadows of the prison bars. The Mother is crying.

MOTHER: This *would* happen to us! It's not enough your father was a drunken good-for-nothing but you had to turn out rotten too . . . a highwayman. It's all over the newspapers! I've already warned them out there they shouldn't get the idea that we can pay for that train! What with? The lady where I work . . . when she saw your picture . . . oh, she was so frightened! I thought she was going to fire me. Work, work, work, so that you'd have a chance to study and now look! I should have let your father beat you whenever he wanted to. He was right! It's all my fault for having spoiled you. But what I want to know is why the hell you were so stupid! . . . you and that idiot girl! Why did you have to stay there, huh? What's the matter, don't you know how to run? But you just stayed there looking until the police came and arrested you.

POLO (*quietly*): It wasn't the police.

MOTHER: What?

POLO (*quietly*): It wasn't the police. It was the engineer from the train.

MOTHER: And you couldn't run? What are your legs for? (*She starts to cry.*) Just when I was going to buy you shoes out of next month's pay! . . . The lady I work for, she knows a good lawyer. But heaven only knows how much he'll cost. And the newspapers say that the train was worth half a million dollars! (*She loses her temper and starts to shake him.*) Oh, you're so stupid! I should beat you to death! Look at him! Sitting there so . . . so . . . meek as a lamb! Snot-nosed, idiot louse that you are! Now look what you've come to? (*She breaks out sobbing.*) Now they're going to keep you here for I don't know how long! Thrown in with all those filthy criminals. Your father was right! I spoiled you! Keeping you tied to my apron strings! I miss you all the time. I've even thought . . . God forgive me . . . why didn't God take one of your other brothers instead of you! But that's the way it is when you love someone . . . we always love the ones we shouldn't. Oh, Polo, how are we ever going to get you out of here? How will we ever do it?

Darkness.

The Newsboy enters. Instead of print his newspapers are now covered with stains that resemble Rorschach tests. He holds them out so the audience can see them and cries.

NEWSBOY: Get your *Daily Press*! Latest news in your *Daily Press*. Schizoid children induce a public trauma! One moment of unconsciousness causes a five-hundred thousand dollar shock! The *Daily Press*! Get your latest news! *Daily Press*! (*He walks off.*)

The first Professor enters. He dresses meticulously.

PROFESSOR: Our century has tended to place increasing and specific emphasis upon collective problems. In a way, it's only natural. We live massively, that is to say, in masses. Industrialization, syndicalization, the enormous urban problems, all these summon before our eyes great human conglomerations, great conglomerations of . . . (*He smiles.*) *of individuals.* And it is here that we discover our real nucleus, in the self, that complex self composed of many layers wrapped one within the other like . . . well, like the petals of a rose. We are intricate beings and the word "complex" has taken such roots in our everyday speech that it is used . . . well, even by the average patient . . . ah, what I mean is the average *man*! We use this word as though we were referring to the very gears that move and control the strings and fibers of our everyday behavior, gears that lead us to the very source of traumatic nuclei. And it is our duty to make the patient aware of them and thus guide him until he discovers for himself the secret reasons that lie hidden behind his impulses, the unconscious controls, the frustration of our acts, very much in the manner of some sort of explicit formulation. And our most neutral conversations manifest the weight of hidden content which, when interpreted correctly, leads us to a proper diagnosis of all aberrational conduct. Let us take, for example, this terrible act, difficult to understand, when one tries to explain it as a conscious and rational deed. Two adolescents derail a train. Well, it just so happens that there are certain antecedent factors that will permit us to explain concretely the hidden and submerged impulses that gave rise to the case. Now, as we formulate them, we shall see how the *whole* matter becomes logical and coherent! (*He moves to one side.*) Polo is in the telephone booth endeavoring to extract a coin from the telephone. Toña stands guard. Now I want you to observe the symbolic content of the phrase "*stands* guard." (*We see Polo and*

Toña as described.) Keep in mind please that telephones are symbols of *sexual* communication.

TOÑA: When I was a little girl, I noticed that dogs *did . . . things* with each other. You know, "things." That is . . . until my mother came and threw a bucket of water on them to separate them and then made me stand guard so that they wouldn't come together again. Therefore, now I stand guard in order to interrupt the communication. Hurry and get the coin out. There's a man coming to use the telephone.

Polo joins Toña. A man enters.

(*Fiercely.*) It's broken. You can't use the telephone.

The man walks off, frustrated. Polo goes back and extracts the coin.

POLO: My father drinks and he always wants to beat me. I don't love him. I got the coin out of the phone. I'm glad I interrupted the communication. With this coin I'm going to buy a banana and I'll give it to you.

TOÑA: But I want sesame candy! My father always gave me sesame candy.

They act out the coin-flipping scene at breakneck speed. They resemble a silent movie.

PROFESSOR: Now they're trying to lose the money they've obtained as rapidly as possible. This of course reveals the symbolic nature of their act as well as their hidden guilt and desires for self-punishment.

Maximino enters and Toña hangs on his arm.

TOÑA: You're my father image! I want to ride with you on your motorcycle.

PROFESSOR: Motorcycles are also sexual symbols.

POLO: And I too want to ride with you on your motorcycle.

PROFESSOR: Abnormal sexuality is really normal in all human beings. Incest, fetishism, homosexuality are, normally speaking, latent in all of us. They are simple stages that we outgrow, unless, of course, we encounter traumatic elements along the way that produce a regression.

MAXIMINO: My motorcycle is busted.

POLO: What happened?
MAXIMINO: I cracked up and the piston's all bent.

Toña laughs.

PROFESSOR: Did you notice her laughter?
POLO (*passionately*): She doesn't know anything about motorcycles. I do! Pay attention to me. Me! Pay attention to me!
TOÑA (*to Maximino*): Your trouble is that your motorcycle is
all worn out! And now I'm looking for an excuse to touch
your body!
POLO: Don't touch him!

She removes the wallet from Maximino's pocket.

TOÑA: Hey, you look pretty good in this picture. Give it to
me. Write something on it. I'll keep it.
PROFESSOR: Fetishism.

Maximino writes.

POLO (*truculently*): You prefer her to me and you spell
friend with a "ph." I want that picture for myself . . . but
I don't dare ask you for it! I'd like to blow you up . . .
both of you . . . her and you.
TOÑA: I hate your sweetheart. I hate her! I'd kill her! I'd
like to pluck her eyes out! She's cross-eyed! She's horrible!
(*She spits.*)
PROFESSOR: So we witness the birth of a first destructive impulse. Note the association of sweetheart and worn-out
motorcycle.

Maximino leaves.

Now, here we are at the dump next to the railroad tracks.
I don't believe that it will be necessary to point out that
by nature there exists within each and everyone of us a
veritable garbage dump!

*The garbage dump . . . but now the various plants and
objects are in distinct sexual configurations. Toña and Polo
dance and sing.*

Observe the very mechanism of the dance. Notice the mu-
tual release and discharge of the libido! Polo fluctuates

between virile and passive attitudes. Toña is alternately both mother and lover!

The dance comes to an end. Polo thrusts up the broken piece of the engine. It now has a very "suspicious" shape.

POLO: Hey, here's part of a motor. I'm going to take it to Maximino.

TOÑA: Blood! Look! I've been deflowered!

POLO: I saw a movie in which the superego fights sadistically and triumphs.

TOÑA: On Sunday *I* went to see a symbolic realization of masochistic incest. Later on I dreamed about all manner of pleasures . . . but my self-censorship woke me up . . . screaming with guilt! Naturally, I've forgotten all about it.

POLO (*balancing on the rails*): Tightrope walkers are like a dream of flight come true.

PROFESSOR: Dreams of flying are simply realizations of sexual impulses.

TOÑA: I identified with a bareback rider who rode a galloping horse while standing on one foot! My father took me to the circus!

PROFESSOR: Horses are sexual symbols too.

TOÑA (*very excited*): Bears on bicycles, horses at a gallop! A circus full of all kinds of male beasts! Virginal flowers pursued by all kinds of large wasps with huge stingers that sting and draw blood! And over there . . . there's a round tub as empty as my womb . . . a tub in which we can plant flowers!

Polo goes to lift the tub. He can't.

POLO: This womb is fascinating and frightening . . . maternal!

TOÑA: I'm scared of it too. It frightens me.

POLO: We must roll it to the other side of the tracks.

PROFESSOR: Tracks, communication . . . an identical symbol with that of a telephone! Now we are going to witness the reconciliation of all contradiction . . . as in dreams! The *impulse* that forces us to cross tracks of life! Get the symbol? And at the same time the impulse that forces us to obstruct the path.

Polo and Toña go around and around the tub, screaming.

POLO: Incest! Libido! Maximino!
TOÑA: Defloration! Maximino! Father!
THE TWO OF THEM: Womb! Jealousy! Crime!

We hear the approaching train.

PROFESSOR: Psychology! Whenever man's conduct appears to be inexplicable . . . psychology will lay it bare!

We hear the terrible sound of the derailment.
Dim out.

Flashes of lightning.
Blackout.

Lights dim up upon the Newsboy. He is peddling news-papers that are printed in red on black.

NEWS VENDOR: Latest news! Latest news! Routes of communi-cation disrupted! Derailment! Significant protest against in-justice to the workers. Read your *Daily Press*! Today's *Daily Press*! Read your *Daily Press*! (*He goes off.*)

The second Professor enters. He dresses somewhat care-lessly and a bit out of fashion.

PROFESSOR: The individual cannot be judged except insofar as he is judged in the context of his fusion into the collec-tive. The isolated individual does not exist. We are *social* beings. Robinson Crusoe lived solely in relationship to a society from which he had been accidently separated. We are all of us witnesses of the event commented upon so extensively in the press. It is without any question a clear expression of class struggle. Protagonists: two children of the proletariat.

The scene in the telephone booth is repeated.

TOÑA: Hurry up. Here comes a petit bourgeois.

The man walks in.

The telephone is out of order. Since the telephone company is a monopoly it gives very poor service. The phones are always out of order.

The man becomes angry, curses the telephone, and then goes away. The children laugh at him.

PROFESSOR: Notice the workings of ingenuity, the best recourse and most typical weapon of the people. Here, in the presence of this machine, which is not at her disposal or within her proletarian economic reach, the girl expresses her first gesture of rebellion.

Toña beats the telephone and shakes it and gets the coin.

TOÑA: What will we buy?
POLO: Bananas. They're full of nourishment.
TOÑA: Sesame candy. They have more calories!
POLO: We didn't eat enough breakfast.
TOÑA: That's typical of the capitalist society in which we live!
PROFESSOR: Now, notice how devalued currency and diminished purchasing power give rise to a compensatory interest in gambling! The addiction to gambling is a typical symptom of underdeveloped countries! Gambling becomes the vice of the proletariat.

We see in pantomime the tossing of the coins and the purchase of the jicamas.

TOÑA: Aren't you going to school?
POLO: I can't.
TOÑA: Why?
POLO: Because of the exaggerated economic demands imposed by a bad educational system. The expenses of bus fare and the demands of the teacher . . . How can I?
TOÑA: There are not enough local schools and the teachers behave that way just to scare us off.
PROFESSOR. We are now going to encounter a living compendium of the youthful aspirations of a young worker.

Maximino enters. His clothes are very clean, impeccably ironed. He is radiant.

An authentic representative of his class: exploited, socially responsible, self-sacrificing, incorruptible, fraternal, vigorous, alert. By his example he plants within these children the highest ideals and principles.

MAXIMINO: Where do you plan to spend the rest of the morning?
POLO: We'll look around . . . we might go down by the railroad tracks.
TOÑA: It's just a garbage dump down there!

POLO: But you can find useful things sometimes and you can see the train go by!

PROFESSOR: In Maximino's expression the children can read his disappointment at how corrupt syndicalism has betrayed the workers to the power of capitalism. How it has made it possible for the trains in which our very own revolution was carried forward now to be loaded down with the goods of the monopolies!

They examine each other's faces. She sees Maximino's wallet.

And now the young girl asks for a photograph. She's not one to enthrone the false idols of a cinematographic industry . . . an industry devoted exclusively to the ends of rank imperialism! *She* is going to cherish the image of a comrade!

TOÑA: Who's this?

MAXIMINO: My sweetheart.

TOÑA (*looking at her carefully, then speaking cautiously*): She's cross-eyed. One eye points to the north and the other one to the south!

MAXIMINO: What do you mean by that?

TOÑA: It's just that . . . she's a little middle class, and her ideas couldn't help but be cross-eyed. You'd better watch out.

Maximino goes off very worried.

PROFESSOR: And now we will witness a sample of those dances with which capitalism manages to corrupt the true spirit of the people.

Toña and Polo do a ridiculous dance. The dump is now altered and instead of sexual symbols, one makes out the trade names of many Yankee products: chewing gum, soda pop, etc., etc.

The authentic expression of joy in these children should be something other than this . . . something like . . .

Toña and Polo dance a jarabe tapatío[2].

Note that the dump is an eloquent symbol of what it means to have undisciplined industry and production. It is proof

---

[2] The *jarabe tapatío* is a popular Mexican folkdance.

positive of the false values that capitalism fosters and creates. And now, behold the fraternal relationships between these youngsters and the downtrodden proletariat.

Male Scavenger comes on, very sick.

MALE SCAVENGER: Please, won't you help me. I'm so sick! I need help.

TOÑA: Yes, why don't you help him. They don't have social security.

POLO: Neither do we. That's only for the privileged few.

They exchange a comradely good-bye with the Scavenger. Presently they see the tub and are amazed. They give each other a conspiratorial look and then return to examine the tub more closely.

PROFESSOR: We are now witnessing the uncertain gestures and signs that reveal the birth of a social conscience. Extreme contradictions produce extreme results.

TOÑA: Leave that tub alone. It frightens me.

POLO: Fear is a springboard of all revolutions.

TOÑA: One must fell a certain number of trees in order to preserve the forest.

POLO: Who can blame the woodsman for leveling the forest in order to sow the ground with seed.

We hear a hymn. The children push the tub with heroic gestures. We hear the train and the sounds of the derailment.

Darkness.

Lightning flashes. Only this time the flashes of lightning last a bit longer in order for us to perceive quite clearly that the children are posed in heroic and statuesque postures, while the Scavengers and the other persons of the neighborhood loot the train in a triumphal procession. Maximino enters and completes the heroic and sculptural tableau.

PROFESSOR: Man is Economy! All of Life rests upon the infrastructure of economy. There is nothing inexplicable in this act. It is typical of its class. Even down to the lack of true intellectual direction.

Dim out.

The lights come up on Maximino and Toña seated under the shadow of prison bars.

MAXIMINO: But how stupid can you be? Whatever made you think of derailing a train?

TOÑA (*quickly*): Nothing. We just wanted to see what would happen.

MAXIMINO: Well, now you know! Didn't it ever occur to you that someone might be killed?

TOÑA: Later . . . but then it was too late. That's why we didn't run away. We were so scared we couldn't move. We just stayed there, like statues. And it was a mess! Oh, it was real ugly.

MAXIMINO: Well, what did you expect? The engine half turned over. Three whole freight cars rolled over and broken open. And then the whole neighborhood came out and stole everything. Do you know how much that little game of yours cost? Half a million dollars!

TOÑA (*she thinks*): How much is that?

MAXIMINO: How stupid can you be?! I tried to see if I could get you out by paying your fine but—fat chance. Your joke was too damned expensive. (*Pause.*)

TOÑA (*truculently*): There's some girls in jail with me that were arrested because they threw boiling water on a man, when he came to collect the rent. They claimed they didn't do it on purpose. . . . What do you think? . . . And then there's a girl who used to sell marijuana. And there's another one who used to make her living by showing off little girls . . . naked . . . you know. Then the mothers of the little girls caught her. But she says that the little girls like to show off that way. . . . What do you think? . . . And then there's another one . . .

MAXIMINO (*desperately*): Don't you have anything to do with them, do you hear! Don't you talk to them! None of them!

TOÑA: But they're nice girls . . . and they're a hell of a lot sharper than the girls at school. They nearly died laughing when I told them I derailed a train.

MAXIMINO: You see! I don't want you to talk to them anymore! They're just a pack of stupid bitches . . . pigs . . . and criminals!

TOÑA (*sadly*): Is that what the papers say I am?

MAXIMINO (*putting his arm around Toña*): . . . Well . . . anyway, don't have anything to do with them! (*Pause.*)

TOÑA: At night . . . I'm scared. I wake up . . . I don't know where I am! And my cot smells of pee because the girl that had it before used to wet her bed. You know, they won't tell me when I'm going to get out of here. Some of the girls say I'll be here for years! Imagine.

MAXIMINO: We'll get you out of here. You'll see . . . Oh, now, don't cry! (*He tries to make her feel better.*) Anyway, you're famous now. Your picture's been in all the papers and everything! If you're lucky they'll give you a job in the movies!

TOÑA: Fat chance! My pictures were awful; they didn't even look like me!

MAXIMINO: You looked fine! Here. (*He takes out his wallet.*) See. I've got your picture.

TOÑA: You've got it in your wallet! Oh . . . I didn't see that picture, it was so small. Hey, what if little cross-eyes sees my picture in your wallet? Hey, let me look at her picture. See, see. Look at her close now! Is she or isn't she cross-eyed?

MAXIMINO: No more cross-eyed than you . . . No! She's not!

TOÑA: No?

MAXIMINO: Well, she just looks that way because . . . well, because of the way she's standing. See. She's looking off to the side.

TOÑA (*taking advantage of the attention he has paid her*): Why don't you get rid of that picture? Just keep mine, huh? (*Pause. They look at each other. Toña speaking in earnest.*) Just mine? Huh?

MAXIMINO: All right. From now on I won't carry any other picture.

TOÑA: Swear?

MAXIMINO: Promise.

TOÑA (*hugs him weepily*): And come to see me whenever you can. I want you to come and see me lots and lots and lots of times!

He embraces her.

The lights shift and come up on the dump. It is a night scene. The Scavengers of the previous scene plus two more, male and female, are seated around the fire.

FIRST SCAVENGER: It may be poor and rickety but I'll say one thing about my house, it's warm. I built it myself out of some boards I found . . . and some old broken boxes. I made the roof out of some sheet metal I stole from a chicken coop over there. Yep! Well . . . when do you plan to come and pay us a real visit?

SECOND WOMAN SCAVENGER: That's up to you.

FIRST SCAVENGER: Well . . . in honor of your company I'm going to dedicate this little old song to you. (*He sings, accompanying himself on the guitar.*)

> You're a rose of the few
> That bends with the dew
> It's a pity you're dry now
> You're nothing but thorns, ow!
> The light of your eyes . . .
> Bright as cloudy skies!
> And the curves of your legs
> Are as graceful as kegs!

SECOND WOMAN SCAVENGER: If you're going to insult me . . . I warn you!

FIRST SCAVENGER (*laughing*): Pass me the bottle. (*He drinks.*)

SECOND SCAVENGER: The next thing you'll be telling me you got the tequila from the train too!

FIRST SCAVENGER: In a way we did . . . we sold a little bag of chick-peas!

FIRST WOMAN SCAVENGER: We got the tamales by trading off a few pounds of sugar.

SECOND WOMAN SCAVENGER (*intimately*): You can tell the master of this house is a very important man! He has a way with money . . . doesn't he!

FIRST WOMAN SCAVENGER: I'm pretty good at that myself.

SECOND SCAVENGER: Well, they're right, you know, when they say it's better to have bad company than no company at all!

FIRST WOMAN SCAVENGER: Go on, say whatever you like . . . it's water off a duck's back to me!

FIRST SCAVENGER (*sings again*):

> Your sweet little voice
> Makes the tomcats rejoice!
> Teeth brighter than pennies
> But you're missing so many!
> Your throat's like a stream;
> Your songs flow like a scream!

And your breath is as sweet
As the smell of your feet.

They all shout and applaud.

FIRST WOMAN SCAVENGER: If you can sing that about me, just think what I could sing about you. Nah, I didn't like the song.

FIRST SCAVENGER: Really? Didn't you like it? Not even a little bit?

FIRST WOMAN SCAVENGER: Now why should I like to have things like that sung to me? What are you thinking of?

FIRST SCAVENGER: Hey, come on. Snuggle up a bit. It's cold.

FIRST WOMAN SCAVENGER: No, thank you, I'm very well where I am.

FIRST SCAVENGER: You snuggle up a little closer and you'll see. Come on, come on, snuggle up.

FIRST WOMAN SCAVENGER: I don't know why you're making such a fuss about my snuggling up . . . (*She does so.*) when you turn around and sing nothing but insults to me.

FIRST SCAVENGER (*putting his arm around her*): Later on I'll sing very pretty to you, very pretty! You'll see, you'll see!

SECOND SCAVENGER: How about sharing that bottle? 'Cause my little woman and I . . . we got to warm up, too, huh? What do you say, my little old sow? (*He gives her a hug.*)

Darkness.

Lights come up on Maximino talking on the telephone at the garage.

MAXIMINO: What happened? Well, no, no, I couldn't go. Well . . . there wasn't a telephone around. I couldn't let you know. No, I . . . think whatever you want. I didn't say I'd stay here. Yes, working . . . but someplace else. . . . What do you mean where! If you want to I'll give you the address and you can go and check up on me! . . . Look, I'm going to hang up because the boss gets mad if I talk on the phone too long! . . . Well, then don't talk to me anymore if you don't want to. . . . That's your business! . . . Well, sure I do. But you said that you didn't want to talk to me and that's your business. (*He makes a gesture of impatience.*) Oh, call me back then and ah . . . ah . . . Hello? Hello? All right, good! Good! (*He slams the phone down on the hood.*) Goddamn cross-eyed bitch.

Three projections appear on the backdrop: A rose, a rose petal, and the fiber of a rose petal seen under a microscope. An Announcer of the master-of-ceremonies type enters—very energetic.

ANNOUNCER: Ladies and gentlemen! A very good evening to you! I am here with you this evening to put a few questions to you. Now! To begin with . . . which one of you ladies and gentlemen can tell me what this is! (*He points at the rose with a long pointing stick.*) We stand before the image of a flower of a dicotyledonous bush of the rosaceous family. But! on the other hand it might be something utterly different. It might be one of those *divine* roses which, among cultured and refined people, is taken as the favorite symbol of the human architecture. Let's see . . . Now! let's see! Young lady? Or you, sir? It's one or the other! It can't be both! Won't anybody answer? (*He pauses briefly in disappointment. Then he doubles his vitality.*) Very well, let's get on with it. Our job now is to reject quite definitely and conclusively all false images. Look at them carefully, there are three of them and only one of them is authentic. The other two should be stricken from the books so that they will be forgotten forever. And any person who divulges them should be pursued by law. All those who believe in these false images should be suppressed and isolated! . . . Kept under constant surveillance! . . . Pay very close attention now. It is supposed that this is a rose. Is it? It is supposed that this is a petal. Is it? And it is supposed that this is the fiber of a petal seen under a microscope. Is it? First hypothesis: without petals there are no roses. Look at this one. Take its petals away, what's left? No rose, that's sure! It has never existed. There has never been anything but petals. Second hypothesis: a petal in and of itself is nothing. When have you ever seen a petal grow like this? What stalk produces petals such as this? And who can tell if there are two or three petals missing in a rose? No, there are no petals, there are only roses. Third hypothesis: there are neither petals nor roses. There exists only a union of cells that form fiber. Suppress this and you've got nothing. And that fiber is composed of primal matter, live matter. And that matter isn't really matter, it's energy. There is no matter, there are no petals, there is no rose, no perfume, no nothing.

There is only a fusion of miraculous fictions. One of them is called a rose, others have different names. One miracle after the other, everywhere you look. Without the least possibility of rational explanation. (*He points to the three images.*) If you accept one of these images as certain, as real, all the others will be false. Because no one would dare pretend that there are several answers to one question. Any intellectual could tell you that one answer precludes the others and that's the way things are . . . and we *are* among intellectuals, are we not? Now, which is the true image? This one, this one, or this one? Any persons answering correctly will be the recipients of a magnificent prize, which they may claim after the show is over in the offices of this theatre. You have ten seconds to answer. Ten seconds. Here we go. Ten . . . nine . . . eight . . . seven . . .

Dim out.

The News Vendor enters with his newspapers. Now they are printed on parchment or vellum or any very ancient paper. We can make out not only letters but also hieroglyphs and magical signs.

NEWS VENDOR: Get your latest news! Latest news! All of it true . . . the total truth! Learn about all things and choose the most convenient! They all add up to the same thing. They're all the same. News. Get your latest news. (*He goes off.*)

The Medium comes on from upstage. She is dressed in white with some small touch of vivid color. The cloth of her garments is filmy. It weighs nothing at all and seems to float in the air.

THE MEDIUM: Now it's time to shout the news! . . . such as springtime! eclipses! . . . or to investigate algebraic propositions and find them decorated with snails and petals! But I should talk less and cleave to my subject. Now it's my turn to explain the accident.

Toña and Polo enter balancing on the railroad track.

There they are changing into all that surrounds them. They *become* the dump, the flowers, clouds, amazement, joy . . . and they *understand* . . . they *see*! That's what happened. That was it. (*Pointing with a small flashlight. The Medium indicates the flowers.*)

We hear Women's Voices.

WOMEN'S VOICES:
>   I have strength . . .
>   I have promise . . .
>   I am beautiful . . .
>   I am the labor of the universe . . .
>   Flies love me.
>   . . . and I welcome the wasps and bees.

The children dance. The dump begins to glow from within. It shines, it sparkles, as if it were covered with jewels.

MEDIUM: With gestures such as these we pray for rain! With rhythms such as these we summon and arouse fertility! This is how we call upon the sea and air!

The dance stops. Polo raises a metal object.

POLO: This came from a mine! To give it shape, it took the total effort of all the peoples of this world! It's resting now but even so it hides energies, surprises, and changes . . .

TOÑA: There's a spell in the air of violent news: explosions and changes, but there is no death. Flies and wasps buzz back and forth guarding the secret of flight.

MEDIUM: They look at signs like children learning the alphabet. They are looking at arrows that indicate directions, paths. They are searching for crossroad signs, signs . . .

TOÑA: I'm so happy! . . . and I love my body. It's good to be alive! Oh, it's good to be alive! My mother works with the sick and the dying but I'm healthy. Thank you!

POLO: I am my parents' child and I will relive their life. My father, his salary, his vices, and his fate. My mother's love is a destiny.

TOÑA: Discovering the joy in my body will not be easy . . .

POLO: My whole life can be predicted.

TOÑA: Easily . . . so easily!

MEDIUM (*smiling and shaking her head*): We can't tell what gestures our hands will make from one moment to the next!

A column of light falls upon the tub full of cement.

VOICES: Each step turns a corner. Each step makes a journey. Between one choice and the next there are many roads. We always find ourselves some place else and not where we meant to be . . . nor do we know how we got there. Can we tell what fruits our acts will bear? Some plants bloom before others and some trees grow very slowly!

TOÑA: Look! Look, that tub would make a wonderful planter. You could put a big plant in that one.

They start to push the tub. They hesitate and then they make up their minds. In the meantime we hear Voices, single and in chorus.

VOICES: Choice is only one face of a coin forever flipped in the air! Freedom is an act of madness! But so is choice! And freedom becomes the shape of the gesture in which we choose freedom.

They begin to push the tub toward the railroad tracks.

There's beauty, too! And the free circus! And the long paper tails that practical jokers pin to the asses of comets! There's day and there's night! Waves! Light! Fiestas! The kangaroo and armadillo! The rainbow and the echo! Everyday life! Thanks.

They push the tub onto the tracks where the train will pass. We begin to hear joyous laughter all around. We hear the racket of the derailment, which gradually turns into music. There is a great shout of joy! Colored lights dance about everywhere. All the figures in the play run on. Maximino, the Scavengers, the street people, the Peddlers, the Professors, the Announcer, the parents, those who dreamed, everyone. They embrace, they kiss, they dance chaotically.

MEDIUM (*shouting*): You *know*! . . . a sudden and amazing change occurred! But do you *know* how Polo came to own his own garage? And what Toña's wedding looked like?

The characters begin to dance in order. There is now a certain symmetry to their movements.

Well, that . . . you've guessed it . . . that's another story.

The pattern of the dance has become more clear and definite.

(*Asking in the manner of a teacher.*) : And now, what about the light from that star . . . extinguished for so many years?

TOÑA (*she answers the question with the memorized reply. She has her arm around Maximino*): It kept flowing into the telescope . . . but all it meant to say, all it ever meant to speak, all it meant to reveal . . . was the humble existence of the hairy hunter who was drawn by his friend, the painter, on the walls of an African cave.

The dancers have now taken hands and they have formed a kind of solemn chain. They pass from hand to hand combining in precise and complex figures.

MAXIMINO: And now, all of us . . .

TOÑA: For a long time . . .

POLO: Let us listen to the beating . . .

TOÑA: In each and every hand . . .

MAXIMINO: Of the mystery . . .

THE MEDIUM: Of our single hearts . . .

The chainlike dance continues. The light has been growing more and more intense and bright as though by heartbeats. It is at its brightest when the curtain falls.